Liaison

ALSO BY JOYCE WADLER

My Breast: One Woman's Cancer Story

Liaison

JOYCE WADLER

BANTAM BOOKS
NEW YORK   TORONTO
LONDON   SYDNEY   AUCKLAND

LIAISON
A Bantam Book / October 1993

Grateful acknowledgment is made to The Guidebook Company Ltd. for permission to quote from Chinese Days *by Angela Terzani © Angela Terzani 1988.*

All rights reserved.
Copyright © 1993 by Joyce Wadler

BOOK DESIGN BY ELLEN CIPRIANO

Library of Congress Cataloging-in-Publication Data

Wadler, Joyce.
    Liaison / Joyce Wadler.
      p.   cm.
    Includes index.
    ISBN 0-553-09213-8
    1. Boursicot, Bernard. 2. Civil service—France—Biography. 3. France—Officials and employees—Biography. 4. Shi, Pei Pu. 5. Spies—China—Biography. 6. Female impersonators—China—Biography. 7. Espionage—China—History. I. Title.
JN2737.W34   1993
354.44′00092—dc20
[B]   92-31384
                                            CIP

Published simultaneously in the United States and Canada

Bantam Books are published by Bantam Books, a division of Bantam Doubleday Dell Publishing Group, Inc. Its trademark, consisting of the words "Bantam Books" and the portrayal of a rooster, is Registered in U.S. Patent and Trademark Office and in other countries. Marca Registrada. Bantam Books, 1540 Broadway, New York, New York 10036.

PRINTED IN THE UNITED STATES OF AMERICA
RRH 0 9 8 7 6 5 4 3 2 1

In memory of my father,
Bernard Wadler,
a realist

# CONTENTS

Liaison

Here is the Palais de Justice. They used to bring me here, the secret police: seventy, eighty kilometers an hour through Paris, racing through the streets; they thought the Chinese were standing on the street corners to save me, waiting to shoot. "Monsieur Boursicot, Ambassadeur de Fresnes," *they said when they brought me in before the judge. They chained my hands and also my feet and put me in the back of this truck, with one car in back, one in front, sometimes a motorcycle alongside. On the way to court it was okay, but always, on the way back to prison, I would throw up. The trial itself I do not remember very well. I was so full of drugs. They said this in all the newspapers. I was told it later. They did not let me read the papers myself. They thought it would disturb me. You know the sorts of things they say:* "For an accountant, he did not know how to count." *Or that I lie.*

I go to parties. They say, "Everybody needs to be famous once." "Does spying pay well?" *I was not spying for money. I was not spying for the secret of the washing machine. I was a diplomat. I had a life. New York, Belize, Paris, Marrakech, the same year I was arrested. Three continents the year before. I wanted to be Mr. Onassis, with a plane to take me to New York or Harry's Bar. Forgive me for speaking like this, I am drunk. Then four years in prison while he,* "The Living Treasure of the Beijing Opera"—*no, never mind, if they had caught me sooner, if they had caught me in China, it would have been twenty years in prison. Then I was a really great spy.*

Ah, there, beside Notre-Dame, there is the Hôtel-Dieu, the hospital where they took me when I committed suicide. There was blood on the walls, there was blood on the floor. My lawyer came for me in prison; they said to him, "If you recuperate your client, you will be lucky."

No, no, this is what I mean—Je me suis suicidé, *I committed suicide, I mean this precisely:*

When he took me in his arms I was lost.

$\mathcal{P}$ROLOGUE

There is a little alarm that goes off in us, a small inner voice that senses danger, and on Thursday, June 30, 1983, on a busy commercial street in Paris, Bernard Boursicot, an attaché in the French Foreign Service who had always dreamed of being a man of distinction, is hearing that alarm in his head.

He heard it earlier that week, returning from his post in Belize, when a man he had known for fifteen years at the Foreign Affairs office on the Quai d'Orsay had been cold to him. It is giving him the old problems: He is drinking too much and smoking too much and he cannot sleep.

It is odd. Usually Bernard returns to Paris as a hungry man sits down at the table. Old friends, good food, all-night bars, the possibility of a little late-night adventure—he approaches it all with cheerful greed. In the arena of love, he tends to get what he wants, too. It is not, at thirty-eight, that he is a handsome man by Parisian standards: His face is a bit too round; at five seven, a hundred and eighty pounds, his belly, he sometimes thinks, is a little too round also. But his shoulders are broad, his hips narrow, and he has a grin—when his energy is high—that announces to the world that whatever the sport, he is game.

But this morning, walking down Avenue Bosquet on the Left Bank, dressed for his holidays in loafers and jeans, all Bernard feels is the tension.

He tries fighting it, telling himself he has every reason in the world to feel good:

He has a new post in Scotland, which will keep him just close enough to and just far enough away from Paris. He has a new car awaiting him at a shop that caters to diplomats. And best of all, after years of struggle, Bernard has been able to get his sixteen-year-old son, Shi Du Du, or as he prefers to call him, by his French name, Bertrand, out of China. Tomorrow Bernard will take Bertrand down to his family in Brittany and show him off.

Bernard is terribly proud of Bertrand. You can see at a glance that he is of mixed blood, but it is clear to Bernard the boy has his own wide face, his brown eyes, his adventuresome nature. He rushed back to Paris when Bertrand arrived from Beijing nine months earlier and introduced him to his friends. He is less proud of Bertrand's mother, Shi Pei Pu.

"She has gotten old," Bernard thought when Pei Pu came to greet him at the airport in her usual guise, dressed as a man. Though she wants very much to be included on this outing to meet Bernard's family, she is not. She is his old love, he will provide for her, but it is finished between them. Already, over the years, he has given too much: television sets, tape recorders, Grundig radios, four Rolex watches, because Madame must have only the best. He is the only spy in the history of the world, Bernard often thinks, who *paid* to spy. Even now, he is paying: Pei Pu has heard of an apartment on Boulevard Saint-Germain, owned by a wealthy Chinese friend, which might be had very cheaply, and Bernard has agreed to go with her early this evening and look.

"I will meet you as planned," he told her the night before, calling her at home from a phone booth near his borrowed studio.

And she answered as she had since even before they had become lovers in the spring of 1965.

"You are still my best friend."

Her best friend—her best resource—but no matter, he has Bertrand; four boys in his family, two married with children, and *he* is the only one to provide his mother with a grandson. Bernard still remembers how happy she had been to meet him, coming up from Brittany with a breakfast mug with "Bertrand" stenciled on the side. Bertrand recognized her the moment she got off the train.

"Grandma!" he yelled.

There is something to blood.

Then suddenly, on the busy shopping street of Avenue Bosquet, they hit him. One man in sneakers tackles him from behind, another from the side. Bernard thinks it is a holdup and in his panic flings his wallet and address book down the street. Then, as they try to drag him into a car, Bernard grabs a tree and holds on. People are stopping to stare.

"What are you doing to that man?" one yells.

Now two more of them are on him and one is flashing a badge with his picture on it, and at last Bernard realizes who they are.

"Come with us, we just want to talk to you," one says, and the moment he gets into the Renault they slip on the cuffs.

"Say nothing," he tells himself as they tear up the street, north toward the Seine. "Nothing, like Sorge."

There is an organization in France called the Direction de la Surveillance du Territoire, which seeks out internal threats to national security, and in the winter of 1982, operating, as they would later report, they found "within the normal surveillance of the activities of the Chinese diplomatic representation in Paris" something that piqued their interest: the relationship between Bernard Boursicot, identified in their files as "a civil servant at the Ministry of Exterior Relations posted abroad," and "a Chinese national living in Paris, later identified as Shi Pei Pu."

Shi Pei Pu, according to D.S.T. intelligence, was a man of forty-five who made his living as singer, writer, and voice teacher. He had arrived in France from Beijing with his teenage son on October 8, 1982, at the invitation of the Maison des Sciences de l'Homme, a government-funded research institute for social studies, to give lectures on Chinese opera. Shi Pei Pu had once been a star of the Beijing Opera, and in France was having great success, starring in two network television shows. A delicate man who was only a few inches over five feet tall and had strikingly tiny hands, Pei Pu, as was traditional in Beijing Opera, performed both men's and women's roles. In one TV production, "The Messenger from Beijing," he appeared as a shepherdess awaiting news of her lover in a dreamlike fog beside a bridge.

"Watching the ocean, I guard my sheep and wait for a messenger to bring me news," Pei Pu sang in a high-pitched voice. "Oh, wait! My eyes see a horse at gallop!"

Backstage, Pei Pu had played the prima donna. He complained of fatigue and spoke often of a heart condition. He reappeared once, after an absence of a week, with scars around the eyes. When the producer asked if Pei Pu had had a face-lift he was, as usual, vague: Pei Pu just laughed. But after all, Pei Pu was a star. His teacher before the Cultural Revolution, had been Mei Lanfang, the greatest Beijing Opera actor in China. Mei was so exquisite in the female roles that made him famous that his students spent months mimicking the smallest details of his style: the movement of his wrist as he executed any of the fifty gestures of a kimono sleeve symbolizing feelings from love to subterfuge to pain; the proximity of his knees and sway of his body as he portrayed an empress taking tiny steps on bound feet.

The D.S.T. had the opportunity to learn a good deal about Beijing Opera as Shi Pei Pu went about his work on "The Messenger from Beijing":

They had tapped the phones.

It was impressive to be the subject of a one-hour television show nine months after arriving in a new country. Even more impressive was Pei Pu's circle of friends. He was seen going several times to the embassy of the People's Republic of China. He attended dinner parties with some of the highest-ranking members of the French diplomatic community. One evening the man who had served as ambassador to China only the year before had personally dropped Shi Pei Pu off at his apartment.

Most interestingly to the D.S.T., Shi Pei Pu's home, a sixth-floor studio in a weathered old building on Boulevard de Port-Royal on the Left Bank in Paris, was owned by a Foreign Service employee named Bernard Boursicot. Boursicot was a loose cannon in the organization, a working-class kid with a tenth-grade education who was viewed by his superiors as something of a maverick. It was never anything serious, nothing even that solid, just talk that followed him post to post around the globe: black-market dealings in Mongolia, his contract dropped at least once in his career, an enthusiastic drinker, a Romeo. He had been posted in the French embassy in China in 1964 for one year as an accountant and later spent three years there as an archivist. He had defense secret clearance, giving him access to some classified documents. He had also—for reasons unknown—twice visited the Chinese embassy in Paris.

He was posted in Belize, but since the arrival of Shi Pei Pu in Paris in October 1982 he had made two trips back to Paris. In mid-June 1983 he returned again.

"The surveillance under which Shi Pei Pu was placed," reads a D.S.T. report of July 2 from Commissaire Divisionnaire Raymond Nart, "revealed that Bernard Boursicot was living with Shi Pei Pu. The decision was made to call in Bernard Boursicot in order to receive explanations concerning this situation. The service suspected a cooperation between Bernard Boursicot and the Chinese intelligence services through the intermediary of Shi Pei Pu. Bernard Boursicot was arrested on June 30, 1983, at 11:40 on the street during a surveillance operation."

Bernard is shaking as the car speeds across Paris and he is afraid they can see it.

"I am a diplomat," he wants to say, "you cannot touch me," but he can't speak. Everything is spinning around him; his mind is racing so quickly he feels he is seeing sparks.

"They're going to ask me about Pei Pu. They're going to say, 'What is this Chinese doing in your place?' " he thinks. "Say nothing, be strong."

They tear east across Boulevard Haussmann and then, three blocks from the Ministry of the Interior, turn right onto the Rue d'Argenson, pulling up before a five-story building protected by a metal gate. Bernard can see no street number on the building and no name. The gate opens and they drive down to a second-level basement. From there the police take Bernard through a series of corridors and lead him into a large room. They do not speak. Just like the Gestapo, Bernard thinks. Somebody takes off the cuffs.

The man who seems to be in charge is a middle-aged, beefy guy in a blue suit and tie, who introduces himself as Nart. He has the beginnings of a belly and his hairline is receding and he looks tough. There are three others with him, dressed very much the same. "Nice suits," Bernard thinks, "They're dressed for a big day."

"Sit down," somebody says. Bernard does, jamming his hands in the pockets of his jeans to stop them from shaking, but they will not.

The cops seem to know a lot about him. They have a picture of Bertrand talking to a neighbor near the apartment, but they won't let him look at it, just pass it around in its plastic case. They shoot questions and accusations at him all at once.

"You were at the embassy of France in Beijing between '69 and '72 and in the embassy of Mongolia from '77 to '79 and there are five hundred documents missing."

"You went to the Chinese embassy and you saw the cultural consul in February '67 and again in April '68."

"Who is this mysterious Shi Pei Pu who is living at your place?"

"There were no documents missing in my time," he wants to tell them, but his thoughts are scattered and wild. Nothing could have been missing from the embassy, and if something was, there was no way they could prove it. But at the same time Bernard remembers the slides of him and Shi Pei Pu and Bertrand he had taken on his last trip to China and the letters on top of his desk at the apartment and he fears this might be proof enough.

"You're homosexual!" somebody is saying.

"Says who?" says Bernard, able for the moment to be tough.

"Perhaps we could bring in some of your friends for questioning," somebody else says.

"Bring in anybody you like," he says, but he knows who they mean and he is scared.

And then they are waving something in front of him.

"What about the plane ticket you got from the Chinese in April '71?"

April 1971—the time during the Cultural Revolution when Pei Pu had been sent to the countryside and Bernard had refused to give the Chinese any more documents until Pei Pu was allowed to return to Beijing. He thought he had won that round, but now he sees he did not: The Chinese had bided their time until they no longer needed him, and then given him up. The words come out of him unstoppable, like a moan:

"*Aaaah, les salauds ils m'ont vendu!*" Bernard cries. "The bastards have sold me."

The game is over.

"I did nothing for money," Bernard says.

"Who is Shi Pei Pu?" somebody asks.

Nothing to do but let it all go:

"If you want to know the truth, Shi Pei Pu is a woman," Bernard says.

Silence. They are stunned. Perhaps they think he is joking. Why, after all, wouldn't they?

"Aaah, that's why she's with her son," one of them says finally.

"It's my son," says Bernard.

Silence again. But briefer.

"And what about the papers?" the senior man asks.

"There were no documents," Bernard wants to say, but he cannot.

"One letter of Sihanouk," he begins. "Some telegrams of Marshall Green . . ." and on and on, into the afternoon.

It is interesting to see what happens to a man's signature when he is held by the police for forty-eight hours without an attorney and by his own volition his life falls apart.

In the early afternoon on Thursday, Bernard Boursicot's first day in police custody, his signature on the bottom of each page of his typed confession is cohesive and controlled, the letters of his name connecting one to the other as the letters in a name should. By nine-thirty that evening, after ten hours of questioning, the letters are starting to separate. Friday morning, when Bernard gives the police a list he had made in the night of additional documents he had given the Chinese, his handwriting is barely legible, like the writing of a child, or a man whose mind is unraveling and who is progressively unlearning everything he knows. For years, Bernard Boursicot says, he has been a spy.

His confession runs fifteen pages, single-spaced. Bernard admits giving the Chinese information on the Soviet Union, Southeast Asia, Japan, and Laos in the early and late 1970s. The Chinese were particularly interested, he said, in papers arriving in Beijing from the French embassies in Washington and Moscow. They had specifically requested information on the secret visit of American national security adviser Henry Kissinger to China in 1971, to prepare for talks regarding the opening of American-Chinese relations.

He insists that none of the papers was classified or top secret.

He also frames his espionage activities within the context of a love story. That story is far more important to him than the documents. It is how his formal confession begins:

"In October 1964, I was assigned on a contractual basis to the French embassy in Beijing where I functioned as the accountant. At the end of December 1964, at a party given by the First Counselor of the French embassy, I made the acquaintance of Shi Pei Pu, who was presented to me as a Chinese writer of about twenty-six years of age. He spoke French and we hit it off. . . .

"Je vous precise des maintenant qu'en fait, il s'agit d'une femme qui se faisait passer pour homme. . . ."

"I wish to make it clear to you that this is about a woman who has passed for a man," he says.

He reveals the secret he promised Pei Pu he would never tell: that she had been forced to live her life disguised as a man. He tells why. He says that after learning Pei Pu's secret, he and Pei Pu had become lovers and that when he returned to France at the end of his first stay in 1965, it was without the knowledge that his mistress was pregnant. He told of returning to China in 1969, when Mao's Cultural Revolution was in full force, when Red Guard teenagers were beating government leaders with "Quotations from Chairman Mao Zedong" and intellectuals were being sent to work camps for "reeducation." There were suspicious deaths and forced suicides. It was so bad then that a Chinese would not say hello to an old French friend in the street. Everything foreign was suspect. Despite the dangers, Boursicot made contact with Pei Pu. When their relationship was discovered by the Chinese authorities, Bernard, in order to protect his mistress and child, became a spy.

"I gave [the Chinese], on my own initiative, a sealed letter that I had taken from the mailroom of the embassy . . . a letter from Siha-nouk, who was then in Beijing, addressed to Senator Mansfield via the French diplomatic bag," he says. "I thought that in this way I could gain time and prolong my relations with Pei Pu and that the police would close their eyes. . . .

"I didn't act for personal gain, but for my family. I wanted to save my son and his mother, who constantly risked their lives. I was always motivated by the hope that they could leave China. My only regret is to have been placed in a situation where no other alternative was proposed to me. I never in my life wanted a clandestine role in an information service."

"Elle est tombée enceinte"—*"She* became pregnant"; *"Elle m'a dit qu'il e'tait dangereux de la recontrer"*—*"She* told me it would be dangerous to meet."

The prisoner is obviously sincere. Taken before a judge and indicted for "having relations with intelligence agents of a foreign power of a nature which would do harm to the military or diplomatic situation of France or its essential economic interests," Boursicot waives his right to a lawyer and reiterates his statement to police.

"I gave information only in the hope of one day being able to get my child out of China. I was successful in this since my son is now living with me."

The police take him to Fresnes, the gloomy maximum-security prison on the outskirts of Paris, and early the next morning, a Saturday, climb the six flights of stairs at Boulevard Port-Royal to interrogate Shi Pei Pu.

The boy Shi Du Du, a tall gangly teenager with deep black bangs falling over his eyes, opens the door. The police send him from the room. The studio is large and dark. The curtains are drawn. The floors are covered with Oriental rugs, the walls with long, narrow Chinese paintings and calligraphy. Shi Pei Pu, in a man's shirt and baggy trousers and a wig of wavy black hair, looks pale and weary and speaks of poor health. The police call a doctor and allow the suspect to be questioned at home. The voice is unusual for a man's: high and breathy. Pei Pu sighs often and smiles sadly. "An extraordinary tale, I know. Who could know better than I?" the smile seems to say. The story is told like a Chinese fairy tale. "I was born into a family of Mandarins, high-ranking *fonctionnaires* . . ." Pei Pu begins. Though knowledge of espionage is denied, the odd little creature admits she is Bernard Boursicot's mistress and the mother of his child. She has indeed gone through life in disguise.

The D.S.T. are professionals, matter-of-fact in their reports, but they cannot keep a note of excitement from this file:

"Shi Pei Pu was raised, right from the start, as a boy by her mother," the police report of July 2 reads. "Her true nature was hidden from everyone until this day. . . . Today, Shi Du Du is ignorant of the fact that Shi Pei Pu is a woman and his mother. . . . Shi Pei Pu says she was ignorant of the fact that Bernard Boursicot was turning over documents. . . . This is possible."

One week later, they return and arrest Pei Pu anyway.

"I will never be able to stand prison," Pei Pu says when taken before the judge.

The story breaks July 5, shortly before Pei Pu's arrest.

Le Monde, the French newspaper of record, treats it as a minor item, giving it only a few inches of space: a Foreign Affairs employee has been charged with espionage for giving information from the French embassy in Beijing to a Chinese woman friend.

The tabloids, fascinated by Shi Pei Pu's disguise and delighted by this story of secret love, banner it on the front page.

"SPY FOR LOVE," screams one headline, while another paper reports that Bernard Boursicot, while in China, provided documents to his secret Chinese wife, the Beijing Opera singer Shi Pei Pu.

French friends of Shi Pei Pu's, some of whom have known him for eighteen years, are astonished. Shi Pei Pu likes an aura of mystery. He tantalizes China scholars by promising to tell secret stories of this famous literary figure or that. They wait and wait—he rarely tells. He has a tendency, some are beginning to think, to embroider a tale, though perhaps this is to be expected of a man who made his living as a librettist. But Pei Pu is also a man of stature in China, an artist, and if he had surprised some old friends by coming to France with a son, there is no secret about it: The boy was adopted. Nor is there any mystery about Shi Pei Pu's gender: Pei Pu is effeminate, probably homosexual, but Shi Pei Pu is a man.

Two days later, no one is certain what Shi is.

"ESPION OU ESPIONNE?" reads the headline in *Le Monde* on July 8.

"French judicial authorities remain perplexed today after questioning, on the 7th of July, the Chinese lyric artist Shi Pei Pu who claims to be a woman, since he [she] has the appearance of a man," the story reads. "Forty-six years of age, he [she] was the lover of M. Bernard Boursicot, a chancellery attaché, who has been held since July 2nd charged with passing information to foreign agents. Two medical experts have been ordered to determine sex."

Friends of Bernard Boursicot's, the half dozen to whom he has confided that Pei Pu is a woman and the mother of his child, are dumbfounded. It is true that Bernard often stretches the truth for a good story: Let him find himself on the same plane as British Prime Minister Margaret Thatcher, no matter that he is in tourist and she in first class and he doesn't get within ten feet of her, and next thing you know he's talking about the time he flew out of New York "with" Margaret Thatcher. He can be—especially when drinking—histrionic. But he is not crazy, he is not delusional, and he is hardly inexperienced sexually. The rival of Shi Pei Pu, when Bernard was in his twenties, had been a beautiful French girl who is now a doctor in Paris. Bernard had adored her body; she had taken her baths in front of him. Bernard had recently proposed marriage to a Polish girl. She remembers an exquisite seduction far off in Mongolia: a man who bundled her up in his fur-lined overcoat against the freezing winter and played *La Traviata* back in his room. Bernard has also had a significant liaison with a man. Bernard certainly knows—my God, anyone knows—the difference between a woman and a man.

On July 14, 1983, the findings of the doctors who have examined Shi Pei Pu are made public. And Bernard Boursicot, as he has always wanted, in press reports becomes a man of extraordinary distinction who will soon be known round the globe:

The greatest sexual buffoon of the century. The man who made love to another man for eighteen years and did not know.

Bernard Boursicot, sedated in his prison cell, hears the news on the radio two weeks after his arrest.

"The Chinese Mata Hari, who is accused of entrapping a French diplomat into spying, is a man."

"It's not possible!" Bernard yells. "It is unbelievable! It's a lie!"

He refuses to believe it when his lawyer comes to see him the following day and says he has seen the newspaper reports. The papers lie, Bernard says. The police lie. Get the medical reports.

He refuses to believe it one week later when the lawyer announces that he has seen the medical reports and the newspapers are correct: There is no sign of surgery. Pei Pu is and always has been a normal man. Order another examination, Bernard tells his lawyer. Order a blood test to prove the parentage of my son. He insists to prison psychologists that Pei Pu is a woman. He sends tender letters to Bertrand.

"Your father who loves you," he writes.

Two and one half months after his arrest, when Bernard is taken to a closed hearing prior to trial before investigating judge Bruno Laroche and told that Shi Pei Pu has admitted he is a man, he refuses to believe him either.

"I must tell you that I am astounded by this declaration," he says, in a lengthy and sexually explicit statement. "I have always considered Shi Pei Pu a woman ever since we had sexual relations together, that is to say from May or June 1965. I have seen him naked on a number of occasions between 1965 and 1978. . . . Contrary to what Shi Pei Pu declares, when we had sexual relations we were not always in the dark. . . . I never had relations 'against nature' with Shi Pei Pu."

Eight months later, locked in a prison cell, he removes the blade from a plastic disposable razor and begins slicing at his throat.

Love

1

I t is difficult to imagine a more exciting place to be than the People's Republic of China in 1964. In January, President Charles de Gaulle announces the French government has decided to recognize China, and one month later the French open their embassy in Beijing, becoming the first Western power to do so since the Korean War. In the summer, Chairman Mao Zedong attacks the Soviet Union, formerly China's greatest ally, with a speech entitled "On Khrushchev's Phony Communism." And on October 16, the Chinese make what is interpreted as their most aggressive and independent gesture: They detonate their first atomic bomb.

But the big thing on twenty-year-old Bernard Boursicot's mind on October 24, 1964, as he boards the Aeroflot plane in Moscow for the last leg of his thirty-six-hour journey from Paris to Beijing for his new job as the accountant in the French embassy, is his overcoat.

It had looked wonderful back in Brittany when his uncle had given it to him: royal blue, double-breasted wool with an air of adult prosperity, even if it was fifteen years old. Now, as Bernard suddenly finds himself among a group of new passengers, sixty or seventy French students, confident and laughing and dressed far more casually than he, he stares down at his lapels. They are very old-fashioned, he realizes. His huge wool coat suddenly looks like what it is: a rich uncle's hand-me-down. He takes off the overcoat and stuffs it clumsily into an overhead compartment, feeling everyone around him is staring at him as he does so. Ten hours, he tells himself, and he will actually be in China. He hopes to hell nobody finds him out.

The plane lands in Beijing in mid-afternoon. The airport buildings are newly built, squat, and ugly, and there is an ominous precursor of a nation holding itself aloof and apart: At the huge international airport, Bernard's is the only plane. To Bernard that only heightens the sense of adventure and excitement. So does the fact that Ambassador Lucien Paye, a former Minister of Education, is waiting on the tarmac to greet the students. He is a broad-shouldered man with a ruddy face and a jovial style; his interest in Bernard is perfunctory.

"Aah, Boursicot," he says. "We've been waiting a long time for you —there's a car waiting," and then he turns back to the students, leaving Bernard with an embassy driver and a fellow with a monocle and a notebook named Jacques Marcuse, whom Bernard takes to be a press aide.

There are few cars on the highway as they make the eighteen-mile trip into the city, only an occasional bus or truck, and looking out at the men and women working the land with their mules, Bernard feels a comforting wave of literary recognition—aah, yes, the red dirt of Pearl S. Buck. He also feels shy, and is happy to let Marcuse, who seems to be a very sophisticated man, do the talking.

"Interesting people, the Chinese," he says, removing a box of matches from his coat pocket and trying unsuccessfully to light his pipe. "They can build an atomic bomb but they can't make a box of matches. How old are you, by the way?"

"Twenty," says Bernard, wondering what it is about him that makes people always ask.

"Same age as I was when I first came to China," Marcuse says.

They arrive at his home, where a Chinese servant in a white Mao jacket opens the door.

"You'll stay for dinner, of course," Marcuse says. "I have a small story to file and we can have a drink and have dinner. We'll have dinner at the Spanish time. I'm very fond of Spain. I used to go horseback riding on the Costa Brava. Have you been?"

What Bernard has ridden in Spain is his thumb, hitchhiking, but he nods like a man who's been around. Dinner is superb—duck, prepared by an old cook who was trained before the revolution. Impossible to get decent help from any of the young people, Marcuse says. The days before the revolution in 1949, now those were the days in China. Playing polo on sturdy little Mongolian ponies. Casinos and opium dens. Terrible poverty, yes, but even with that the Chinese seemed a freer and happier people; they laughed then. And Beijing was a wonderful city, a jumble of narrow streets and Chinese courtyard houses. It had not yet been ruined.

After dinner, Marcuse takes Bernard to the Beijing Hotel. They drive down Changan Avenue, the Avenue of Eternal Peace, the main street in Beijing. Everything is so big, so echoingly large and empty. Changan Avenue measures eight lanes across. Tiananmen Square, in the center of the city, is ninety-nine acres, the largest public square in the world. Beyond one red-walled gate of the square one can see the outlines of the curving roofs of the palaces of the Forbidden City. The hotel, just off Changan Avenue, is the grandest Bernard has ever seen: Columns carved with dragons and painted in yellow and red and green are at the entrance; the floors in the lobby are marble; there are rows of blue and white Chinese pots filled with red chrysanthemums.

Then, walking across the lobby, Marcuse spots someone he knows.

The voice he uses to greet the second-ranking man at the French embassy is relaxed and easy.

"Aaah, Monsieur Chayet," Marcuse says. "Let me introduce your new accountant, Monsieur Bernard Boursicot."

Bernard's heart stops for a second.

"The game is up," he thinks, but it is okay. Chayet does not recognize Bernard's face or name.

"You had a good trip in to the city?" Chayet asks Bernard when they arrive at his rooms.

"Oh, yes, I came in with the press attaché," says Bernard.

"Ah, no," says Chayet. "Monsieur Marcuse is not the press aide. He is a journalist for Agence France-Presse."

Bernard's face turns red—the first thing out of his mouth, he thinks, and it's got to be a mistake. He fumbles for something to say but is lost. Within moments, as if she has spotted his discomfort, Mme. Chayet, a slim, elegant woman, breaks in. There is a movie at the International Club, she says, a group is going—will Bernard join them? Bernard is exhausted but he does not know how to say no.

He is relieved when he can finally retreat to his room. It is a fine room. The furniture is heavy and ornate, the bathroom enormous, and when Bernard opens the double windows he can see the red walls and curving yellow roofs of the Forbidden City. The view is marvelous. A moat surrounds the palaces; there are four towers in each corner of the sprawling grounds, and here and there little white carved stone bridges arch over streams, glowing softly under the moon. It is like looking at an illustration in an adventure book when he was a boy in Vannes. He cannot believe he is in China. But he is still more worried than excited. He feels guilty about the way he got here. He recalls with embarrassment referring to M. Marcuse, who everyone seemed to know was an important foreign correspondent, as an attaché. That this is the first impression he has made with the minister councillor makes him feel awful. He thinks of what his mother used to say about how to behave during those moments you are not sure of yourself: *"Il faut tourner sa langue sept fois dans sa bouche avant de parler."* "Roll your tongue in your mouth seven times before speaking." He will watch himself. He will not make such a mistake again.

"Why did you leave home?" one sometimes asks a man who grew up in the French countryside, and the answer comes back: "I left home because I was tired of eating soup." Meaning, "I was tired of fish every Wednesday and Friday, tired of the priest in his skirts, tired of the routine of homely things." Even a festive occasion, a communion lunch, which in Brittany is a ten-course affair, with first the champagne and oysters, then the fish, then the pheasant, then the roasted meats, then the salads, then the cheese, then the fruits and the cakes and the cognac, could become a heavy and oppressive thing. A meal such as this in Brittany just after the Second World War is common. If a daughter of a successful farmer in a village outside the old walled city of Vannes got married, the whole village would be invited for the wedding breakfast and after the ceremony at the church everyone followed the bride and groom back to the farm, singing. Then one sat down to a wedding lunch for which two cows had been killed.

Bernard Boursicot's family was not successful. His father, Louis, had been a salesman—just like Willy Loman, out there with a suitcase and a smile, Bernard would think later, reading an American play, except that in his father's case he had only the suitcase, never the smile. He lost his inheritance in a traveling sales venture that failed as large shops came in. He was a proud man—he had been in the Resistance during the war—and he hated working for others. Nor did he stay with a job for long. He could not bear following orders. He had many trades: handyman, gardener, cop, but eventually he always quit. The early 1950s are a boom time in France, all the Boursicot men are making money, five strong brothers, each one successful, except for the father of Bernard. Everybody in town knows it, too. Louis the Loudmouth. Louis who is fond of his wine. A good thing his wife can sew, some say, or what would they do with four young sons in the house? As for leaving home, Bernard wants to get away from the provinces from the time he is a boy. He dreams of romance. It drives his father crazy.

"Life is not a fairy tale!" Louis screams. "Get your head out of the clouds!"

Bernard cannot. Movies to him, as a child, are as real as life. When he sees the film *Samson and Delilah* he weeps. *The Count of Monte Cristo, Lord Jim, The Brothers Karamazov;* when they call on Bernard in school he is never there, he is off dueling for a lady's honor or lost on the Russian steppes. He is not an unintelligent boy. He has a talent for languages, excelling in English and Spanish; he reads books that are advanced for his age. But he reads only what is of interest to him, ignoring his studies, and on vacations he goes hitchhiking. When he turns eighteen and is two years behind at school they throw him out. That suits Bernard fine. The army rejects him, too. They classify him as *"défaillant psychisme—X 5,"* giving him a psychological deferment. He fakes the psychological tests, he will later say—he does not want to serve in the military. When an invitation comes from an old school friend whose father is working in Algeria, he grabs it.

His first trip abroad. Bernard remembers it so well: hitching the thousand kilometers from Vannes to Port-Vendres. Buying a fourth-class steamship ticket for Algeria for forty francs that gives him a spot in steerage—a chair and a blanket are ten francs extra so he does without. His first look at Oran, high on a cliff over the harbor, with its ocher hills and palm trees and paths winding down the hills like lace. Bernard loves Algeria, the veiled women, the sinuous streets, the history. Algeria has not been independent long. One can still see bullet holes in buildings from the war that took a hundred thousand lives. Yet the French Foreign Service people still live splendidly. Bernard's friend Bertrand whose father is assistant consul general, lives in a two-story villa overlooking the city, with a cook and driver and maid. When Bertrand's father arranges for Bernard to tour the country with an assistant, he is treated like a prince. Bernard also goes along with Bertrand when he is invited to the beach at Trouville with the family of the consul general, Claude Chayet. Trouville is a ramshackle little town, a few miles of beach with a stretch of weathered villas and a post office and a bakery. It bears no resemblance to the elegant French resort adjacent to Deauville for which it was named. But Bernard is excited to be in the presence of so important a man as M. Chayet. He has, Bertrand tells him, just spent four years as *conseiller d'ambassade* to the French delegation to the United Nations in New York. His father and grandfather were diplomats. His three children, who are Bernard's age, are fluent in English. Of course, when the visit is over, it is impossible for Bernard to remain in Vannes. At nineteen, dreaming of adventure, he returns to Algeria and gets a job as an accountant in the bureau of Anciens Combattants et Victimes de la Guerre, the French war veterans' office. A year later, Algeria having paled, Bernard returns to France and makes his way to Foreign Office headquarters in Paris, hoping for a spot in some exotic place as accountant or clerk. The war veterans' office is a division of the Foreign Office. Bernard has civil service experience.

The man in personnel who interviews him does not seem particularly interested. Can Bernard speak German? he asks. No? What a shame; there is a spot for an accountant in Bremen. Is Bernard really only twenty, or has he misread the form? Frankly, he doesn't have a thing. He does not ask Bernard the reason for his military deferment—how much time can one spend on a clerk, after all?—and Bernard sees no reason to volunteer the information. Then they are interrupted. Another man, who seems to be the interviewer's boss, steps into the room. There is a problem that requires immediate attention. The newly opened embassy of France in China needs an accountant. The name of the *premier conseiller* is mentioned.

"Monsieur Claude Chayet," the man says.

"Chayet?" says Bernard, as if recalling an old friend.

The atmosphere in the room changes.

"You know him?" one man asks.

"I went with him to the beach in Trouville," says Bernard.

Eight weeks later, nervously guarding the secret of his little deception, he is on his way to Beijing.

The French embassy is located in northeast Beijing, in the outskirts of the city, at 10 Sanlitun. The ambassador's residence is next door. As Bernard, nervous and wearing his new suit, reports for his first day of work, he sees Ambassador Paye. Paye has a reputation for being an easygoing man but, Bernard knows, he had originally been against having so young and inexperienced a person as Bernard on his staff. Only the urgency of getting an accountant had made him change his mind. Now, from the look he gives Bernard, it seems he still has doubts.

"Twenty," he says. "Aaah, well. You will do for now."

And yet things do not go badly. There are only about two dozen people at the embassy and there is little for Bernard, in his first weeks, to do—Yu Tong, a Chinese national who has been handling the accounts and will train him, is on sick leave. Bernard, with time on his hands, reads the accounting manual and soaks up the stories around him. He is observing, he tells himself, like Proust. There is one case that particularly intrigues him: A French citizen, thirty-seven-year-old Jean Pasqualini, born in Beijing to a Chinese mother and a Corsican father, has been in Chinese labor camps for seven years, on charges of spying. His Chinese wife, though she loves him, has divorced him so that their two sons will not be made outcasts. Pasqualini, in his years of confinement, has come close to death. The French are working for his release. Bernard is fascinated when he hears his boss, consul Jean Colombel, negotiating on the phone with the Chinese.

"The weather is so nice between our two countries," Colombel says. "And yet, we still have a cloud in the heavens. . . ."

In his off hours, he explores the city. Much of the old city is gone, as Marcuse warned. The *pailoo,* the triumphal arches in marble and wood erected in honor of emperors and nobility, are fast disappearing. They symbolized the old feudal society, Mao believed, and when he took power in 1949 he ordered them torn down. Many of the old palaces and traditional courtyard homes were also destroyed. The rickshaw runners, who lived an average of six years after assuming their trade, are also gone, replaced by bicycle-drawn pedicabs. *"Pousse-pousse,"* the French call them.

Yet there is still much that is beautiful in Beijing. Bernard explores the palaces of the Forbidden City. He visits the Palace of Heavenly Purity where the Last Emperor, Pu Yi, had forty years earlier been married, as a boy. He is fascinated by the traditional Chinese house, a one-story building constructed about a central courtyard, hidden behind three walls. The exterior wall is high and encircles the property; the next two walls, about six feet high, are ceremonial walls with circular gates, designed to keep out evil spirits. Bernard is enchanted with this notion, that the spirit world is a real world, powerful enough to require barriers of brick and mortar. Walls also intrigue Bernard. They heighten a sense of mystery. There is no way a passerby can get a sense of the life within. But Bernard tries. He studies conversational Chinese, learning enough to ask directions, have a polite conversation about the weather, and understand a phrase here and there in the talk around him. While his French colleagues socialize among themselves Bernard often goes off alone on his bicycle into the old quarters. Foreigners are so rare that often the Chinese stop what they are doing and stare at him, but that does not dissuade him. Bernard talks with the peddlers; he soon has a regular *pousse-pousse* driver with whom he shares Gauloises. Late at night they ride about the streets. Bernard studies the old ladies in trousers and black velvet caps, tottering along on their bound feet, inhaling their hand-rolled cigarettes as if they are a drug, and he makes up stories about them: They are thinking of the old days, he is convinced.

But finally Bernard is frustrated. For while he can chat with a merchant or cab driver, it does not lead to anything. There are no shared meals, no going for a drink, no invitations home.

There are other walls, invisible, around the Chinese. Social relationships with foreigners are frowned upon by their government. There are a few Chinese employees at the embassy whose ties to the French date back to the forties and who are viewed as special friends: Antoine Yu, who does the accounts with Bernard and whose father had worked in the embassy before the revolution; his brother Odilon Yu, who teaches Chinese to the ambassador and M. Chayet; San Chan Liu, an intellectual in his early sixties, who translates newspaper articles. But all Chinese employees, at the embassy or in private homes, are screened and selected by the Chinese government's Bureau of Foreign Services for Diplomatic Personnel, and the veteran diplomats are aware that the Chinese must report everything they see to their work unit chiefs.

Beijing is a segregated city. Before the revolution, the diplomats of the nations which had once occupied Beijing had lived in their own neighborhood, the legation quarter, southeast of Tiananmen Square. The streets were lined with pink mimosa, the buildings were a mixture of opulent European styles, and the French compound was particularly impressive: a tall red gate at the entrance, flanked by two stone lions. Chinese were not permitted to live in the quarter, nor could their police enter. Now the Chinese tell the foreigners where to live. Arriving in China, the French are assigned rooms on the fifth floor of the Beijing Hotel—the better, Bernard realizes, for the Chinese to keep an eye on them. As housing becomes available, they are moved to the district of Sanlitun, a neighborhood so far from the center of town it has been nicknamed Siberia. Minister councillor Chayet, who lived in Beijing as a boy when his father worked in the French ministry, has, by virtue of this old relationship, been given something very special: a traditional court-yard house for him and his family. But Chayet understands the social restrictions. Though he and his Chinese teacher Odilon Yu have known each other since they were children, and Odilon may be invited to the occasional French reception at home or at the embassy, Chayet under-stands that he will not be invited to Odilon Yu's home. Such an invita-tion could make Odilon politically suspect. Chayet does not even know where Odilon Yu lives.

The European community, to Bernard, is as insular as Vannes. When the French arrived to open their embassy earlier in the year, there were only fifty-five French nationals living in all of China. Now, with the embassy staff and exchange students, the number of French in Beijing is still under one hundred. The British, who recognized the People's Republic in 1950, have a small consulate. Finland, Denmark, Sweden, and Switzerland have some diplomatic personnel posted in Beijing as well. The Americans, who do not recognize the country, are not permitted entry.

There is little entertainment. Theater consists of revolutionary ballets featuring girls in Red Army uniform or operas and plays which glorify the worker's struggle. *A Bucket of Manure*, the story of a woman who wants to use manure for her private garden plot but is convinced by her husband to bring it to the communal field, is typical. A foreigner can go to the International Club, in the old legation district, where a dance band wheezes out fox-trots learned before the revolution, but it is not a cheery alternative. Travel is difficult: Foreigners cannot go more than twenty-five miles outside Beijing without permission. Nor is Mao's China a place for illicit pleasures: Drugs, prostitution, even horse racing are forbidden.

Foreigners are forced to amuse themselves. They show films, which arrive via diplomatic pouch from Europe; they have endless cocktail and dinner parties. Sunday mornings some attend Catholic services in a convent, the only Catholic facility left in Beijing. Bernard, who was raised Catholic but is now an agnostic, attends for companionship.

Bernard has a few acquaintances: François, the tutor of the Chayet children; Françoise, tutor to the children of second embassy councillor Yves Pagniez; Nicholas Komaroff, a French linguist in his early thirties who works for the Chinese as a translator and editor at the Foreign Language Press. He is also befriended by Augustin Quilichini, the fifty-one-year-old embassy consular agent. Augustin had arrived in China in 1934 as a soldier and married a French-Chinese woman, Thérèse. During the sixteen years the French embassy had been closed, the couple stayed on in China, where Augustin lived in a fine old house on Changan Avenue and served as consular agent, looking after French interests. Now Augustin takes a fatherly interest in Bernard, bringing him to his tailor, inviting him to their house.

But Bernard does not have any close friends and he is conspicuously uncomfortable with his coworkers. Foreign Affairs employees, particularly those of rank, are a well-educated and privileged group. Their style is the opposite of Bernard Boursicot's. While they prize discretion and understatement, Bernard blurts out the first thing that comes into his head. They have attended the best schools in France: the École Nationale d'Administration, which has graduated finance minister Valery Giscard d'Éstaing; the Institut d'Études Politiques; the École Normale Supérieure, which has trained intellectuals and teachers, including Jean-Paul Sartre. Bernard was expelled from school in tenth grade. The manners of the embassy staff are perfect. Bernard is visibly awkward.

He fusses over his appearance and showers twice daily but still appears unkempt. When he is excited or drinks he flushes, perspires, and talks too much. A buffoon, some people consider him.

One day in the embassy, the secretary to whom he gives the accounts to type tells him that another secretary is spreading the story that his feet stink.

A few days later, the story reaches the minister councillor:

"Your bath facilities—they are in working order?" he asks Bernard.

Bernard becomes very self-conscious—he changes his socks three times a day.

There is something besides adventure that is eluding Bernard in China. It is love. Bernard has never been in love but he knows what it entails: agony, longing, desperation, barriers.

"What I'm looking for," he had written in his journal before departing, "is something creative which will provoke in me both the feelings of fright and of vitality. . . ."

He had also listed what was wrong with his life.

"I should be doing more sports; I should be living with a woman; I should be working night and day; I should be reading and writing furiously; I should be meeting lots of people; I should leave all mediocrity out of this journal . . ."

But a magnificent love affair provoking a great emotional flood of "fright and vitality" is not working out. The truth is, Bernard has never made love to a woman. He has never even had a steady girl. He had had a schoolboy crush on the girl next door when he was eleven—her father had been a civil servant in Africa, they had a big white Peugeot parked in the yard. It was all tied up in his mind: the pretty girl, the savannas of Africa, the shining car, a great erotic escape fantasy. He had lain in his bed on humid summer afternoons aroused, thinking about her, but he had been too shy to approach her. In high school, he had taken out a girl once or twice just to show that he could, but nothing ever came of it. In Algeria, when a friend took him to a whorehouse and it could not have been easier, he could not go through with it: Nine dinar bought a woman there, but the women, some French, some Algerian, were fat and middle-aged. They sat in a big room on low Moroccan settees, pink and green light bulbs in the lamps behind them, and hoisted their dirty gowns up to their hips, showing fat thighs with varicose veins. Seeing a nervous boy from the old ruling class in the company of older Algerian men amused them. They toyed aggressively with Bernard.

"Tu vas venir avec moi?" they'd asked, jiggling a fat leg.

Bernard found them repulsive. But sex, he often found himself thinking, was a dirty game. You could not get away from it in a boys' school. At night in the dormitory, the prefects patrolled the floors and the bathrooms, suspicious and knowing. At confession, all the priests asked the same questions: "Did you touch yourself? Did you touch another boy?" Bernard always said yes, even though he had not, because he had done it in his mind.

At sixteen Bernard meets a young man we shall call François. He is one year younger, but in Bernard's mind a far greater social success. He is one of the best soccer players at school. He always has a girl. He is tall and slim, and when Bernard sees him on the soccer field in his tight white shorts he finds himself looking at François' strong legs and firm, muscular ass. Bernard is good-looking too. Five feet nine inches tall, he has clear skin and a muscular body with a swimmer's broad shoulders and small waist. Bernard does not, however, consider himself handsome. He considers himself short. He also thinks he is stupid about sex. François has a magazine collection of naked women. He has kissed the prettiest girls in school. He brags of having made love to an older woman of thirty-five.

One day François shows Bernard some of his magazines. A few days later, they go to a deserted movie theater. The exit is unlocked, the theater is dark and full of spiders. François shows Bernard some pictures of naked girls and when Bernard is hard François turns his back to him and they have sex.

It is not difficult. François is supple, accommodating, and it seems to Bernard he has had experience—he comes to this meeting with toilet paper in his pocket. The act itself, however, Bernard finds disappointing. Maybe it is like your first whiskey, he thinks; it takes a while for it to be good. Or maybe it is that afterward, Bernard is disgusted.

"Did you touch yourself? Did you touch another boy?"

Now he has, and if anybody knew it would be awful.

And yet he does it again. Maybe once a month, sometimes with François, sometimes with other boys. There is something exciting about it, and despite the guilt afterward, he starts to enjoy the act. He is particular in his tastes, too: a boy must be good-looking, muscular, and slim, with a nicely designed penis. Bernard never kisses his partners. Kissing is between men and women; he cannot do it with a boy. The truth is, he knows he should be doing nothing with boys. He feels so strongly about it that when he turns eighteen, he makes a promise to himself: He will stop sleeping with boys; it is a schoolboy's game. He will stop masturbating, too.

Coming to China, Bernard tries to keep that promise. But he is desperate to lose his virginity, he wants very much to have a steady girl, and he is finding it difficult even to get a date. He may tell the students he tries to pick up after church that he is a diplomat, but he is merely a contract worker, hired for a thirty-month period, and the girls can recognize a clerk. The more they look down at him the more he exaggerates, and that makes it even worse.

"I boasted a lot about my work and I regret it," he writes in his diary, in early November, after an evening with two French girls.

And of the outing: "I think Roselyn finds me attractive but it's Catherine I desire."

It is the old problem of the romantic: The one you can have does not interest you, the one you cannot have, you must. Bernard does not give up easily, either. A week later he is speaking of "this Catherine who haunts me, who tomorrow I will try to have."

When Catherine rejects him, he takes out Roselyn, "who can feel the passion."

Bernard never makes love to either girl. He tells himself it is because he does not care to: The girls do not offer sufficient challenge to interest him. There has to be some obstacle, some difficulty, for real love. Also, there is something very ordinary about these girls.

In the French community, meanwhile, the girls give Bernard Boursicot a nickname.

"*Bourricot*," they call him, "the donkey."

2

I n winter in France there are diversions for the loneliest man. When it is too chilly and damp for the parks, one can go to the movies, or browse in a bookstore, or sit for hours in a café. Bernard, as the temperature dips into the twenties and a cold wind blows the yellow dust of the Gobi across Beijing, is without those comforts. Moved from the Beijing Hotel to a small apartment in the diplomatic district, unable to kill time in the streets and parks, he feels particularly alone. The Chinese rush past him bundled up in padded blue cotton overcoats, with surgical masks to protect their faces from the biting wind, as if he is an invisible man. The French, denied their walks and picnics, throw more cocktail and dinner parties, and Bernard, even when he is invited, finds himself feeling like the odd man out. He is, in a sense, a double outcast: cut off from the Chinese, a misfit among the French.

He's tired of China, he decides. The diplomats are nothing more than pretentious civil servants, saving for retirement. He shouldn't be here. He should be where he wanted to be when he got this appointment.

For the truth is, Bernard has another secret. He has, over the years, been in correspondence with the French explorer Fernand Fournier-Aubry, whom he read about as a boy of sixteen in a magazine piece called "Adventure Is My Job."

"There's no resisting the winds of adventure" is Fournier-Aubry's philosophy. "When it blows I feel it and I obey. As far as possible, I try not to think and simply follow my instincts."

He has been a forester in Gabon and the Amazon, a shark hunter in the Pacific, and has traveled in Afghanistan with opium thieves. His life, if you can believe it—and Bernard does—sounds like something out of a boy's adventure story: When he was a young man in Africa, he claims, he was so beloved by a tribe that the witch doctor asked him to permit the women to come to his bed so they might have his children. When he saw another European mistreating his African workers, he beat the man with his whip. His style was marvelous, too. Returning to France from Gabon with his first fortune, he bought a cream-colored Hispano-Suiza and ordered a suit to match. Even the name he used was fantastic: Capitaine Tropic.

Most boys, reading about such a man, would have done nothing. Bernard had written Fournier-Aubry telling him how much he admired him and later made four pilgrimages to his family home in Monte Carlo. At eighteen, Bernard even managed a fleeting meeting with his hero, who was back in France after traveling in the Amazon. Bernard longed to join him. His trip to the Foreign Affairs office in Paris, before coming to China, had really been to see if there might be an opening in the embassy in Brazil, so that he could get from there to Fournier-Aubry. When he learned there were no openings in Brazil, he grabbed the most exotic available spot: China.

Now Bernard writes Fournier-Aubry again.

"If you need me, I am ready, you only have to call," he says, making a point of saying he is now at the embassy of France in Beijing, where he suggests life is grand.

His true feelings are recorded in his diary.

"What am I doing tolerating this empty life?" he writes in early December.

And later, "Will take a bath and look at this unused body."

But such is the round of parties in Beijing in late December that the most melancholy accountant cannot remain at home. The British invite the French to a Christmas party with Scottish dancing. The French are not surprised: Just like the British, they say, to invite them and then try to flummox them with that Scottish business. Well, *they* will deal with that: The Quilichinis find someone who knows the absurd dance and they throw a pre-party party so the French can learn it. Bernard feels like an idiot trying to master it, first holding up the left foot, then the right, and feeling twice his bulk. The forced intimacy also puts him off. Why put your hand on the shoulder of someone you don't know or like as if you are buddies? It does not reflect the nature of human trust, particularly among diplomats.

"I'm the worst," Bernard writes in his diary.

Nonetheless he goes to the British party. And it is not so bad. He meets a blond British secretary who looks like Julie Christie, and he is pleased when she gives him her number. He has talked very little to the girl, but he is impressed by her looks and the number of people who surround her—it is a coup, he feels, to get the number of such a good-looking, popular girl.

Just before Christmas he is invited to another party, which *premier conseiller* Claude Chayet is throwing for the French students at his home. Bernard takes the British secretary. He feels good arriving with a beautiful girl on his arm, and he is excited to be at the Chayets' Chinese house: the courtyards and spirit walls make an evening special.

It's a terrific party. There is music and people are dancing. Bernard feels awkward with the British girl, but he takes her coat when they arrive and goes off to fetch her a drink—if he has learned anything in diplomatic life it is to make sure the lady has a drink. When he comes back, the lady is happily amusing herself on the dance floor.

Bernard is not that eager to dance.

But then he does see something that interests him: a Chinese guest —the only one Bernard has ever seen at a private party. He is a slightly built man in his mid-twenties, wearing a Mao suit, and is quite short, really no taller than a girl. His French is fluent and he is the center of attention, yet there is something about him that seems tentative and shy. Bernard also sees, among his colleagues, a solicitousness that is markedly out of character.

"May we get you a drink, Monsieur Shi?" "May we get you something to eat?"

Bernard is curious. He waits a bit, then walks over.

"Why aren't you dancing?" he asks. "There are a lot of beautiful girls here."

"I don't really like it so much," the young man says and turns away.

Bernard goes to the dance floor. His date is chatting with some other young men; she has perhaps the same utilitarian view of Bernard that he has of her. He doesn't really care. There are other girls with whom to dance. But his mind is still on the Chinese man. Fifteen minutes later, he returns to him.

"It isn't difficult, dancing," he says. "You should try it."

"My health," the man says. "It won't permit it."

They introduce themselves: Bernard Boursicot, Shi Pei Pu. Pei Pu tells Bernard he is a member of the Beijing Writers' Association and that he is a writer of operas and plays. He also teaches Chinese to François, the vivacious tutor of the Chayet children, who has invited him to this party, and to Mme. Eliane Richard, wife of Robert Richard, the commercial councillor. Bernard is impressed. Robert Richard had organized a commercial exposition between France and Beijing in 1964, before diplomatic relations had been established, and is considered responsible for the most successful aspect of Franco-Chinese relations: trade. Mme. Richard, in Bernard's opinion, considers herself even grander than the wife of the ambassador. Bernard doubts she even knows his name. That this man is Mme. Richard's private tutor is something. Also, Bernard has never met a writer.

Bernard has a Chinese teacher, but this doesn't stop him from making a suggestion now.

"Well, if you are a Chinese teacher, maybe you could teach me," he says.

"Perhaps," says M. Shi, going off.

Not good enough. The party is breaking up. Bernard, looking across the room, sees Pei Pu writing down his address and phone number for one of the French students. He walks over and snatches it out of the student's hands.

"This must be for me," he says.

The young man and Pei Pu are speechless. Pei Pu writes his name and address for the young man again. Then he goes into the street, where a *pousse-pousse* is waiting.

Bernard follows him.

"Remember, I want to see you," he says. "I will call!"

· · ·

Bernard doesn't call the next day, though he wants to. He waits three days, playing it cool, then phones Pei Pu. They arrange to have dinner. It is the week before Christmas and there is little work to do. Bernard puts in an appearance at the embassy in the morning, but in the afternoon goes skating on the great lake in Beihai Park. Skating by the British chargé d'affaires, he falls and hurts his wrist. Worse, he feels like an idiot—why does he always have to fall on his ass in front of high-ranking men? By the time he meets Pei Pu in the Covered Market, a street of small antique shops and dusty bookshops unchanged by the revolution, his wrist is swollen. The restaurant Pei Pu has chosen cheers him. It's on a little street, up one flight of stairs, and there are no other Europeans. The waiters look like Buddhas in white Mao jackets; the food is delicate and delicious. Pei Pu is treated with great respect.

"I came here," Pei Pu says, "with Mei Lanfang."

Bernard says nothing. *Il faut tourner sa langue sept fois dans sa bouche avant de parler.*

Mei Lanfang, the greatest actor in China, says Pei Pu. When he died four years ago, there was a national day of mourning. Mei performed Beijing Opera and was Pei Pu's teacher—before he had become a playwright, Pei Pu says, he had been an actor and singer. At seventeen he had even enjoyed some fame. He and Mei had eaten in this restaurant often in 1959 and 1960 during the great famine. A bag of rice, then, says Pei Pu, was more valuable than gold; he was always glad to be invited to eat with Mei because it left more food for his mother at home. Now he is twenty-six and no longer performs. He writes plays about the workers. His tone suggests that the workers are not a subject of very great interest to him.

Pei Pu speaks a bit of his growing up in Kunming, the capital of the southern province of Yunnan, north of Vietnam. He has, Bernard gathers, a very cultivated family. Pei Pu's father, who is dead, was a professor; his mother, who lives with him now in Beijing, was a teacher. Pei Pu has two older sisters; one is married to a famous painter, the other was a table tennis champion. He has an uncle, Ting Hsi Ling, who is a cultural vice-minister and who has traveled abroad. Pei Pu as a boy had a bicultural education: He was taught by French missionaries, which is how he learned the language. Later he received a degree in literature from the University of Kunming.

Then Pei Pu notices Bernard's swollen hand. He stops his stories and insists they go at once to a hospital. The waiting room is crowded, but the staff, spotting a foreigner, quickly moves Bernard to his own room to wait: One cannot be a foreigner in China and expect to be treated like everyone else. Even so, it takes a long time to see a doctor. The injury turns out to be only a sprain, but Bernard is moved by Pei Pu's concern. Except for his mother, no one has ever taken care of him.

The holidays come. There is a sit-down dinner at the home of one high-ranking diplomat on Christmas, a black-tie party at the home of Ambassador Paye on New Year's Eve.

"According to the young ladies, you're the best dressed of the twenty- to thirty-year-olds," Augustin Quilichini tells Bernard, but he is not convinced. He makes a point at midnight of wishing all the gentlemen a happy new year and kissing all the ladies, which he knows is the correct thing to do, but privately he is glum.

"Many *faux pas* for me," he writes in his diary.

But with Pei Pu, he feels relaxed—perhaps because Pei Pu is kind to him. Bernard makes no entries in his journal of their first meeting in December, but by January he mentions meeting Pei Pu two or three times a week. Pei Pu shows him restaurants and parks and shops unknown to other foreigners. He teaches him about paintings and ceramics and encourages him to buy. He tells stories of the emperors and of palace intrigues: His family, he suggests, was related to the Last Emperor.

It would seem, with Bernard's history, that there must be, in this friendship with an exceedingly delicate man, a sexual undercurrent, but Bernard denies it—those days are over, he says and were they not, this delicate little man would hardly be his type. Nor are there indications in Bernard's diary of a sexual attraction to Pei Pu. Unlike his meetings with the French girls, Bernard's entries regarding Pei Pu are limited to the barest facts, and for such an important friendship they are surprisingly brief:

"Meet Shi Pei Pu three o'clock; go to the Temple of Heaven, then a restaurant, then to the movie *Spring in February* . . ."

"Wait for Shi Pei Pu at a place where they sell milk and brioche. We visit an art gallery and do a tour of the Forbidden City."

"Rendezvous with Shi Pei Pu."

A sexual attraction? It never crosses his mind, says Bernard: It is Pei Pu's stories that make him so interesting, and the marvelous way he tells a tale: He speaks slowly, in a whispery, almost breathless voice, as if what he is saying holds some wonder for him too. When he speaks of his lonely childhood—for his sisters were much older than he—it sounds like a poem.

"I took for my friends the birds and the trees and the moon and the stars," he says.

He elevates the ordinary to the marvelous. They go to a restaurant and Pei Pu tells Bernard the cook served in the palace of the Last Emperor. They go walking on Coal Hill, the park north of the Imperial Palace, and Pei Pu shows Bernard the locust tree from which the last Ming Emperor, Chong Zhen, hanged himself in 1644 after enemy troops entered the city and his own eunuchs turned on him and prevented him from fleeing the palace grounds. He also tells Bernard of his life in the Beijing Opera, where actors and actresses often portrayed the opposite sex on stage. His teacher Mei Lanfang was the finest of all the female impersonators, Pei Pu says. Pei Pu himself, at sixteen, played a woman's role in *The White Snake,* the story of an immortal white snake who comes to earth in the form of a beautiful girl and falls in love with a mortal man. He sang the role so well that afterward a man came to see him from the audience.

"Oh, what a golden voice you have," he said.

The man, says Pei Pu, was Mei Lanfang. Pei Pu became a favorite pupil, traveling with him, accepted as a member of his family. Two of Mei's children were actors. His son played women on the stage, while his daughter portrayed men. Both are now famous. But Beijing Opera, with its tales of lovelorn aristocrats and cunning demons, is out of favor. Only last summer, at the government's Beijing Opera Festival on Contemporary Revolutionary Themes, Beijing mayor Peng Zhen said that Beijing Opera "prettified the exploiting classes and uglified the working people." Now theater is to extol the workers. Mao's wife, Mme. Jiang Qing, who had been an actress in the 1920s, is overseeing the creation of new works and Pei Pu says he has updated some pieces.

Bernard once attended a Beijing Opera performance and he could not bear it. The music is piercing, atonal, and monotonous. There is no scenery. Everything is dependent on symbolism and the actor's skill. "Small as the stage is, a few steps will bring you far beyond heaven," the actors' adage says: With a few gestures one can create a universe, but you must understand the code. An actor raising a foot symbolizes that he is entering a house. Walking in a circle means undertaking a long journey. The movement of a sleeve signifies remorse. Occasionally props are used, but they have their own language as well. That actor is a general, someone explains to Bernard, that one the enemy; you can see the difference in the masks. Bernard sees no difference at all. Now the horse jumps in a stream; you can tell because there is the word "water" on a sign. It drives Bernard crazy, and among Westerners he is not alone, for Beijing Opera requires a complicity between audience and performers far more demanding than the Western stage. Assistants carry props on- and offstage during a performance, dressed in black to signify that they are invisible. The Chinese do not see them because they are not supposed to see them, but the Europeans do and are distressed.

"How long is Beijing Opera?" someone asks Bernard.

"Too long," he says, and when Pei Pu invites him to one he has cowritten, Bernard does not go.

Bernard is not Pei Pu's only French friend. Pei Pu visits regularly with M. and Mme. Richard at the Beijing Hotel. He takes the Chayets on a visit to the Ming tombs at midnight—during which a soldier, seeing a foreigner with a Chinese, stops the car. He enjoys spending time with tutors François and Françoise, and Françoise also studies Chinese with him. Bernard himself introduces Pei Pu to his friend Komaroff. Komaroff is impressed and somewhat curious about this friendship. He works closely with the Chinese as a translator and never sees them socially.

But it seems to Bernard that he and Pei Pu are best friends, telling each other things they reveal to no else. And yet sometimes Pei Pu turns abruptly silent. He tells Bernard that when he was a famous young actor women pursued him, but that he had nothing to do with them. When Bernard asks why, Pei Pu becomes irritable.

"You cannot understand," Bernard remembers him saying. "You couldn't possibly."

He says friendship between a Chinese and a foreigner is doomed. He frets often about his health; he cancels dinners on short notice claiming fatigue; he tires easily on walks.

Even something that should be cause for fun—the arrival from Hong Kong of Bernard's new bicycle, a light, smooth piece of equipment compared to the bikes in Beijing—Pei Pu views fearfully.

"C'mon, try it," Bernard says.

"I don't ride bicycles," says Pei Pu. "But when you leave, I will buy it from you."

So Bernard at last has a friend—but he still hates embassy life. These people, he thinks, have no interest in China. All they do is complain about their servants and talk about the houses they will buy when they retire.

Nor are his employers entirely happy with him.

In the beginning of the year, Bernard falls behind in his accounting, and the normally easygoing ambassador is furious. He bursts into Bernard's office one Friday, knocking ledgers to the floor.

"This place is a mess," he says.

A high-ranking friend at the French Embassy warns Pei Pu about Bernard, and Pei Pu passes the comments along to Bernard.

"He's the lowest person in the embassy, a little accountant," Pei Pu tells Bernard she has been told.

"I have a very important job," Bernard says. "I pay the ambassador."

But inside, he hurts.

Even social events with Pei Pu seem to go badly. One evening the children's tutors, Françoise and François invite Bernard and Pei Pu over to the house—perhaps Pei Pu put them up to it, Bernard thinks, because he's sure the cultivated pair don't like him. They listen to French music and talk about Beijing Opera and then Pei Pu tells a story about one of his most famous roles: "The Shadow of the Willow," also known as "The Story of the Butterfly." He begins it just like a gentleman about to give a piano recital. A smile, a pause allowing for the audience to settle in and the pianist to hear his inner song, and then the music:

Long ago in China, Pei Pu says, there lived a beautiful and intelligent young lady named Zhu Yingtai. The daughter of a learned man, she wishes very much to attend one of the imperial schools that prepare students for national exams, but being a girl she is not permitted to do so. It troubles her, particularly because she has a brother who does very badly in school. She begins to dream.

"If only *I* were a boy," the girl thinks, "I could be number one."

She makes a plot with her brother: They exchange clothes and she goes off to school in his place, pretending to be a boy. Zhu Yingtai is a brilliant student. She also becomes close friends with a handsome boy, Liang Shanbo. They share a bed and come to love each other very much, though Liang Shanbo does not understand the strange feelings of attraction he feels for this boy. Zhu is very much attracted to Liang, too. She yearns to tell him her secret, but she is afraid of endangering her family. Then Zhu's family calls her home. They have found her a husband. Anguished, the girl returns to school and reveals her identity to her friend. Liang, though disturbed by the news, is relieved because he now understands his feelings for his schoolmate. He declares his love for her and asks her to marry him, but Zhu, though she loves him, cannot disobey her family.

"It is too late," she says.

She returns to her home. Distraught, Liang takes his life. Zhu's family tells her she must go on with the wedding. The girl agrees, but says she first must go to her beloved's grave. She sees now there is no way she can love another.

"My wedding dress will be my burial dress," she says, and beneath the willows shadowing Liang's grave, she throws herself on his tomb and dies.

Her family, finally understanding how much their daughter loved Liang, buries her beside him. The souls of the two lovers turn into butterflies and they fly away together to live in everlasting happiness. And as the willows under which Liang and Zhu are buried grow, the branches intertwine.

It is a wonderful story, wonderfully told. But Bernard, though he enjoys Pei Pu's stories when they are alone, this evening makes fun of the story and interrupts. He is not invited again.

Then in mid-March he gets the letter he has been dreaming of for four years: Capitaine Tropic invites him to join him on an expedition in the jungles of Brazil.

The address is unknown to Bernard: "Territorio ile Rondôniol, Brasil," the envelope and paper so light they are practically tissue.

"Your letter, after having made six trips around the world, has found me in a corner of the jungle of the Amazons, a vast region of woods and plantations," Capitaine Tropic writes. "If your intention is to be useful and live the great adventure, we are on the same wavelength."

Bernard can't believe it. And yet, now that escape *is* possible, he suddenly has doubts: His contract is not one-third finished. The government has brought him here at great expense. His boss Colombel, seeing him buckle down after the ambassador's reprimand, has told him if he applies himself he may have a career with the Foreign Service.

Bernard does not know what to do. He calls up Pei Pu and goes for a walk with him in the railroad station. It is a big marble station, but it is not busy; they are quite alone.

"I'm thinking I will resign," Bernard says.

Pei Pu, though he is supposed to be a friend, seems unable to think of this in terms of anything but their relationship.

"So," he says, as if the decision has been made and was inevitable. "I will not see you anymore. I am sad."

Bernard feels bad. But he has dreamed of adventure all his life, and if he does not accept this invitation, who knows if Fournier-Aubry will ask again? He resigns. Then, Pei Pu morosely accompanying him, he goes to the post office and wires Fournier-Aubry that as soon as the embassy finds a replacement, he will join him.

Bernard is a little blue himself. Is it only when one decides to leave a place that it becomes more pleasant? While he awaits word of a replacement at the embassy a raise comes through for Bernard, and in April he is told he will carry the diplomatic pouch on one of the twice-monthly trips to the consulate in Hong Kong. It sounds to Bernard like a vacation, not work: a special travel allowance, first-class hotels, and the famous nightlife of Hong Kong. Bernard knows exactly what he will do there. He will at last rid himself of his virginity.

"*Me réveille songeant* . . . ," he writes in his diary on April 30, the day before his departure. "I wake up daydreaming of the women I will find in Hong Kong."

It is an excellent trip. Bernard first flies to Canton. It is May Day, the big workers' holiday, and there are fireworks and celebrations. Ber-

nard wants to get out in the street and be part of it, but he is too serious
about his responsibility to leave the diplomatic pouch. He watches from
his hotel window. The next day he takes the train across the border to
Kowloon, on the Hong Kong peninsula, and then picks up the ferry to
Hong Kong island. He delivers the pouch to the French consulate.
Then he checks into the elegant Embassy Hotel in the financial district.
He has, he thinks, the best job in the world: five days of liberty, on
salary until the pouch from Paris arrives to be carried to Beijing.

   He goes out to buy condoms and find a girl. The second is not so
easy. He walks for two hours until, finding himself in a seedy strip near
the ferry station, he sees two pretty Chinese girls. He strikes up a
conversation, inviting them to the movies. Then he goes home and
changes his socks. In the evening, he meets the girls at the Princess
Cinema. The movie is *The Spy with My Face,* a spoof consisting of a few
episodes of *The Man from U.N.C.L.E.,* an American television series.
Bernard has no interest in it at all. He concentrates on the prettier girl,
trying to decide how much time should elapse before he takes her hand.
When he does, she takes it away and her friend gives him a dirty look.
Afterward, the girls do not speak to him. They just hail a taxi and
leave. Bernard goes back to the hotel dejected. A boy, he notes in his
diary, follows him back. A week later Bernard is back in Beijing. The
highlight of his stay in the capitalist center of vice will have been
making friends with another Frenchman, a twenty-six-year-old student
named Daniel who is traveling around the world, and going with him to
see *My Fair Lady.*

Pei Pu, when Bernard returns, is moodier than ever. There is a nice
interlude when Bernard's new friend Daniel visits Beijing for ten days.
Daniel is a quiet, intellectual young man who is making his tour on an
educational grant. There is, Bernard feels, something very decent about
him—something that makes him sensitive to people who need help. Pei
Pu likes Daniel, too. He shows him the city and takes him to the zoo,
and Daniel, who wants to be a writer himself, is fascinated by this
Chinese librettist. Still, something is troubling Pei Pu. Bernard sees it
one evening when they are in Beihai Park, rowing on the North Lake. It
is one of the prettiest spots in Beijing; there is an island on the lake with
a white Tibetan pagoda. The park was once the site of Kubla Khan's

palace, and lovers sit on the benches about the lake. With the long days of summer, the park is open late. But as Bernard rows with Pei Pu, telling him about his trip to Hong Kong, Pei Pu seems nervous. He also, says Bernard, does something that makes Bernard feel very odd: He puts his hand on Bernard's and tells him that he is his "nice friend." Bernard wants to move his hand, but he does not. Perhaps sensing his discomfort, Pei Pu removes his hand and goes back to what is becoming a familiar litany:

"You are my friend, but you do not understand China, you don't understand me. When you leave, I will lose my best friend."

It has the ring of lovesickness, but Bernard does not see this. He is busy looking elsewhere for love—he is, after Hong Kong, even more anxious to find a girl.

In May, he gets his chance. As he walks along Changan Avenue, a young Chinese man comes up to him and flashes a picture of a pretty girl. Officially prostitution may have been wiped out, but it is clear she is being offered. At eleven that night, Bernard returns. The young man gestures to him to sit on the handlebars of his heavy bicycle. They drive through narrow streets to a small shack. Inside, the lights are dim. The man walks to a bed and pulls down the blanket. A girl, in her underwear, is lying there. The man leaves. Bernard approaches the girl. She is his age and frightened. He moves his hand gently over her arms, trying to soothe her, and when he does, his hands come up against a knife. She is clutching it in one hand, half hidden beneath her hip. Bernard runs outside. The man seems to be nervous now, too—he must be an amateur, Bernard thinks; he is more worried about getting Bernard away from his neighborhood than collecting a fee. He drives Bernard back to the center of Beijing, pedaling frantically. Bernard gives him thirty yuan —the equivalent, he later learns, of three weeks' salary.

The next day, Bernard tells Pei Pu.

"You must not do this," Pei Pu says. "It is very dangerous in China."

Soon afterward, Pei Pu invites Bernard to his home for the first time. It is understood by both that the visit is not something the government would approve. To Bernard, this makes it particularly exciting. Pei Pu takes some precautions. He tells Bernard to wait for him at the eastern gate of the Forbidden City in early evening when there will be fewer people. From there, they walk a few blocks east, to Nanchezi, a long, narrow street of courtyard houses with deep red gates. Tree-lined streets are rare in Beijing, but Nanchezi is so narrow and lush that the trees form a dappled green canopy. At Number 25, Pei Pu stops and takes Bernard through three circular gates, to a paved courtyard. There are three little houses around the courtyard. Pei Pu's mother lives in one, Pei Pu in another. Pei Pu's home is clean and spare. To the left of the entranceway is a little bedroom with a canopy bed with mosquito netting; to the right are a writing table and chairs and a stove. Incense burns and the lighting is low. A bulb shines through a red lamp shade, tinting the room blood amber, deep and unnatural. Bernard has the feeling of having entered a temple. Pei Pu disappears and a few moments later returns with his mother, a diminutive, gray-haired woman in her sixties.

"*Ni hao,*" she says. "How do you do?"

She stays only long enough to serve tea. Pei Pu seems concerned about Bernard's presence, so he stays just a short time. But he is excited. Some people spend years in China and are never invited into a private home.

A few days later, Bernard invites Pei Pu to dinner at a restaurant. Bernard does not tell Pei Pu there will be another, but he arrives with a strikingly beautiful French-Vietnamese girl he has met at an embassy party. Bernard has no plans of seduction. He could never succeed with such a girl, he feels. When Pei Pu arrives and sees the girl, he is at once irritable. He finds fault with the food, he finds fault with the service; his mood does not improve until they put the girl on the bus.

Bernard keeps talking about her as if he doesn't notice his friend is jealous.

"But don't you find her beautiful?" he says.

The following week Pei Pu and Bernard go walking near the entrance to the Forbidden City in one of their favorite places, a courtyard beyond the main gate where five marble bridges arch across the Golden Water Stream. It is a beautiful evening, mild and not yet dark—the tiles of the Forbidden City are moon gold. It is a night when one feels close to emperors and legends, when one can remember the boy emperor Pu Yi, kept prisoner in his own palace; when it is possible to think of spirits like the White Snake goddess who come to earth to make mischief in human form. It is a perfect setting for one of the old stories, and as they stand on the bridge Pei Pu again tells Bernard the story of the Butterfly: the young girl who dresses as a boy; the boy who falls in love with her not knowing her secret. He played that role on the stage, Pei Pu reminds Bernard; it was one of his favorites.

Then, as Bernard remembers, Pei Pu holds up his little hands:

"Look at my hands," he says to Bernard. "Look at my face. That story of the Butterfly, it is my story, too."

And then, in the shadow of the Forbidden Palace, as Bernard recalls it, Pei Pu tells another story: Pei Pu's mother, as Bernard knows, had two daughters before Pei Pu was born but there were no sons. Sons are far more important than daughters in a Chinese home. With the birth of a third child imminent, Pei Pu's paternal grandmother, who ruled the household, made a decree: If Pei Pu's mother did not at last provide the family with a boy, Pei Pu's father would have to take a second wife. Pei Pu's mother was terrified. She did not want to lose her position in the household to another wife. Pei Pu's father was upset also—his wife was his one great love; he could not bear to see her unhappy. And then Pei Pu's mother gave birth to Pei Pu. And Pei Pu was a girl baby, yes, a girl. So Pei Pu's mother and father and the midwife made a pact: They agreed to lie to the grandmother and raise Pei Pu as a boy. So it was. Pei Pu had lived disguised as a man, struggling to be something against nature, telling no one the secret. It was far too dangerous, in modern China, where men and women were supposed to be equals, to admit that one had given in to an old, feudal sense of values. But now, Pei Pu is telling Bernard. In doing so, Pei Pu is trusting Bernard with her life.

It is an incredible story—and yet Bernard accepts it as if there is no adjustment to be made, no space to bridge, in learning that your best buddy is a girl. He is surprised and yet he is not. It is as if somehow all along he has known this. The strongest feeling he has is one of compassion.

"You are my best friend. I will tell nobody," he says.

But later, as he goes home in a *pousse-pousse* through the side streets on the hour-long trip to Sanlitun, the full impact of the story hits him. The familiar streets under the moon seem like a stage-set in a black-and-white movie. Everything has changed.

Pei Pu is no longer a friend; he is a woman and nobody else can see it, and now it is another romance Bernard will have with this person. Pei Pu trusts him so much, he—no, *she*—has told him and him alone her story. As Pei Pu is a woman, Bernard must save him—no, *her*—and deliver her from China. He must care for her and protect her and later on must do everything to help her restore her personality. He must make her a woman again, even if it is necessary to marry.

This delayed reaction is volcanic.

"Revelation!" is the one word Bernard writes that night in his diary.

A few days later Bernard starts thinking about making love to Pei Pu. He does not feel a great passion; it is rather something he feels he and Pei Pu have to do: You are a woman, I am a man, we love one another, therefore we should have sex. It is almost like a clause in a contract.

"If you are a woman, we should sleep together," he says.

Pei Pu does not say yes, but she does not say no either.

"Not now," Bernard remembers her saying.

"Whenever you think it is possible," he says.

They set the date, finally, for the eleventh of June, at Bernard's apartment. Bernard can think about nothing else for days. The day of the rendezvous, he counts hours. Pei Pu arrives at his apartment at six o'clock.

She is not dressed for an evening of love, in soft, pretty, feminine things—how can she be? She is dressed like a young man, wearing a leather jacket and a Mao suit; she wears her secret story, thinks Bernard. Moved, he goes to her and kisses her on the neck, gently. Then he starts to undress her.

"Let me do it," she says, taking her clothes off, down to her underpants.

Naked, Pei Pu has tiny little breasts and is indeed rather plump. Bernard's touch seems to frighten her. He is somewhat nervous, too. He goes into the bathroom and puts on one of the condoms he bought in Hong Kong; he comes back to Pei Pu and lies down with her and starts to caress her.

Pei Pu catches his hand.

"Let me do it," Pei Pu says, guiding him.

It is over quickly and Bernard has to admit to himself that this first time with a woman is not so erotic as it had been with boys—perhaps because all the planning had made them tense, perhaps because he was so worried about Pei Pu. He goes into the bathroom to get rid of the condom and when he comes out he finds Pei Pu in her underwear with blood on her leg. He feels terrible that he has hurt her.

"My poor friend," he says, taking her in his arms. "My wife."

3

The movies are right about love—it changes everything. Bernard, except for some odd, inexplicable feelings of tension which once or twice come over him shortly after the affair is begun, feels wonderful. He is lover and hero and savior. Pei Pu adores him. Even the Foreign Service seems to be aiding love: The staff is put on a summer schedule and Bernard has to work only two afternoons a week. The rest of the time he is with Pei Pu. He is even more careful, now, to hide their love affair. He hires a *pousse-pousse* to the Forbidden City, so no one will know his true destination, then walks two or three blocks to Pei Pu's house. When he arrives, he kisses Pei Pu the way a man kisses his wife when he returns home, though not when her mother is there—the Chinese, Bernard feels, are prudish. Pei Pu's mother does not speak French and Bernard still cannot understand much Chinese, so Pei Pu translates. Mme. Shi dotes on Pei Pu. She does all the cooking and cleaning. Pei Pu, in turn, says her mother is her closest friend. If the word "comrade" as used by the government reflected the feelings that Pei Pu and her mother have for one another, it would be a very fine thing, Pei Pu says. After lunch, Pei Pu's mother leaves, and Pei Pu and Bernard make love under the mosquito netting on Pei Pu's canopied bed. The sex is not entirely satisfying to Bernard. It is hurried, and Pei Pu often seems to prefer to be at least partially dressed. Oriental modesty, Bernard assumes, and the more universal fear that her mother might walk into the room. Pei Pu does not allow Bernard to caress her as fully as he would like, either, and she likes to be in control.

"Let *me*," she always says.

It does not matter that much to Bernard; it is his love for Pei Pu, his knowledge of her secret, that binds them. When the lovemaking is over they sit for hours and talk. They like the same kind of stories. Pei Pu's education by French nuns has given her a knowledge of Hugo and Balzac and de Maupassant. Despite the growing government restrictions on what constitutes appropriate entertainment, Pei Pu has been exposed to foreign movies. A few years earlier, her boss at the Beijing Writers' Association had screened some American movies to help his people with screenwriting. Bette Davis starred in some. Ignore the content, study the structure, the boss said, for the movies of course reflected a decadent capitalist system. Pei Pu could not ignore the content. She was mesmerized by Bette Davis: those eyes, that haughty style, that way she swept across a room. Her favorite movie is *The Old Maid*, in which Bette Davis plays an unmarried woman in America who has a child by a soldier. When the soldier is killed, Bette Davis gives the child to her cousin so that it will not be marked by scandal. The child does not know Bette Davis is her mother and regards her with contempt. It makes Pei Pu cry. What greater pain can there be for a mother than to be unable to reveal herself to her own child? Bernard's favorite is *Jules and Jim*, the tragic story of a woman and the two friends who love her. Bernard cannot stop talking about it. Are there love affairs so powerful that they can only end in death? Is whom we love a question of fate? He has bought a tape recorder in Hong Kong, and he and Pei Pu often listen to Jeanne Moreau singing the film's lilting, bittersweet love songs. Back in France, British rock singer Petula Clark has a hit with "Downtown" and Bob Dylan has made the charts with "It's All Over Now, Baby Blue." In Beijing, at student parties, they're dancing to the Beatles and the Rolling Stones. Bernard does not care for rock music and he despises folk. He likes torch songs. He likes melancholy, sophisticated, cigarette-after-sex songs: the smoky voices of Juliette Greco and Edith Piaf; the dusky, sad tenor of Léo Ferré singing "Paname," his love song to Paris. If Bernard and Pei Pu have a song, it is that: of

walking along the banks of the Seine among the chestnut trees, of
beauty that gives flight to tedium and melancholy.

> *"Paname*
> *Quand tu t'ennuies tu fais les quais*
> *Tu fais la Seine et les noyés*
> *Ça fait prend l'air et ça distrait."*

They speak, as they lie in bed, about marriage. Bernard says he will
go to his ambassador and ask him to help. Pei Pu tells him not to go, he
recalls. It is too soon to reveal her true nature. There could be a scandal.
It might even be politically dangerous.

But she does allow herself to dream with Bernard. She talks about
the day the two of them will go to Paris: They will walk through the
Luxembourg Gardens; they will visit the Louvre; they will go to the
Paris Opéra.

"I will be a normal woman then," Pei Pu says. "And you will be
proud of me, because I am not so ugly."

She loves French things. One of the diplomats has given her a
bottle of Chanel Pour Monsieur, and she keeps it in the middle of her
bureau, unopened—like a little Buddha, thinks Bernard. Then he feels
bad for making fun of her. Of course she loves perfume; she has never
been able to indulge herself in feminine things. He wants to make it up
to her. Pei Pu will not let him buy her pretty lingerie, but Bernard goes
to the Friendship Store, which is open only to foreigners, and brings
back other gifts: duck, pork, great containers of cooking oil, so that her
mother will not have to stand in line—Pei Pu herself never shops. He
has the floor painted lacquer red.

So sweet, these hot, dry Beijing afternoons—while the diplomats
brag about acquiring this painting or visiting that temple, Bernard
knows the greatest treasure is his. He is a member of a Chinese household; he is involved in a love story of a dimension that no one at the
embassy will ever know. The secrecy is pleasant, too. Not all secrets tax
the soul; some carry with them a not unpleasant feeling of power and
control.

And yet for Pei Pu, Bernard is learning, the secrecy is a terrible
thing. Pei Pu never drinks tea when she is away from home, she tells

Bernard, because she might be forced to use a public bathroom. When she worked as an actor, she could not share a room. She has taken hormones in an attempt to change her appearance, and she fears she has injured her health and is now perhaps not quite like other girls. Nor can she participate in sports. If Bernard goes swimming, in a secluded canal Pei Pu finds for him, Pei Pu sits on the bank.

"I would like to do these things you do," she says, "but I cannot."

Her life, Bernard now sees, is a charade. Pei Pu plucks her hairline, making it look as if she is balding, because an uncle once said she had hair like a girl's. She puts a handkerchief in the front of her trousers to suggest a penis—Bernard often notices it when they make love. She worries that other people will notice the feminine curve of her spine or her little breasts, so that Bernard, when they go walking, begins to worry, too.

"Can't you stand up straighter?" he scolds. "Walk like a man."

Then he feels bad.

"I do want to marry you," he says. "You know that."

Bernard never, he says, doubts her nor does he fear that anyone in the French community knows they are close.

But there is one thing that bothers him—at least three people mention to Bernard that they believe Pei Pu is a homosexual. One is another member of the French Community who has been invited to Pei Pu's home.

"I don't like these kinds of people myself," Bernard recalls him saying one evening, giving him a lift back to the diplomatic compounds on his motorcycle, "but it is very common in the theater."

Bernard says nothing. He hates any reference to homosexuality; it reminds him of what he did as a schoolboy, and if people think his friend is a homosexual they may think he is one too.

Nor does he feel there is any basis to the man's theory. The reason Pei Pu seems feminine, Bernard knows, is that Pei Pu *is* feminine. But he is sworn to secrecy; he cannot tell.

His friend Komaroff has told Bernard the same thing.

"Your friend Pei Pu is a pederast," he says.

"He's not," Bernard says. "He just seems that way."

Later, he repeats the story to Pei Pu.

"People don't know the story of my life," Bernard recalls Pei Pu saying calmly, but after that her relationship with Komaroff cools.

It is not always a perfect love affair. Pei Pu is still sometimes moody and difficult, but now Bernard knows why: He sometimes sees the bloodied rag in the bucket.

"It's your period, right?" he asks.

Pei Pu is embarrassed then.

"Oh," Pei Pu says. "You saw."

They are now a bit more relaxed with one another, Bernard says. Pei Pu is nude more often. Bernard no longer wears condoms when they make love, because they are uncomfortable, and when one loves, one must love fully, without barriers. Anyway, he knows nothing can go wrong.

It is frankly making him feel good, this double life. Tell the people at the embassy he is going swimming, then spend the afternoon with Pei Pu; in the evenings, go over to the International Club and talk politics. Pei Pu seems to know a lot about powerful people and it amuses Bernard—what was it one of the higher-ups called him, "the lowest-ranking member of the embassy"?—to drop, say, the news that Premier Zhou Enlai would *not* be attending a reception at the Guinean embassy, information the Guinean officials would not know.

"Diplomats," he says often, at embassy cocktails. "I know more about China than the diplomats."

Juggling two lives is fun. When his twenty-first birthday arrives, on August 12, and friends at the embassy ask him to dinner, he accepts with pleasure. Then he goes to Pei Pu's where there is another feast with his second, hidden family.

But of course, it does not always work out so smoothly. A week later, when the weather turns very hot, Bernard books a reservation through the official China Travel Agency at the Yellow Sea resort of Beidaihe, on the easternmost shore of northern China. Pei Pu cannot go but she comes to the railroad station to see Bernard off.

"Kiss me," Pei Pu says, "and I will tell you something very important. I don't know if you will accept it or not. It is difficult and our lives are going to change. It is dangerous also. I think there is something in my belly."

Bernard does not know what to say. He loves Pei Pu, but despite what he has told her he is not ready to marry.

"We'll see about this when I come back," he says.

Beidaihe, a five-hour train ride away, is luxurious for Maoist China. Created by homesick Europeans in the 1880s and modeled after the seaside resorts of Brighton and Deauville, it is now a resort for high-ranking government officials and foreigners. Villas with wide Victorian verandas, as well as dozens and dozens of small cottages, nestle among the sand dunes and pine trees. At West Beach, the area set aside for foreigners, there are three fine restaurants, including a branch of Vienna's famous old Kiessling & Baader café. Bernard, preoccupied with Pei Pu, is for once not interested in exploring. He heads out to the beach to think.

He notices her at once: a slim, pretty French girl with long brown hair and an air of privilege. It is a conspicuous mark, privilege: a lifetime habit of speaking one's mind without concern, an air of confidence that can border on rudeness. Sylvie, at twenty, has every reason to feel special in this community. Her father was a boyhood friend of Ambassador Paye's; a cousin is the wife of the Moroccan ambassador to Beijing; Sylvie is living with them at the embassy as tutor to their children. She attends dinner parties and embassy functions to which Bernard is not invited. More than a few French diplomats are curious about the fact that on some occasions the cultivated and charming Zhou Enlai seeks her out at parties. The reason is simple: Sylvie grew up in Angers, where Zhou, as a young man, spent two years working in a factory. A number of high-ranking Chinese government people, including Vice Premier Deng Xiaoping, had studied in France in the twenties and retain a sentimental attachment. Sylvie loathes Angers. She graduated from convent school at sixteen and wanted to go to medical school, but her parents felt she was too young, so she had traveled. When she first decided to go to China her mother opposed it. Now that Sylvie is here, studying Chinese at Beijing University, she cannot say she is happy. The Chinese, in her opinion, are racist; she is segregated in classes for foreigners. She finds the diplomatic community stuffy.

Sylvie likes Bernard at once. He is outspoken, direct—independent like herself. He fetches a bottle of gin from his bungalow and they take a good-sized piece out of it, talking into the night: of cultural affairs minister André Malraux, whom Sylvie met when he came recently to China, of politics. Sylvie is not attracted to Bernard—but in a day they are best friends.

"*Tongzhi,*" they call one another, Chinese for "comrade."

Bernard tells her he has some very serious problems. And yet, though he does most of the talking in this new relationship, he does not reveal what the problems are.

"You're going to help me," he says repeatedly. "I don't know when, but you're going to help me."

At the end of the week, he returns to Beijing with Sylvie and the family of the Moroccan ambassador and, after dropping his things off at home, goes to Pei Pu.

Pei Pu has not gotten her period. Neither Pei Pu nor Bernard can decide what to do. Abortion is legal, even encouraged, in China, but it goes against Bernard's Catholic upbringing. It also puts Pei Pu at risk, exposing her secret. But Bernard still does not feel ready for marriage. He cannot tell this to Pei Pu. They quarrel continuously. When Bernard says an abortion is best, Pei Pu says she cannot go through with it; when Pei Pu says she has the name of a doctor who is not a Communist and might be trusted with her family secret, Bernard tells Pei Pu abortion is murder.

Bernard has sworn to keep Pei Pu's secret. But the pregnancy is too much for him to deal with alone. He goes to the Moroccan embassy, just down the street from the French, and tells Sylvie.

Sylvie is stunned. But when she has time to reflect, she accepts the story. It is strange, yes, but then everything in China is strange; the men go about dressed the same as the women, so much is hidden, who knows what really goes on?

Sylvie knows Pei Pu, too. They met at the home of Claude Chayet and she remembers it clearly because Pei Pu is the first Chinese she has seen at a private party. Later, she notices Pei Pu at French embassy functions. A few days after Bernard tells her the secret, Sylvie sees Pei Pu in the diplomatic quarter. She looks Pei Pu over closely: The face is smooth, the hands are tiny, there is no Adam's apple.

"Yeah," she thinks. "It's possible. There is no doubt."

Pei Pu finally tells Bernard to make the decision. He spends a dreadful night. The next morning Bernard calls Pei Pu from his office. Fearing the embassy phones are tapped, he speaks in veiled terms:

"Get rid of it," he says.

A few hours later Pei Pu calls back and tells him she has taken care of the problem herself and is feeling sick.

As soon as he can get away from the embassy, Bernard goes to her house. Pei Pu is lying in bed, in a white shift. She looks haggard. Her mother is beside her and with them is her aunt, the wife of the high-ranking minister. She is a cool, imperious woman who seems to know their secret.

"Remember *Madame Butterfly*," Bernard remembers her saying. "It is not a good story for our people."

Bernard wants to get a doctor but Pei Pu will not allow it. That night, back at his own apartment, he has nightmares that Pei Pu is dying. He has thought until now he is an atheist, but he finds himself trying to make a deal with God: If Pei Pu survives, he will never allow this to happen to her again.

The following evening, Pei Pu grows worse. Her breathing is at times labored, and in the corner of the room he can see a pail with bloodied rags.

"We have a doctor at the embassy," Bernard tells Pei Pu. "I can get him."

Pei Pu refuses.

Bernard is frantic. Though it is two in the morning, he finds a pedicab and goes to the Moroccan ambassador's residence, where he wakes up Sylvie. He says Pei Pu is hemorrhaging to death from a self-inflicted abortion and she must come with him at once. When they arrive, Pei Pu is lying in bed, an elderly Chinese woman beside her. Sylvie sees some bloody rags in a bucket, but Pei Pu appears very much recovered.

In a week, Pei Pu is back on her feet.

But Bernard is sick with guilt, sick with love. He visits Pei Pu every evening and afterward goes to Sylvie's and speaks of Pei Pu.

"My wife," he calls her, and he talks of her so ceaselessly, so obsessively that Sylvie sometimes falls asleep. Never, she thinks, has she seen anyone so intensely in love. It also seems to her the couple are taking some chances. Once or twice, she sees Pei Pu going into Bernard's apartment. Very dangerous, she thinks, because government buildings are probably being watched, though Pei Pu could be going in his official capacity as language professor.

Pei Pu, Bernard recalls, is now often melancholy. Neither of them is interested in sex. Sometimes Pei Pu speaks of suicide, saying she does not want to be autopsied, because that will reveal her secret. She also says if Bernard leaves, she will take the boat to Shanghai and throw herself into the water.

When Bernard is assigned to carry the pouch to Hong Kong in October, it is a relief to get away. He is more worldly now than on his last trip and, thanks to Pei Pu, more sexually confident. When he checks into the hotel, he asks the doorman to send him a girl. The next day, guilty, he buys Pei Pu some beautiful gray gabardine for a suit and picks up a carton of Kools for her mother.

In Beijing, he and Pei Pu resume making love, though now, concerned about the abortion, he is even more careful with her.

They also manage to get away for a long weekend on Armistice Day in early November. They choose the harbor city of Tianjin, sixty miles southeast of Beijing, for which it is easy for foreigners to receive a visa. As a cover the two friends invite an elderly secretary from the embassy, whom Pei Pu has nicknamed "Mme. Blue Hair." It is a lovely weekend. The French and British have been trading in Tianjin since 1860, and part of their legacy is the Tianjin Hotel, the former Astor. It is done in baronial style: marble floors, chandeliers. At the reservations desk Bernard is nervous: One cannot check into a hotel room without a letter from the China Travel Agency, and he has no letter or reservation for Pei Pu. He brazens it out, pretending there has been an error and Pei Pu is his interpreter.

"You take one room," he says to Mme. Blue Hair, "and I don't think it is necessary for us to spend money on a third hotel room for Pei Pu. We can share a room."

The rooms are huge: the ceilings double height, with two large beds. The first night, Pei Pu disappears into the bathroom for a very long time and when she comes out it is heavenly. They make love three times that night. And for the first time, they can spend a night together, though Bernard, awakening from time to time, never finds Pei Pu sleeping. Like a little nocturnal cat, she lies smiling and watching him.

One week later, in Beijing, the bad news comes. Bernard is told his replacement is arriving and he will be leaving within the month. And Pei Pu tells him she suspects she is again pregnant.

"This time," Bernard says, "no abortion."

"I don't know," Pei Pu says. "I am not sure I will keep it."

Bernard has never hit anyone. But suddenly he slaps Pei Pu hard across the face.

"You won't touch our baby," he says.

A moment later, horrified by what he has done, he takes Pei Pu in his arms and cries.

"So," says Pei Pu, "you do love your baby."

Bernard cannot bring himself to tell Pei Pu he is leaving. Instead, he tries desperately to extend his stay. He goes to Sylvie and asks her to use her connections. Sylvie speaks to the ambassador of Morocco, who goes to the ambassador of France.

"Don't tell me Sylvie is in love with this boy," Paye says.

It seems as though he will intervene. But as the days pass, Bernard hears nothing from the embassy.

Bernard still cannot tell Pei Pu. Then one afternoon, Bernard recalls, a mutual acquaintance telephones.

"Oh, by the way, do you know Bernard is leaving China?" he says to Pei Pu.

"Oh?" says Pei Pu calmly.

Then, says Bernard, Pei Pu hangs up the phone, falls to the floor, and reaches for her handkerchief, spitting up blood.

"You never told me," Bernard remembers Pei Pu crying. "It is just as my aunt said: '*Madame Butterfly* is not a good story for our people.' "

It takes the evening to calm her. A few days later, she has a request.

"You say you love our baby," Pei Pu says to Bernard. "As you love our baby, I will ask you to do something: Speak into the tape recorder and make French lessons for your child, so he will hear your voice later on and speak French with your accent."

It is a wretched time. Pei Pu clings, Bernard feels guilty, even the political climate about them grows worse. In late November, the vice mayor of Beijing, Wu Han, who is also a playwright, is attacked in the newspapers. Han's play *The Dismissal of Hai Rui* is "a poisonous weed," *The People's Daily* says. The man making the attack is Yao Wenyuan, a friend of Mao's wife, Jiang Qing. The attacks worry Pei Pu. She remembers a time, after a period of freedom, when writers and artists were attacked. She fears a purge.

On December 12, 1965, Bernard says his good-byes at the embassy, then goes to Pei Pu. He tells her if their baby is a boy he would like it to be called Bertrand, and if it is a girl to take his own middle name, Michele.

He receives a farewell gift from Pei Pu's mother: two white porcelain cups with dragons, which once belonged to the Emperor.

He records a last story for Pei Pu.

"Ten more minutes," she says, every time he tries to leave.

He stays until three in the morning. Five hours later, he calls Pei Pu from the airport.

"I will be back," he says. "For sure. I don't know how, just remember I will be back."

"You will always be my best friend," says Pei Pu.

"Bernard, excuse me, the first time you made love to Pei Pu—can you tell it to me again?"

"On the eleventh of June. He comes to the house at six or seven, just before night is falling. I asked for a taxi for the way back, because he had so much blood. I was asking, 'Are you all right?' It was me who was feeling the pain, because he was no longer a virgin and because of the blood. If I go to the hospital and see blood, I turn my face."

"How had you gotten ready for him?"

"We made sex on the floor. I put my mattress on this beautiful wooden floor. I did it instinctively. I closed the curtains."

"Do you remember what he was wearing?"

"I believe he had on top his leather jacket. I started to undress him immediately, to kiss him on the neck, and he said, 'Let me do it,' and he finished undressing, except for what the American boys wear. . . ."

"Boxer shorts. Baggy. Used to wear."

"I went into the bathroom and he was like this"—gestures, legs together—"with a handkerchief, this is a big part of this story, the handkerchief, like Othello, it is always there, and he caught my arms and said, 'Let me do it,' and then he was stopping, 'Oh, oh, not too much,' a very good actor. And then we start again. I don't have this premature ejaculation, this sickness, but I was twenty, it happened quite soon. I went back to the bathroom. When I come back, he is pulling on his shorts, there is a little bit of blood. . . . When I saw blood, I was just like a child, saying, 'Oh, my poor friend.' It was his first time; he told me he never had sex with anybody before.''

"How often did you make love?"

"There was a lot of lovemaking, maybe two or three times a week. And after the abortion, no sex for one month."

"How did you make love?"

"The same way always. He's on his back or side, generally, waiting. We closed the curtains so it was dark. I am always facing him. There is no mouth, no hands, at this time. He said later to the judge his sex was coming inside his body, everything, even the balls, and with his thighs he was able to make me believe.''

"You're sure it wasn't anal sex—you would know that from the guys."

"Yes."

"Was he ever on his belly?"

"No. It would have made me think of homosexuality, I wouldn't have liked it. That was in my mind, 'Never again homosexuality.' "

"Did he know about that part of your life?"

"Maybe I told him. I am sure I had told him. Not in detail, but I told him everything. Maybe at a certain time I told him I had experience at school with boys, but he didn't ask me, he was smart. I saw the pubic hair, sometimes he showed me, for me it was enough. He was closing so well the legs, becoming Marlene Dietrich, and I was not asking more. . . ."

"You saw him naked, then?"

"Yes, but like this." (Puts knees together.) "And after the abortion, I was so careful. Even several times, I said, 'I'm coming,' and I jerked in my hand. I was so afraid of hurting Pei Pu. I believed she had taken so many hormones. 'My condition'—that was his favorite word. 'I wish I could do so many things, but you understand, my condition . . .' "

"I still don't understand why it would have been so bad to reveal himself as a woman."

"Well, first he had a family of high rank, they would lose face, and then he could not leave China because of his mother, for nothing would he leave his mother. . . ."

"Tell me about the night you made the baby. . . ."

"First he went to the bathroom, which was large, and he stayed, I don't know how much time. I was in the bed naked. Then he closed the light and came into my bed and said, 'Isn't it easier this time?' I think he put a type of cream, because he stayed in the bathroom so long. . . . The walls were of double height in this room. I may have asked him to keep the light of the bathroom open, but no, no, all the lights are out. I am sure he had put some cream between his legs. So he drove me the way he wanted and I even enjoyed it. He had spent such a long time in the bathroom, he was very fresh. I believe now he put some cream between his legs and technically he made it, compared to my innocence, very beautiful that night."

"Did he let you touch him?"

"Never. I don't know what he did, maybe sorcery. It was so lovely."

"How did making love to Pei Pu compare to the prostitute?"

"I didn't care so much about the prostitute. I did this like I went to the Hilton to have a good meal. Like I had to do it, with not so much excitement. Maybe I had read too many stories about colonial countries where the people have a good meal, buy an Arrow shirt, have a girl in Hong Kong. I was in the Astor Hotel and I asked the doorman, 'Could you bring me a girl?' She arrived and I slept with this girl and afterward I talked to her. I was making psychoanalysis. 'What about your family life?' 'Why do you do this?' She told me she had a baby; they all say the same thing."

"Were the lights on?"

"Yes, because this was different. The prostitutes generally want light, they are more secure with light. I was not so much excited by the sex."

"How did you make love to her?"

"In the straight way, on top of her, it was very formal."

"Oral sex? Did she make love to you with her mouth or did you do it to her?"

"No, I was thinking it was not polite to do this at the time. Later on, less than a year later, in Rio, I was with a prostitute and she asked my age and I said twenty-one and she asked in Spanish why I was fucking only one time if I was twenty-one and she was doing this to try to excite me to do it a second time. She was a bit fat and I didn't like her so much, that is why I was not excited, but I could not tell her that."

"When you were inside the girl, did she feel different?"

"I don't remember. She didn't excite me so much. Psychologically perhaps I was a bit unhappy to have a prostitute. Paying a girl was not love. Also I believed she was a human being, perhaps her life was sadder than mine. I was a bit shy, this is true. If I have sex now I am much more vicious, I want it tough sometimes, but then I was not believing we could jump this way or that. Anyway, it was not important. Sometimes I had a good meal, sometimes I had a prostitute—it did not matter. What mattered was my story. This is what I am telling you: Pei Pu screwed me in the head. I try to explain about sex, I misunderstood the situation, which is difficult for me even now to describe, how I was so blind. I understand, I explain, but not deeper, not as deep as I would like to know or black or white. I can tell you facts that happened. It is not that I don't want to tell you the truth, it is I only know this, remember this, and believe in this: I was millions of hours from reality. *Années-lumières.* I was having relations and in my thoughts, my dreams, I was light-years away from what was true."

"There is still one big question for me: When Pei Pu tells you his story, you have no trouble accepting it?"

"Yeah, why not? He's dressed the same as a Chinese girl, the men and women all dress the same. He shows me his hands, his hands were not the same as a man. His face was without any hair. A few days later, I say to him, 'Well, as you are a woman, we can make love.' *I* say this. But years after, I believe Pei Pu *wanted* me to say this. He told me so many times this story of the butterfly. He prepared the field very well."

"But if someone tells you they are a woman after you have related to them as a man, you can't just switch over like that. How do you make the adjustment in your head?"

"Because I was not knowing."

"No, we may have the language thing here. Listen: You know me as a woman and one day I say I'm a man. Would you buy it?"

"No, it is not possible. You have to be Pei Pu and you have to be in China and men and women have to dress the same way, no perfumes, and you have to be such a person as to create such a story. In 1965 I was searching for love all over, and Pei Pu tells me this beautiful story and I was prepared to fall. . . ."

"He has been your man friend and then he becomes a woman—"

"No, no, he was my friend, he was an actor in a difficult condition and he explained to me this story of why he was so shy, why he was not enjoying life ever, why he was never laughing, why he—"

"What do you mean, 'friend'?"

"He was not a sex person. He was like, uh, like somebody who had come down from the clouds. He was not human. You could not say he was a man friend or a woman friend; he was somebody different anyway. You don't feel man friend or that he was not a man, you feel he was only a friend who was coming from another planet and so nice also, so overwhelming and separated from the life of the ground. He was not my man friend; he was my friend who had some mysterious story, which I could not know at once. I would ask him and he would say, 'Let us talk of other things, please.' For me, he was very attracting."

Are there men so convinced from childhood they will become someone of importance that they save every scrap of paper, no matter how trivial, as if in preparation for the biographer? Is this some sign of an egomania that may one day become malignant, making one reckless, self-absorbed, vulnerable to the manipulations of others, or merely an indication of a boy who is unable to clean up his room?

Whatever, Bernard is such a young man. He has documented his life from the time he was eleven or twelve, saving railroad tickets, communion invitations, Christmas cards, fliers for a new restaurant in Vannes. Coming back from China, he has more: his pass to the Friendship Store, snapshots of him and Pei Pu, airline ticket receipts. There are also the treasures from his shopping expeditions with Pei Pu: dozens of vases and Oriental rugs and pieces of calligraphy, shipped free of charge by Foreign Affairs. His mother and two younger brothers, seventeen-year-old Alain and thirteen-year-old Lionel, are awed as he unpacks his treasures in their little house in Vannes. His father, Louis, is not. He is a big man, well over six feet tall, with the long face and rough looks of the actor Fernandel. He is always upset when Bernard leaves a secure civil service post. He is angry with Bernard now, comparing him with his brother Roland, one year older but already working as a technician in the nearby town of Rennes.

"You had a good job in the civil service and you quit it?" says Louis. "Just like Algeria? How many more jobs are you going to quit?"

His mother says nothing and pretends not to hear.

Bernard tells none of them about Pei Pu.

Her letters start arriving almost at once. A postcard mailed five days after his departure with a photo of an empty pavilion near North Lake, where Pei Pu and Bernard had often gone rowing; a letter asking him if he might manage to write once a week. In February, as if her pain is growing, comes the loneliest note of all.

"We have been separated two months already, how long it seems to me. During that time there have been lots of celebrations: Christmas, New Year's, Spring Festival, and one birthday, which you have forgotten.

"I still remember all the things we did together last year. But I think we can still see each other, even if we are very far away now, if you do not forget me.

"I have not gone out very much except to go to my office or, once in a while, the theater. I write all the time or I talk with my only friend —the tape recorder."

Bernard reads and rereads each letter and writes her once a week, feeling a little uncomfortable and guilty. But he is determined to get to the Amazon.

In late March he goes to see Fournier-Aubry, just returned from Brazil, who is staying at his sister's home in Monte Carlo.

Fournier-Aubry is sixty-four, a big man, well over six feet tall, with a square jaw. A thick scar cuts the left side of his jaw, his right leg is injured, and he walks with a cane. He seems an irascible old goat. He takes Bernard at once from his sister's villa on Avenue Grovetto, which with its closed shutters and smell of starched linens seems to cramp him, and goes lurching and limping down the hills of Monte Carlo to the Café de Paris. Broke his leg in Jaguarão in an accident on an overloaded pirogue, the explorer explains. Figured if the leg had to come off he'd have a fake one made in aluminum, hollow, with a little locker for whiskey, heh-heh. Didn't come to that, thank God. The Café de Paris, on the Place de Casino, is the smartest spot on the Riviera, a Belle Époque jewel overlooking the casino, with brass rails and stained glass windows, but the clientele doesn't seem to impress Fournier-Aubry. Caged dogs, he says, dismissing the lot. Just got back from Paris, where he had tried to get funding for a forestry development on the Amazon. No interest. Bankers are just more caged dogs. The Rue de la Paix is nothing but one long kennel. When the drinks come, he finds fault with them, too. It is impossible to get a decent Pernod in France anymore, he says.

He launches into a monologue on his plans that Bernard finds difficult to follow: harvesting the rare woods of the Amazon as he had done in Africa in his youth, taking care not to ruin the topsoil, an intricate program in which the Indians will share in the wealth.

"I am thinking of a concession of six hundred thousand acres," he says.

"That's big," says Bernard, unable to follow what Fournier-Aubry is saying but savoring the style of the man.

"I've had two this size already," Fournier-Aubry says.

He tells Bernard about the clothing, equipment, and guns he will need for his life in the jungle. He tells him where he can book a freighter. Bernard waits for him to bring up the subject of salary. He does not. Bernard brings it up himself, as casually as he can. He is getting a little short of funds, he says, though he has brought back paintings from China, which he might sell. Fournier-Aubry gives him the name of a friend in Paris who can help: one Mary Meerson. Then he's off.

Adieu et bon vent, "Good wind for your sails," he says—they will meet in the jungle.

The name Meerson means nothing to Bernard—though as a man who loves movies, it should. Mary Meerson is the companion of Henri Langlois, the founder and director of the Cinémathèque Française, the most influential film library in the world. The New Wave filmmakers who are the stars of the French film industry—François Truffaut, Alain Resnais, Jean-Luc Godard—spent much of their university days watching the old American and European films shown daily at the Cinémathèque.

Langlois and Meerson are also among the famous eccentrics in Paris. They are grandly indifferent to finance, extraordinarily disorganized, almost theatrically unkempt and overweight. Langlois, at fifty-one, is a gargantuan figure. His chin is a fallen parenthesis in the folds of his neck; his shoulder-length hair is stringy. Mary, who is twelve years Langlois' senior, is of such a heft that when Buster Keaton comes to visit, she in her enthusiasm can lift him easily off the floor. She changes the story of her life often and is dramatic in her affections: "Darling," she calls her favorites, "dear boy." When Meerson and Langlois go to the café in the morning, they wait in a taxi while the waiter brings their coffee and croissants to them. They keep a running tab at the cafés, which Henri often takes a few months to get around to paying. Like royalty, he never carries cash. They do not permit the real to intrude upon the ideal. When Langlois puts together an ambitious retrospective, such as *Sixty Years of German Cinema* or *The Forgotten Films of Louise Brooks*, he ignores inconsequential facts.

"I am thinking of a program of *The Magnificent Ambersons* and *Intolerance*," he tells the documentary filmmaker Jean Rouch.

"That sounds wonderful, Henri," Rouch tells him.

"Unfortunately," says Langlois, "I do not have *Intolerance*."

It is Rouch, who is making a film on Fournier-Aubry, who had introduced him to Langlois and Mary Meerson. Rouch considers Fournier-Aubry a great adventurer, even if twenty percent of his stories are lies: that he has a short-wave radio transmitter hidden in his wrist-watch, that he can kill a man with his pointed Italian shoes. The man still has great style. When Rouch's wife admires an Afghanistan coat Fournier-Aubry is wearing, he sweeps it off his shoulders with a flourish and drapes it across hers. Mary Meerson is crazy about him, too.

"Our own living Gary Cooper," she calls Fournier-Aubry.

When Bernard Boursicot arrives at the offices of the Cinémathèque at 82 rue de Courcelles, a parcel of Chinese paintings rolled up under his arm, and says he has been sent by Fournier-Aubry, Mary is delighted.

"So you are going to the Amazon with Fournier-Aubry," she says. "You will be rich!"

Bernard is taken with her at once. The phone is ringing with calls from London and Dakar, important people are waiting to see her, and when Meerson examines his paintings her approach is marvelous and odd: She looks only at the fabric on which the works are painted and says it is that which is interesting. But why sell anything? The

Ministry of Foreign Affairs should pay for the trip. It does not matter to her that Bernard is no longer working for the ministry. Bernard should write, Meerson says, and demand the funds. They become, as Bernard remembers it, rather close. Meerson introduces him to Langlois; he is welcome at the Cinémathèque. Why should a woman who can pick up the phone and speak with Jeanne Moreau befriend a mere accountant? Because he is no longer merely an accountant, says Bernard. He is a man going into the jungle with the great Fournier-Aubry.

In such impressive company, Pei Pu is less often on Bernard's mind. He dashes off a postcard every month or two from his cheap hotel room in Paris, and when his parents forward his mail along it is evident Pei Pu feels cut off and hurt. She was glad to get his cards, she writes, but she feels bad that she has no idea where he is living now.

Bernard feels guilty—the woman is carrying their child. Then again, he thinks, maybe she is not. Pei Pu herself, despite the French lessons they had taped, had not been entirely certain she was pregnant when he left. She had also warned him that because he was a foreigner she would have to be careful what she wrote. Now, looking at her letters, he wonders if she is speaking in some sort of code. She reports that her health is fine but that she is eating several meals a day, and some of her friends have said she is getting fat.

Does "fat" mean "pregnant"?

Or she sends an innocuous note that seems to be about her career.

"I will tell you something I think will make you happy: Two plays of mine are being shown simultaneously (the 'Flag' and a play about workers) and soon a third play will be shown. I hope that I will have a better one in July or August."

Is she really saying in July or August a child will be born?

And yet, as Bernard is worrying about Pei Pu, he finds himself deeply and suddenly attracted to another girl. Call her Catherine Lavalier. She is sixteen, slim, with long brown hair. Her face has the strength and calm of Anouk Aimée. At five feet nine she is nearly as tall as Bernard. Bernard meets her at the home of a friend in Paris and decides at once she is the most beautiful girl he has ever seen. They say very little to one another at that first meeting; he knows only that she lives alone with her mother and that she is planning to study medicine. Nonetheless, he decides she is his ideal. The day after meeting her he shows up outside her *lycée* and walks her home. He does this several times. But he never can get up the courage to ask her out on a real date. It would be unbearable, he thinks, to be rejected.

Bernard concentrates instead on his trip to the Amazon. When Foreign Affairs turns down his request for funds for what he describes as "a fact-finding journey to the Amazon," Mary Meerson intervenes, says Bernard. She recalls that minister of foreign affairs Maurice Couve de Murville's daughter Béatrice has worked at the Cinémathèque. Mme. Meerson tells Bernard she will ask Béatrice to help. Years later, neither Béatrice nor her eighty-three-year-old father will recall making the request. Nonetheless, Bernard insists, soon after Mary steps in, he is received at the office of the minister of foreign affairs by a chargé and given two thousand francs and a letter of introduction to the French embassy in Rio de Janeiro. The day Bernard leaves France for South America, Meerson also takes him to lunch with her old friend Jean Rouch. Rouch remembers the lunch clearly: They dine at the Trocadero restaurant, overlooking the Eiffel Tower, and Mary explains her young friend is going to join Fournier-Aubry in the jungle. Rouch can tell at a glance this boy has nothing. He gives him a personal check for one thousand francs.

Bernard arrives in Rio in early August. He has a trunk, two suitcases, several knapsacks, and all his books. He expects to be in the jungle for a very long time. Probably life.

He does not linger long in Rio. He has the doorman at his hotel get him a girl, because that is what a man of the world does. He calls on a wealthy newspaper publisher who is a friend of Mary Meerson's. He introduces himself at the French embassy and catches up on what has been happening in the world in *Le Monde*. The news from China is not good. Seventy-two-year-old Chairman Mao Zedong is exhorting the students to rid themselves of the revisionists among them, "the wolves in sheep's clothing." It makes Bernard nervous. Pei Pu is a woman disguised as a man—if she is found out, will that make her somehow suspect?

Then he heads out to meet Fournier-Aubry, who is waiting for him in the north in Manaus, in the heart of the Amazon rain forest. It is an exhausting trip. Bernard takes a bus to Belém, which is fifteen hundred miles north of Rio. From Belém to Manaus there are no roads, so

Bernard puts his luggage on a paddle-wheel boat heading up the Amazon and splurges on a plane ride to Manaus. There is a thunderstorm as the small plane flies over the jungle and Bernard is frightened, though, looking out the window at the Amazon snaking below him, he feels the old excitement. With a dugout canoe, Fournier-Aubry had told him, a man can travel the length of the Amazon; a man owns the jungle.

Manaus, the capital of the state of Amazonas, on the north shore of the Rio Negro, eleven miles above the Amazon, is a former boom city, full of ghosts and rot. Rubber had made it wealthy at the beginning of the century. The Brazilians had the only supply in the world and extraordinary fortunes were made. Plantation lords sent their shirts to Paris to be laundered. The opulent opera house, the Teatro Amazonas, had taken seventeen years to build and Jenny Lind had come to sing. Then, in 1923, a British businessman smuggled some rubber plants out of the country and the monopoly was lost. Now the economy is in a slump. Fournier-Aubry is living in a large, run-down wooden house. It is almost devoid of furniture, but there is a maid.

"If you want to screw her, you can, but you have to pay her," Fournier-Aubry says to Bernard.

And, "You didn't bring a tape recorder? You should have."

Perhaps, Bernard thinks years later, when *Papillon* is such a big seller, Fournier-Aubry was right: He had as many adventures as that convict and he had strong opinions, too. In Gabon in 1918 he had known Albert Schweitzer, and he tells Bernard the great humanitarian would cure only his own people; when one of Fournier-Aubry's woodcutters was hurt he did not do a thing. He says that the French, who are uninterested in his business ventures, are fools. When the Americans come in, with their big Cadillacs, then the French will invest. He lurches around the city with a bell attached to his cane, and when he arrives somewhere for an appointment—even with an important man like the governor of Amazonas—he pounds his cane on the carpet. "Tell them Bouglione is here," he hollers, after the biggest circus impresario in France. "Tell them Buffalo Bill!" He loves making trouble. Another Frenchman is there, and one day when he is writing home, Fournier-Aubry reaches into his pants and pulls out a pubic hair and presents it to the Frenchman. "Give my regards to your wife," he says. He has stopped drinking for reasons of health, but for Bernard's twenty-second birthday he makes him and a visitor a special rum drink with roots and lime. When Bernard conks out, Fournier-Aubry is still talking.

But finally, it seems to Bernard, all he does is talk. Rather than go off into the jungle with a machete at his side, he is meeting with government officials and businessmen. And to sit around and watch someone try to get a business started is not very interesting.

"Bernard is a wandering Jew," Fournier-Aubry says one evening, sensing his restlessness.

Perhaps it is true. At any rate, now that Bernard has finally arrived in the Amazon he does not like it. Up close, the jungle is far less inviting than from a plane. In a plane, you can't see the mosquitoes. And having been dreaming of the Amazon when he had been with Pei Pu in China, he finds himself, after less than two weeks in the jungle, thinking of Pei Pu. The ominous remarks of Chairman Mao are echoing in his head. Now Bernard has a terrible dream:

Pei Pu's mother is weeping. She begs him to come back. Pei Pu is in danger. He sees himself back in Beijing, trying to find her, pounding on doors.

He wakes up in a sweat.

The next day he tells Fournier-Aubry he has to go. He is almost out of money. He has only enough for a fourth-class ticket on the paddle-wheel boat from Manaus to Belém. The journey takes five days. Bernard sleeps on the straw mattress Fournier-Aubry has given him. The Indians sleep on hammocks; they are traveling better than he. He does not eat because he cannot afford to. When the Indian cook, preparing supper on deck, sees Bernard eying the stew he takes an old tin can for Bernard and fills it up. In Belém, Bernard wires Mary Meerson's wealthy friend saying delicately he is having some trouble getting back to Rio. She wires a first-class ticket on Varig Airlines. One week later, Bernard is there.

The news of China at the French embassy, where he arranges a loan, is not good:

In early August, he reads in the back issues of *Le Monde* that Mao has announced a sixteen-point resolution for reform, "A Cultural Revolution," which includes reforming education and the arts and "criticizing the ideologies of the bourgeois." Thirty-five million copies of a book, *Quotations from Chairman Mao Tse-tung*, will be printed and distrib-

uted by the end of the year so that all the people can study Mao's
thoughts. The Red Guard, the militant youths spearheading the revolution, have put up wall posters. "To rebel is justified" is their slogan.
They demand that the sayings of Chairman Mao appear in all public
places and that intellectuals go to work in the villages. They call for the
people to renounce perfume, jewelry, cosmetics, and "nonproletarian"
clothing. The old arts must be abolished. Books not reflecting Mao's
thoughts must be burned. A number of European writers are cited as
particularly objectionable. Victor Hugo is "a bourgeois who strived to
preserve the capitalist order." Balzac is "the advocate of a reactionary
theory of mankind." Red Guards are breaking into homes; they are
forcing former professors to walk through the street in dunce caps.

Bernard is terrified: None of this, he feels, can be good for Pei Pu.

He is desperate to get back to her. He books passage on a freighter
to France, and in the meantime walks the streets of Rio, easily making
friends. He stays several days with someone he has just met.

Bernard is now finished with boys. It is not even a struggle to resist,
he says. Yet at least one of his hosts, a former assistant to a famous
composer, is clearly gay. He strikes up a conversation with Bernard in
the street and when, after a few days, he propositions Bernard, Bernard
does not leave the man's house.

"I like boys," he tells Bernard.

"I don't so much," says Bernard and sleeps on the living room
floor.

His new friend continues to tease.

"*La petite Francaise*, the 'little French girl,' " the man calls him. He
takes him to the narrow, bustling Avenida Copacabana, a rainbow of
humanity, Bernard thinks, where boys stand on every corner, some
white, some black, some whose skin is the color of café au lait. The
composer suggests that Bernard get himself one. Bernard declines. That
part of his life is over, Pei Pu is on his mind, and anyway, the way these
boys live their homosexuality is too public.

Bernard stays three weeks with this host. One day he goes off alone
to the movies. The picture is *Dr. Zhivago*. From the moment it begins,
in the empty, barren plains of Russia, where the boy Zhivago sees his
mother buried, to Zhivago's adulthood in Moscow, when his life is torn
apart by revolution and he is forced to go to war and leave his wife and

child behind, Bernard feels he is seeing his own story. The plains of Russia are like the barren countryside outside Beijing. The scene in which Zhivago and his family cross the steppes of Russia packed like cattle in a monstrous black train—he has traveled in trains which look like that in China. Dr. Zhivago leaving his wife—that is what has happened with him and Pei Pu. The Russian radicals forcing the wealthy from their homes—that is like what is happening in China now. Pei Pu may have faded for a time in his memory, but with the movie she is more vivid, more real, than she has ever been. Bernard sees the picture a dozen times. He goes to the theater at two P.M. and leaves at midnight. He drinks the spirit of the movie, he will say later, like bubbles of champagne.

And every time he sees it, one thought goes through his head:

"I will save you, Shi Pei Pu."

5

In late November 1966, Bernard is back in France. Perhaps Fournier-Aubry is correct that he is a wandering Jew, doomed forever to travel: After waiting six years to be with his hero, Boursicot stayed ten days. But Fournier-Aubry is wrong to think that because Bernard did not bring a tape recorder he is indifferent to documentation. Bernard returns to France with nearly every scrap of paper he acquired: phone messages, the telegram from Mme. Meerson's friend informing him she'd sent an airline ticket, the mimeographed farewell from the captain of the freighter he takes back to France. Pocket trash of interest to no one, except if memorializing the life of a hero.

He takes the first job he can find in Paris, cleaning house for a wealthy elderly woman who lives near the Arc de Triomphe, and tries to get news of Pei Pu.

There is very little. Sylvie, who returned from China in August, says Pei Pu is no longer seen at embassy functions and things are bad in Beijing. The old Chinese "friends" at the embassy have disappeared. It is so dangerous for Chinese to have any contact with foreigners that her own longtime Chinese instructor, passing her in the street, does not acknowledge her. Crazy things are happening. Green traffic lights now mean "stop" and red means "go" because red is the color of progress. Roving bands of Red Guard teenagers break into people's homes with the blessings of the government. She glimpsed Pei Pu once in the street but they did not speak. Bernard does not ask Sylvie if Pei Pu appeared to be pregnant. Pei Pu had been angry when he had confided in Sylvie after the abortion, he recalls. Also, Bernard gathers that Sylvie is tired of this story.

When a letter from Pei Pu finally arrives, in early January, it reads as if written for a censor: Pei Pu tells Bernard that while she did not want to move, last month the Housing Bureau gave her and her mother the opportunity to change houses. Their new apartment has two rooms. Pei Pu reports that her mother, who thinks of Bernard often, says it's a pity they did not have this apartment when Bernard was in China—they could have cooked so much better for Bernard.

She includes her new address. Though they have made contact, Bernard is troubled. Pei Pu would never have left her house unless forced; she loved that house. He writes back, taking his cue from Pei Pu's style, saying he hopes her health will be good and permit her to participate in the important work of the Chinese people.

Meanwhile, he can see in the papers, not even diplomats are safe. Families of Soviet embassy personnel leaving Beijing have to crawl under a portrait of Mao to get to their plane. In February, Pei Pu's great friends the Richards accidentally bump into a Red Guard loudspeaker car while driving in to the French embassy and are pulled from their car and forced to stand in freezing weather for seven hours as Red Guards curse them. In a few days there are angry wall posters: "The bastard Richard must compensate and apologize or bear the consequences," wall posters on the embassy say. The Richards, who worked so hard for good relations with China, leave Beijing.

One month later, Bernard receives another letter from Pei Pu. She asks about his work and health, assuring him that whether or not he has a job her feelings for him will never change. She is curious about his life —particularly his love life—asking if he is living alone or *"avec quelqu'un ou quelqu'une."* And then comes the section, Bernard says, that makes him think Pei Pu is trying to tell him something very important.

I rest at home. I regret that I cannot participate much in our
great Cultural Revolution because my kidneys hurt. Every day I

read the works of our Great Chairman. They ask for courage. From time to time I read some of the novels. I especially like *L'Enfant Abandoné*, the book you gave me. (After Victor Hugo's *The Man Who Laughed*.) I am also trying to translate *The Song of Ouyang Hai*, a novel based on the life of a famous soldier. I think it would be done very well if we could translate it together; you could help me correct the mistakes. But I do not think it is possible right now because I feel weaker and older day after day. . . .

"L'Enfant Abandoné" . . . "The abandoned child"—is Pei Pu trying to tell him there is a baby?

Bernard knows he is supposed to discuss this with no one. But he is too upset to contain himself. He meets Daniel, the student to whom he introduced Pei Pu years ago, and though he doesn't know Daniel well, he blurts out the secret.

"What would you say if I told you Pei Pu was a woman?" he asks.

Daniel looks shocked, as if this is some sort of homosexual tale.

Bernard drops the subject.

But he is now determined to get back to China. Since he had asked the Foreign Service to transfer him out, it is unlikely they will send him back, so he goes to the Chinese embassy in the suburb of Neuilly. A French policeman at the door demands identification, but inside it is relaxed. Bernard has tea with a cultural consul and is eloquent in his praise of the revolution. He says he could be useful in the office of the foreign-language press but he is willing to do anything. He does not even have to be paid. He just wants to work with the Chinese people, for whom he has great affection—he even has had personal relations with them.

The Chinese say they will get back to him. When after two months they do not, Bernard goes back to Foreign Affairs. After proving himself in another post, he thinks, perhaps he can get back to China.

There is no problem getting another contract. Bernard is offered a post in either Brussels or Jidda.

"You don't want Saudi Arabia," the personnel man tells him. "It's nothing but desert."

Bernard does. He finds the desert exotic. Two of his favorite movies, *Lawrence of Arabia* and *Exodus,* are set there. He had seen *Exodus* as a sixteen-year-old boy, and it held, for him, a secret passion. He was attracted to Sal Mineo, who played a teenage freedom fighter. For months Bernard dreamed about him, all the while trying to fight the dream.

And so in early May 1967, after receiving defense secret clearance, which allows him access to government documents that are not transmitted in code or are of a military nature, Bernard arrives at the embassy in Jidda, Saudi Arabia, as clerk and accountant.

It is, at first glance, a bleak outpost. The embassy is small, with perhaps a dozen people. The temperature in summer exceeds one hundred and twenty degrees. Alcohol is forbidden. Political parties are forbidden. Contact with women is forbidden. It is forbidden for women to go unveiled. Marxist books are forbidden.

But in a country where so much is forbidden, Bernard quickly sees, there is financial opportunity. Bernard's salary is twenty-seven hundred francs a month and he lives free of charge in the embassy compound. He has far more money than he needs. But he learns a way to do even better. He orders whiskey at ten francs a bottle, brought in with the embassy liquor supply on French army planes, and sells it at six times his buying price. Doing this once every two months, he makes a profit of one thousand francs, which he invests in carpets and gold bracelets. Gold is cheap in Saudi Arabia. There is little else on which to spend money; no clubs, no bars. For recreation, Bernard goes with friends to the beach or the desert. They bring a big water pipe, an Arab boy cooks, and the French—a few teachers, a few embassy attachés—discuss politics.

Talk—that is mostly what Bernard's Saudi Arabia experience is about.

"Wlad, jiba al hedjar!" you holler to the boy—"Come, fix the water pipe," and while he does, you sit around drinking the black Yemenite coffee he has brewed and eating the chicken he has cooked and talk about the merits of socialism.

The chief theoretician is a French schoolteacher named Luc. Bernard, reading in *Le Monde* of the marauding young Red Guards, is concerned about the direction of Mao's government. Luc tells Bernard he is stupid. You spent a year in China, he says, and you know nothing. What is going on in China is not a violation of human rights but the second step of Lenin's October Revolution. Mao's methods may seem brutal, but they are essential now for the ultimate good of the people. The political and economic revolution must come first, then one can restore the rights of the individual. When that time comes, it will be each to his own pleasures without the constraints of church and state. Eroticism should be free, says Luc. Homosexuality, too, why not? I am not homosexual, says Luc, but if I were I would not hide.

Luc has never been to China, but Bernard is converted.

It also excites him when Luc says homosexuality should not be taboo. He begins, he says, to change his attitudes about it. But he cannot bring himself to talk about it with his friend, perhaps because Luc, who is married, so often speaks to Bernard of women. He tells Bernard he should get a wife—it doesn't matter who; women are pretty much alike. He recommends the whores of Damascus and Beirut. Bernard goes twice to brothels but cannot bring himself to buy a girl.

He also begins the dangerous game of keeping company with a seventeen-year-old Palestinian girl who lives down the street from the diplomatic compound. He knows he cannot make love to her—an unmarried Arab woman who has sex can be stoned to death in Saudi Arabia —but she comes to his room late at night and it is pleasant to lie with her and kiss her. There is drama in the danger as well. But finally, for a twenty-three-year-old, it is not enough. And there is the old attraction as well.

The first time Bernard makes love to a boy in Saudi Arabia he has not been consciously looking. It just seems to happen. Looking out the window one night, Bernard sees a man and his wife making love in their courtyard. Aroused, he goes into the street. He believes he is looking for a girl. But somehow he finds a boy, without even knowing he was going out to search.

He enjoys it. But afterward he feels guilty. He has touched the taboo he did not want to touch again. And yet he makes love to boys again. He cannot remember how often it happens, perhaps three or four times, perhaps more. But he does remember that every time it happens he feels guiltier—though not as guilty as he knows he should be. He never discusses it with Luc.

. . .

What is happening with Pei Pu in the summer and fall of 1967, Bernard does not know. In June, one month after Bernard arrives in Saudi Arabia, Pei Pu's letters cease. In China violence escalates. In July, Chairman Liu Shaoqi, "the Khrushchev of China," a constitutionalist who early in the Cultural Revolution forbade his children to break into people's homes, is beaten with *The Quotations from Chairman Mao Tsetung.* In August, Reuters correspondent Anthony Grey is put under house arrest at 15 Nanchezi Street. It chills Bernard. Pei Pu's old house was at Number 25.

In 1968, Sylvie, working as a stewardess for Air France, is often in China. She mails Bernard's letters to Pei Pu in Shanghai or Beijing so there is no foreign stamp, but she is unable to make contact.

Meanwhile, there is disturbing news from Vannes. Bernard's fifty-three-year-old father has been in a terrible bicycling accident. Driving downhill, Louis's brakes failed and he slammed into a telephone pole. He has lost an eye and suffered a fractured skull. In the hospital, doctors learn he has heart problems.

Bernard flies home to France, finding Paris embroiled in a tumult that will ultimately topple the de Gaulle government—the French student strike of May 1968.

And it is, Bernard is thrilled to find, his old friend Henri Langlois who started it. In early February, cultural affairs minister André Malraux and the president of the Cinémathèque Française Pierre Moinot, criticizing Langlois's disorganized ways, had dismissed him as artistic director of the Cinémathèque.

Three days later, three thousand filmmakers and supporters demonstrated in the Trocadero gardens near the Cinémathèque, protesting what filmmaker Jean Rouch, in a passionate speech to the protesters, called the de Gaulle government's authoritarian attempts to control French life.

Langlois was reinstated, but by May a nationwide strike is underway. Leftist students have closed the universities and occupy government buildings. Union workers join them. The normal life of France comes to a halt. The slogan of the students—echoing the Red Guard's "To rebel is justified"—is "It is forbidden to forbid."

Bernard is with the students. He sells the Marxist-Leninist paper

L'Humanité Rouge in the street, taking care to distinguish it from the Trotsky paper *Rouge* and the Communist paper *Humanité*.

"*L'Humanité Rouge, le journal de l'authentique parti communiste revolutionaire Marxiste-Leniniste de la France,*" he yells.

If an acquaintance from Foreign Affairs asks him to dinner, he declines.

"Sorry," he says, "I have to go throw stones at the palace tonight."

Bernard has one month's holiday, but there is far too much going on in Paris to leave. He finds a doctor to write a report that he is sick and spends an additional two months in Paris on sick pay. He makes another attempt to get back to China, going to both Foreign Affairs and the Chinese embassy. When they turn him down, he enjoys the excitement in Paris. He stays at the home of Meerson and Langlois, he says. He introduces Sylvie to a friend from the diplomatic service. "I am tired of diplomats," she tells the young man when he calls. Three weeks later, they marry. He sees the beautiful Catherine, a Trotskyite, leading her contingent from school in a march. He is still too shy to call her for a date.

Jidda, when he returns, is boring. His commercial enterprises have lost their appeal—after buying twenty-nine rugs, Bernard figures he has enough. A desultory affair with his Senegalese maid fails to ignite him. She is crude, she laughs during sex, she is—to put it bluntly—too warm and wet between the legs. He convinces a doctor he is having terrible stomach trouble. In May 1969 he is back in France.

Bernard has not heard from Pei Pu now for nearly two years. He decides that this is a part of his life he should try to forget. He also decides to try a new line of work. Publishing sounds appealing—he has always liked to read. He gets together with a friend and they form a small company. Their offices are two little apartments on rue Saint-Denis, an area distinguished by the number and boldness of its streetwalkers. Bernard is president of the company and lives in one of the apartments. The toilet is in the hall; he bathes in the kitchen sink. His publishing list consists of two books, *Metaphysical Questions of Life* and *The Cult of the Phallus*, with copyrights in the public domain. Bernard reprints the books and sells a few hundred copies through the mail. He makes little money but it doesn't matter—he is collecting half-time sick-leave pay from Foreign Affairs.

Thus having established himself in business, he works up his courage and makes a date with Catherine.

They go to an inexpensive restaurant in the Latin Quarter. Catherine is now a twenty-year-old medical student and is so beautiful Bernard cannot stop staring at her. Her hair is very long, her pale skin perfect. But the evening is not a success. Guilty about Pei Pu, tense about finally being with Catherine, Bernard feels sick to his stomach, and midway through dinner they leave. Still, Bernard wants this girl. Walking her home, he cautiously puts his arm around her. She does not move away. He gets up his nerve and kisses her. She returns his kiss—splendidly, he thinks.

They go to her apartment, a cozy and crowded walkup in a prosperous working-class neighborhood in the Fourteenth Arrondissement. Her mother is away. She invites him into the living room, smiling. He is so nervous his stomach is upset. Catherine makes him tea. When they finally get into her mother's carved wooden bed, he cannot function, so they go to sleep. In the morning, Bernard feels better and they make love. Catherine is magnificent: not a bit of fat on her, smooth and solid, with firm small breasts, a body like a Canova sculpture. Pei Pu always gave orders: "Not there!" "Let me do it!" Catherine is loving and relaxed. They do not have to worry that someone will burst in on them. Catherine soon tells her mother about the affair. Mme. Lavalier has no objections; she likes Bernard. They have much in common. She too comes from the country, quitting school at eleven to work on her parents' farm. Despite her lack of formal education, she has worked her way up from the mailroom of an international oil company to the level of manager, an unusual achievement for a woman. She is a bit puzzled by Bernard: a boy with no family connections who has somehow managed to get to the Amazon. She does not even know what he did in the Amazon; his stories tend to be confusing. He is also very insecure. Yet she likes Bernard. He says what is on his mind, he is funny about the snobs in the Foreign Service, he is warm and kind.

To Catherine, Bernard is different from anyone she has ever met.

He has been to the Amazon and China; she has gone nowhere. Bernard is not her first lover, but he is the first to win her by something other than physical attractiveness or intellect. His words are seductive.

Her father, her first love, had also been a charmer. He was the type who would give you the shirt off his back and then it would turn out to be a shirt he had borrowed—in reality, he was completely irresponsible. There was no financial stability at home. Catherine's father was a gambler. He borrowed money and never repaid it. He couldn't distinguish between the truth and his stories, maybe because to get money he had to tell stories well, to believe his own fiction. He always found a sucker because he was a good actor. It was painful for Catherine because no matter what your father is, you want his love. The marshals repossessed their furniture, the electricity was turned off, the family was evicted from their apartment. When Catherine was eight, her mother decided she had had enough and divorced. She and her children did not speak about their father. It hurt too much.

Catherine heard little from her father. She received some flashy postcards from the Riviera when she was ten: fine hotels, cafés overlooking the sea—her father seemed to have a marvelous life. Then the postcards stopped. Catherine felt abandoned. Nothing was easy. When one teacher learned she wanted to be a doctor she smiled condescendingly. Better, given her background, that she quit school and go to work.

But now Bernard is making up for all of the hurt.

"Love is the essence of life," he writes in her university notebooks. He sings her the love songs of Léo Ferré. He is the most romantic man she has ever met. He gazes at her as if she is a treasure; he talks to her about the marvelous trips they will take. Even the way he lives, Catherine thinks, is unlike other people. One studies, one worries about passing examinations or about paying the rent. Bernard does not worry about such things. Catherine is not sure where his money comes from. With Bernard, it is always a little magical.

They are in love. They talk about living together. In August, Catherine goes to Yugoslavia on a camping trip with friends. She wants Bernard to come, but he declines. He is a bit old now, he says, to live in a tent.

While Catherine is away, Bernard gets a call: It is the Ministry of Foreign Affairs. An archivist is leaving Beijing. M. Boursicot, according to the files, had expressed an interest in returning. Does his health permit?

M. Boursicot's health, suddenly, is excellent. He reports to Foreign Affairs at once for a quick archivist's course. When Catherine returns, he tells her that in two weeks he is leaving for Beijing.

BOOK II

Betrayal

On September 7, 1969, nearly four years after leaving China, Bernard returns.

"I am back!" he writes Pei Pu the moment he is alone, in an apartment in the diplomatic compound. He puts no return address on the envelope. He is fearful, in this political climate, of making a bad move.

He wants to go to her at once, but he cannot. He is not certain she is still living at this address. He has to report to work the day after his arrival and meet the staff, which now numbers nearly fifty. He has to be introduced to the ambassador, Étienne Manac'h, a de Gaulle man who had been in charge of the Asian Department for ten years. After all the handshaking is finished, it is too late to go searching for Pei Pu.

By his third day in Beijing, Bernard has a plan. He'll go to Pei Pu's old house, near the Forbidden City, where he knows the neighbors, and see if they have news. He is careful to cover his tracks. He takes a cab to the center of town and gets out at the Xin Qiao Hotel, an old hangout for foreign journalists and diplomats in the legation quarter. From there he walks the few blocks to Pei Pu's house. The neighbors are educated people who speak English, and Bernard remembers some Chinese. But when they open the door and see Bernard they look frightened and gesture for him to go away. He tries to explain it is urgent, realizing, as he does so, he remembers very little Chinese.

"Ni zhidao shenma difang Shi Pei Pu, Shi Pei Pu Mama?" "Do you know what place Shi Pei Pu and Shi Pei Pu mother?" he asks.

They quickly write out the address. Then they shut the door. The address is the same Pei Pu sent him two and a half years ago:

103, Third Unit

No. 22 Apartment

11th Quarter, Hopingli

A few days later, on Sunday, Bernard leaves the embassy compound and returns to the Xin Qiao Hotel. The railway station is nearby; there are always taxis. He hires a *pousse-pousse* and gives the driver the address. They drive north to the outskirts of the city and Bernard concentrates on the route. It is a tense journey. Red Guard children of twelve and thirteen stand at intersections waving red flags and chanting, "A thousand years to Chairman Mao." After about an hour, the cab arrives at a large housing project. Bernard's heart sinks. The streets have no names. There are row after row of square, ugly cinder-block buildings and they all look alike. Hunting for Pei Pu's building, Bernard realizes people in the street are staring at him.

"Do you know somebody here?" the driver asks in Chinese.

Maybe he's just making conversation, maybe not.

"Take me back to the hotel," Bernard says.

A few days later, he tries again. He puts on a Mao jacket and a worker's cap, with visor and ear flaps. He borrows a bicycle from a friend at the embassy so he won't have to worry about a cab and driver. The bicycle has diplomatic license plates, but Bernard does not consider that. He drives into the city after work and at nine P.M., when the streets are relatively empty, retraces the *pousse-pousse*'s route to Hopingli. He finds the complex, but the address makes no sense to him. Is Third Unit a block? If so, where is it? Where is Number 103? He is frightened. The longer he stays in the street, the greater the chance he will be spotted. He takes a risk: he walks up to a young Chinese woman and asks her for help. She gestures for him to follow. Bernard is still scared. The girl may be taking him to Pei Pu or she may be taking him to the police. They go to one of the apartment blocks. Bernard leaves his bicycle at the stairwell and follows the girl up the stairs to a second-floor apartment. She stands beside Bernard, waiting. He knocks, waiting, worrying. And then he hears the familiar voice.

"*Shuiya?*" she asks. "Who is there?"

The door opens. Pei Pu is wearing a man's shirt and baggy dark blue trousers. Her face is composed. But her voice is trembling.

"*Aaah, c'est vous,*" Pei Pu says.

The girl leaves. Bernard walks inside, his heart pounding. He grabs Pei Pu's mother and kisses her. Then, all restraint gone, he kisses Pei Pu.

"You have come back," Pei Pu says. "My heart changed when I received your letter. I was upside down."

"Is there a child?" Bernard asks. "Do we have a baby?"

"We do," Pei Pu says. "I will tell you later."

It is dark in this new apartment. A worn brown blanket hangs behind the front door to prevent the neighbors from eavesdropping. There is a blanket in front of the window in Pei Pu's bedroom as well. Are the citizens of China now so frightened of one another they are living in the dark? Pei Pu's old furniture and carpets and beautiful wall hangings are gone. The only picture on the wall is a portrait of Mao.

Pei Pu is excited now, trying to tell Bernard everything at once. Times have been awful. She threw the tapes of their French love songs into the stream near the Forbidden City; they were too dangerous to keep in the house. She kept a diary for Bernard so he would have a record of her life, but it is hidden. The child is not here, it would be too dangerous for him, but he is safe. It is dangerous for Bernard to remain now. They do not know the stranger who brought him here. Everyone may know by now there is a foreigner in the building. Bernard must go. She does not know when they will see each other again. She will think of something.

There are a million questions Bernard wants to ask but he can see that Pei Pu is frightened.

He leaves. But despite Pei Pu's warning, he can't stay away. Three days later, he is back.

Pei Pu is nervous when she opens the door.

"You can't stay," she says. "Go away."

Bernard can't. He is desperate for news of her and the child. Pei Pu allows him in. Then, Bernard says, Pei Pu brings out a black-and-white photo of a solemn little boy, two or three years old, with Bernard's square face. Pei Pu shows him the photo for a moment but does not allow him to keep it. She tells him, with some urgency, he must go.

Then, outside the door, they hear shouting.

Pei Pu, terrified, opens the door.

Dozens of people rush into the little apartment, yelling and pointing at Bernard. One man grabs an alarm clock.

"It's a radio," he shouts. "They're spies!"

"Arrest them!" people yell.

Bernard and Pei Pu's mother, in the sitting room, are surrounded. Pei Pu is taken to her bedroom. An hour later three men in army uniform arrive.

One speaks French.

"What are you doing here?" he demands of Bernard.

Bernard thinks fast.

"I am a friend of the Chinese people," he says, "and a great admirer of the revolution. As a friend of the Chinese people, I am also a friend of Comrade Shi Pei Pu, whom I met on my first trip to China, when I was working at the French embassy. He has been teaching me the changes which have taken place in the Great Cultural Revolution under the great leader Mao. . . ."

The man interprets for his superiors.

The officer nods soberly. "Mao is not merely the leader of the country," he says. "He is like the sun in the sky. The sun in the sky at eleven in the morning, giving light all over China and all over the world."

"The sun at noon!" Bernard says.

They talk in this way for a long time, the crowd watching. It seems to Bernard everything may be all right. Then he realizes that Pei Pu is no longer in the house.

"I hope that my visit has not created a problem for Comrade Shi," he says.

"There is no problem," says the officer.

"I mean that he will be taken care of," Bernard says.

"The people always take care of the people," the army man says coolly. "Good-bye."

"Long live Mao Zedong and the Chinese people," says Bernard.

"Long live the Cultural Revolution!" the army man says.

Bernard bicycles back to the compound, terrified. He can't tell the ambassador—if the man is told one of his people has gotten into trouble ten days after arrival, Bernard will be sent back to Paris on the next plane. And what about Pei Pu? Have they found her diary? Is she in prison?

At work in the archives room, Bernard is tense. Any day, he thinks, the police will make their report to the ambassador. But three weeks go by and the ambassador says nothing.

In the first week of October there is a good political sign as well. Anthony Grey, the Reuters correspondent who has been under house arrest for twenty-six months on Pei Pu's old street, is permitted to go home to England. He has been treated horribly: beaten by Red Guards who had mobbed his house, covered with black paint, confined to a room twelve feet square. His cat was hanged before his eyes. He was forced to stand bent at the waist with his hands stretched out for hours at a time doing "The Jet Plane." He was denied visitors.

Emboldened by Grey's release, Bernard decides to try to find out what has happened to Pei Pu. He does not want to endanger her by going to her building. Instead he goes to her neighborhood on his bicycle a few nights a week with his visored hat low on his head and drives around, hoping to spot her. Even this is dangerous. One evening, Bernard sees three men following him on their own bicycles. He turns back toward the embassy. The men scatter. A few blocks later, when he looks over his shoulder, they are following him again.

His obsession with Pei Pu grows. He files his papers at the embassy, he dashes off letters to Catherine. But what Bernard lives for now is finding Pei Pu. Just a glimpse will change his life, he thinks. He does not have to speak to her. He just needs to know she is safe.

Then one evening in late October, he sees her. She is walking with an elderly woman, heading for a bus stop. Bernard pedals slowly behind them but Pei Pu, seeing him, motions him away. He stops and waits. Ten minutes later Pei Pu returns alone. Bernard, with his bicycle, follows a few paces behind her.

"The corner of Wangfujing and Changan Avenue," he says. "I will wait for you there every Thursday at two o'clock."

Pei Pu says nothing and keeps walking.

On Thursday, on his lunch break, Bernard goes to the great intersection. The Beijing Department Store, the city's largest, is on the corner. Changan itself is eight lanes wide. Buses, trucks, workers on bicycles crowd the street. With thousands of people dressed in identical blue jackets and trousers, it is difficult to pick out an individual. Straining to see, Bernard finally spots Pei Pu across the street, sitting on a bench. It would not be safe for him to sit beside her. Instead he goes to a bench and sits under the gray Beijing sky and looks at Pei Pu. Pei Pu, on her bench, does the same. Bernard can barely make out Pei Pu's features; it is impossible to see the expression on her face; yet he feels a greater connection and love for her than he ever has before.

The next week, and every week after, as the temperature drops and winter comes, Bernard and Pei Pu return, sitting across from one another at Changan Avenue. They love each other so much. One day when Pei Pu boards a bus to go home, Bernard, unable to let her go, follows the bus on his bike. Sometimes he writes letters he knows it is unwise to mail. He carries them to their meetings and one day, when no one seems to be watching, passes one to Pei Pu. A woman spots them and screams. Bernard flees. Pei Pu does the same.

"The post office," Bernard says to Pei Pu before getting on his bike and riding away.

The next week, they sit gazing at one another before the towering Main Post Office, several blocks west on Changan.

The hostility toward foreigners in Beijing continues. One weekend Bernard goes walking with an embassy secretary near Dragon Lake, in a secluded park unknown to tourists. They are surrounded by a furious mob and taken to a police station. The charge, as far as Bernard can tell, is trespassing on the people's property. They are detained for hours. The secretary is weeping. Finally, a statement in Chinese is given to them to sign and they are released. When he hears, Bernard recalls, Ambassador Manac'h sends a letter of protest to the Chinese minister of foreign affairs. Privately, he is furious with Bernard.

"You should never have signed! How did you know what you were signing?" he says.

It seems to Bernard, in this atmosphere, he will never get to see his child. And then, one day in spring, the phone rings at his apartment. The caller is Pei Pu. Bernard cannot believe, after the months of hiding, they are speaking. Pei Pu has wonderful news. She has spoken to her unit boss at the Writers' Association of Beijing, she tells Bernard, and has received permission for them to meet two times a week at her home and study the thoughts of Chairman Mao.

Bernard is at her house that night.

"Is it really true?" he asks.

He is aching to speak with her about their child, he longs to hold her, but he is afraid a microphone is hidden in the house and that at any moment the neighbors may burst in again. So he sits across from her in the little living room and Pei Pu reads from *The Quotations from Chairman Mao.*

"Wherever there is struggle there is sacrifice, and death is a common occurrence. But we have the interests of the people and the sufferings of the great majority at heart, and when we die for the people it is a worthy death. Nevertheless, we should do our best to avoid unnecessary sacrifices," reads Pei Pu.

"This is so beautiful, so true!" says Bernard. "Chairman Mao is a poet."

Then they go out in the hall and talk. It is difficult for Bernard to learn anything about their child. When he asks, he recalls, Pei Pu tells him it is a sad story and so he drops the subject. Over the weeks, however, Pei Pu gives Bernard some information. The child was born the summer after he left, on August 12, Bernard's birthday. His features were part European and so, with the hate of foreigners the Cultural Revolution had spawned, Pei Pu sent the baby to the city of Kunming, some eighteen hundred miles to the south. As that became dangerous, the child was sent with a family servant far to the west, near the Russian border. It is cold there and Pei Pu worries about the child's health, but she has no choice. Terrible things have happened. Pei Pu was criticized for her friendship with the French. Pei Pu's sister, the former table tennis champion, was denounced by her own children and sent to work on a pig farm. A pianist friend had his fingers broken for playing reactionary Western music. Lao She, the author of *Rickshaw Boy*, the famous Chinese novel, chairman of the Beijing Federation of Literary and Art Circles, was found dead beside a shallow pond in 1966. The government called it suicide by drowning. Pei Pu is not so sure. Everyone is afraid to write, she says. Only eight miserable plays are being shown, all of them with the imprimatur of Jiang Qing.

Then Bernard and Pei Pu go back inside the apartment.

"There were many terrible things in my life, but this was before our great Chairman changed things, and also Comrade Jiang Qing," Pei Pu says. "Now with the Cultural Revolution, and our eight model operas, I believe there will be a lot of progress."

Two months later Pei Pu tells Bernard she will no longer be his teacher. A man from the Beijing city government is taking over the lessons. Pei Pu says this is good. Let them be the instructors, she tells Bernard; then if a mistake is made, it is theirs.

The following week Bernard finds a thin, serious man in his mid-thirties at Pei Pu's house. He speaks French and congratulates Bernard on his studies. His last name, the only name he gives Bernard, is Kang. He's a low-level cop of some sort, Bernard decides. Kang is accompanied by a plump and outgoing army man named Zhao. They don't seem to be bad people. They discuss the teachings of Mao with Bernard and when they leave Bernard is permitted to visit Pei Pu. Bernard, as time goes by, finds the lessons interesting. Kang and Zhao speak with passion of serving the people, of struggle, of bravery and sacrifice. They say one must know not only the teachings of Mao, but dialectic materialism and Marxist philosophy in order to understand why Mao is working for not only a Chinese revolution but an international revolution.

"International." They use that word often.

Bernard is moved. It is true that his own child has been sent away because of the excesses of the Chinese government. Pei Pu has told him about the persecution of artists. He has seen with his own eyes the fear of the Chinese, their panic to save themselves by denouncing their neighbors. But now, studying with Kang and Zhao, that vision fades. Individual human rights, in his current analysis, have little importance; you can't make an omelet without breaking a few eggs. Bernard now understands the Cultural Revolution. He even explains it to Pei Pu, who he is beginning to feel could use some political enlightenment:

In 1917, during the civil war in Russia, the workers destroyed artwork and palaces just as they had in China, Bernard tells Pei Pu, and playwright Anatóly Lunachársky, the newly appointed commissioner of education, ran after them weeping, begging them not to tear down what was beautiful and rare. This was, however, only an excess of the mo-

ment, as it has been in China. When passions run high, there are sometimes excesses. They are necessary for the revolution. They will pass.

It is Bernard, not Kang or Zhao, who brings up the business of
spying.

"How could I help the people?" Bernard asks after they have been
meeting a few weeks. "If, for example, we had news at the embassy . . ."

His teachers thank him, but insist they could not ask him to under-
take such work.

Bernard insists.

Bernard is working in one of the most important embassies in the
Foreign Service. He has access to the mailroom, where he sorts the
contents of the diplomatic pouch when it arrives twice a month from
Paris. He also works in the archives room, in which the incoming and
outgoing wires of the diplomats are filed. The archives room is in the
embassy's security parameter, a long narrow corridor, protected on either side with bulletproof doors that lock from the inside. Within those
doors is a guard. Every morning Bernard has to request the key to the
archives room from the guard. At the end of the day he returns it. There
is a key for the mailroom as well. Bernard does not have access to every
wire that comes into the embassy. Coded wires marked "Secret" or
"Secret Defense" come over the embassy's telegraph line to the coding
room, which is also in the security parameter. There the wires are
decoded and sent directly to the recipient. Some embassy staffers destroy their wires after reading; some, like the ambassador, may keep
their wires in their own safes or files. Bernard never sees military wires;
they are sent to the military archives, in a separate office in the security
parameter. He cannot read sealed material that arrives in the diplomatic
pouch. But mail addressed to "Ambassador to China," without specify-
ing a name, indicates mail of a general nature, and it is Bernard's job to
open it. And often, after reading their mail and wires, the diplomats
route even important material back to Bernard to file.

Bernard now looks for something he can use to show his devotion
to the Chinese. One evening in May, working late in the mailroom, he
spots it: a letter from Prince Norodom Sihanouk of Cambodia. Sihanouk
is visiting Beijing and considered an ally. But he is writing secretly to

the liberal American Senator Mike Mansfield, the majority leader, in Washington, via the diplomatic pouch of the French. The Americans are considered the Chinese's greatest enemy. The letter is clearly important—it is closed with a red seal. Bernard cannot copy the letter without breaking the seal; he has to steal it. So much the better, he decides. This will make it a particularly good cheese.

The diplomatic pouch is not scheduled for pickup for several days. Bernard puts the letter inside a large manila envelope and slips it under his shirt. He is sweating heavily. He finds a piece of cardboard and places that between his body and the envelope, so the letter does not become rumpled. Then he leaves the mailroom and gives his key to the security guard. He can't wait to see how impressed Kang will be.

The letter is rejected.

"Sihanouk is a friend of China," Kang says. "We don't want to know the secrets Mr. Sihanouk might have with the Americans."

Bernard returns the letter to the embassy. Two days later, the ambassador requests it, saying he wishes to write an accompanying letter.

The close call excites Bernard. He can do anything, he thinks. And even if he didn't grab the right document this time, there will be other opportunities. He has the entire archives department at his disposal. The fox is in the henhouse. *Le ver est dans le fruit.* The worm is in the fruit.

There is a moment when Bernard's new identity as spy makes him feel guilty. Bringing a document to Kang for the first time, making the long bicycle drive to Pei Pu's, Bernard wonders if he is doing the right thing. That is to say the fellow he calls "Bernard from Vannes," the Catholic part of him, feels guilty. But another part, "Bernard the International Communist," feels he must act. And it is not as if he is betraying his country.

"We are not interested in the secrets of France," Kang tells Bernard often. "Our main enemy is not imperialism but the revisionism of the U.S.S.R."

Bernard sees this is true. There had been border skirmishes the year before with the Russians in the northeast province of Heilongjiang, and now Chairman Mao is declaring a Soviet attack is imminent.

"Prepare for war!" the wall posters read.

Mao has instructed the people to dig tunnels from which to escape to the country during the bombing. On the streets of Beijing there are hills of dirt. The ground below, to Pei Pu's disgust, is a huge Swiss cheese.

"They have no idea what they are doing. One day it will collapse on their heads," Pei Pu says. "And if there is an earthquake, watch out."

And of Kang and Zhao:

"Don't give them anything of importance. It could be dangerous."

Bernard ignores her. He is now part of the international struggle. He may one day be as important as the Cambridge Three: Kim Philby, Guy Burgess, and Donald Maclean, the high-ranking British foreign officers who spied for the Russians in the thirties and forties. It's for Pei Pu's good, too.

Bernard buys a Velosolex motorbike for the long drive between the embassy and Pei Pu's. Having no access to the military archives, he cannot give the Chinese information on Soviet arms buildups or war plans, as they had hoped, but he has other valuable material. Reports come regularly from French diplomats in Moscow, routed from Paris, to be filed in the archives. They are of particular interest to the Chinese, for while they still have an embassy in Moscow, their ambassador was recalled from that post two years earlier. Reports also come every two months from the French embassy in Washington regarding talks between Marshall Green, assistant secretary of the U.S. State Department's Bureau of East Asian and Pacific Affairs, and French ambassador Charles Lucet. Bernard also looks for anything on China and Southeast Asia: advisories on political developments in Laos, reports on renewed militarism in Japan and its economic development, newspaper accounts or special reports published abroad.

When Bernard finds something he puts it into his briefcase—for he is growing more confident and no longer feels he has to conceal papers on his body—and passes it to Kang. Kang takes the papers away to be copied. There is an old mimeograph machine at the embassy and Bernard could make a copy himself, but it could be risky. Bernard would have to make a stencil, then a duplicate. Anyway, he prefers the Chinese to believe he's bringing out a valued original. It makes him more daring. Guilt, now, is not a problem. It is like Marlon Brando in *Mutiny on the Bounty*, Bernard thinks: Only the first act of disobedience is difficult. After that, it is easy.

In June, Bernard takes his month's vacation in France. He goes to Catherine straight from the airport, takes her to a hotel in the Latin Quarter, and makes love to her. He brings her carved jade from Tibet. Catherine is well on her way to becoming a doctor—she has worked toward this career for years—but Bernard is so loving she tells him she wants to quit school and return with him to China.

Bernard won't hear of it. He will cut short his stay in Beijing, he says. When he returns, they will live together. On his next vacation, he will take her to Greece.

Bernard flies back to China, stopping over in Bangkok to visit his old friend Sylvie—and to enjoy the whores of Bangkok. On October 1, he joins the Independence Day celebrations in Tiananmen Square. Mao Zedong and Defense Minister Lin Biao stand atop the reviewing stands in front of the red Gate of the Heavenly Peace. The ailing American journalist Edgar Snow, who covered Mao on his famous Long March to victory, is in a place of honor between them. Thousands of schoolchildren in bright costumes march by, their bodies forming a red flag with five yellow stars. They fill the width of Changan Avenue. Bernard sits in one of the lower tiers in the section of the grandstand reserved for the French embassy. Watching the thousands march, he feels a pride that is almost religious. Something tremendous is happening here and he— unknown to the people around him—is part of it.

And yet this double life can sometimes be difficult. Two weeks after the celebration Former Prime Minister Maurice Couve de Murville visits Beijing. On October 14, 1970, he has a long meeting with Mao. There is a verbatim transcript of their talk at the embassy, and Bernard is asked to make copies. It is, he recalls, marked "Confidential," and Bernard finds Couve de Murville a clever statesman.

"I don't understand," Mao had said. "De Gaulle is a very important man and yet there are people who criticize him."

"If he had done nothing," Couve de Murville replies, "nobody would criticize him."

Kang and Zhao want the report. But Couve de Murville is the man who, as minister of foreign affairs, had authorized the money for Bernard's trip to the Amazon. Bernard does not deliver the report. Kang and Zhao do not complain. Bernard gives them plenty of other documents. He also considers his contacts to be good company. They meet at Pei Pu's once or twice a week and eat the excellent supper Pei Pu's mother prepares. Now and then Bernard teases them, praising the Russian Communists over Mao, offering the chubby Zhao American cigarettes.

"It's capitalist," Bernard says, extending the pack of Kools.

"It's a cigarette," Zhao says, lighting up and inhaling deeply.

After drinking, he is careless.

"Criticize anybody you want in front of me, I don't care, except Mao and Lin Biao," he says.

"If I were he," Pei Pu says after they leave, "I would not have forgotten Our Lady, Madame Mao. They know how to eat, anyhow."

When they arrive, she leaves the room.

"I understand nothing of politics, as you know, Comrade Kang," Pei Pu says, disappearing into the kitchen with her mother. "I know only about the opera."

Knows nothing? It is Pei Pu who notes that while the children of the Communist party members wear red badges symbolizing fidelity to Mao, they also wear Rolex watches. When people shout, "Long life to Mao," Pei Pu murmurs, "Everybody has to die sometime." She never stops complaining about the death of Beijing Opera.

"We have a Cultural Revolution, but where is the culture?" she says. "All we have are the eight operas of Madame Mao."

And yet one cannot say that she cares that much about politics, either. Shopping—or, more correctly, making up lists of things for Bernard to buy for her when he carries the diplomatic pouch to Hong Kong or Shanghai—that is what really interests Pei Pu. Bernard brings an electronics catalog from Hong Kong and it's a mistake. It is rare to own a television set in China. Pei Pu wants everything: tape recorders, a Grundig radio so she can listen to the Voice of America, television sets, clocks, a Rolex watch—it seems to Bernard over the years he'll bring her at least four. Pei Pu earns one hundred yuan, or about fifty dollars, monthly, a very high salary for China, and her rent is only nine yuan a month. But since Bernard earns ten times more than Pei Pu, he feels it his duty to help out.

Duty and obligation have begun to override feelings of romance. Perhaps this is the nature of all marriages, Bernard thinks. Or maybe he and his mistress do better in times of danger. For when they could only gaze at one another across Changan Avenue, Bernard longed to save Pei Pu and take her out of China. Now that they are together it seems to Bernard that Pei Pu does nothing but complain. Why can he not spend more time with her? Where is he going? What can be so important about his little job at the embassy? Catherine is not like this. She is a militant Trotskyite and a medical student. She has a full life.

Nor is Pei Pu satisfying in bed. With Kang and Zhao around so much of the time and her mother in the same apartment, Bernard and Pei Pu are lucky to make love twice a month. It is always rushed and Pei Pu is as controlling as ever.

Pei Pu irritates Bernard so, in fact, that one day he tells her he has been seeing a woman in France and if he is unable to get Pei Pu out of China he will marry the French girl.

Pei Pu's reply, as Bernard recalls, is fast and icy.

"Oh?" Pei Pu says. "Then you would go to France and never see me or your child again?"

A big mistake to have told her about Catherine. Now, whenever they quarrel, she throws it up to him.

"I know what will happen," Pei Pu says. "We will come to France, the child and I, and the day we arrive you will say, 'Aaah, but just last week I married a Frenchwoman.' "

Other times, it is good between them and Pei Pu spins wonderful plans. They will go to Paris and Pei Pu will become a great concert singer. Bernard will begin a new life as a journalist. Pei Pu will help make him a great success. Pei Pu loves this idea. One of her favorite novels is Guy de Maupassant's *Bel-Ami*, in which a clever woman works behind the scenes for the men she loves. They are political columnists; she tells them what to write. Pei Pu will do this for Bernard. They also discuss their child. Bernard is prepared to be daring to win his escape. If they can get the child to Beijing, Bernard tells Pei Pu, he can smuggle him to Hong Kong in the diplomatic pouch.

"Yes," says Pei Pu. "And when you opened the bag up, the child would be dead."

Bernard worries about his son, he says. Yet despite his perseverance in finding Pei Pu, Bernard makes no effort to see his child. Pei Pu, he says, discourages him.

"My heart is upside down when I think of our son and so is that of my mother," Pei Pu says when pressed.

Bernard does not want to upset them so he stops asking. He loves Pei Pu's old mother. He carries her up the stairs in their building. Sometimes Mme. Shi reads Bernard's future in the cards.

"You will have success, but you must be patient," she says.

At least this is what Bernard believes she says—for Pei Pu is translating.

•   •   •

At the embassy, meanwhile, the only thing the higher-ups suspect regarding Bernard Boursicot, is that he is totally unsuited for diplomatic
life. He drinks a good deal. He says he knows more about politics than
anyone in the embassy though he is only a glorified mailroom boy.
Once, carrying the diplomatic pouch back from Hong Kong, he brings
back *two* motorbikes, billing the freight—four hundred and sixty kilos—
to the embassy. "An initial good will," his personnel records note, "has
been replaced by a certain laziness."

Also, it is said, he lies.

Fabuliste is the word heard often—not merely a fibber or a fantasist,
but a man who cannot distinguish between fact and fiction.

And yet there are those who are fond of Bernard. They see sponta-
neity and warmth and generosity and a great *joie de vivre* and passion for
China. Bernard Boursicot may not be able to speak a grammatically
correct Chinese sentence, but he knows things they never learned in
school: how to bargain, how to order a beer.

Jean Leclerc du Sablon, the newly arrived young correspondent for
Agence France-Presse, likes Bernard very much.

Bernard is a shy man, Leclerc du Sablon thinks, who tries to cover
his insecurity with an air of mystery. He suggests that he knows some
Chinese people, which Leclerc du Sablon regards as some sort of fantasy—nobody these days can have a personal relationship with the Chinese. He intimates he knows state secrets.

"Someone very important is coming to Beijing," Boursicot tells
Leclerc du Sablon, "but I can't say who."

The visiting dignitary turns out to be Mohammad Yahya Khan, the
president of Pakistan, who everybody knew was coming.

Anyway, in Leclerc du Sablon's opinion there are no secrets to be
had at the embassy, because all anybody knows there is what they read
in the government-controlled *People's Daily*. It's impossible to get anything from the Chinese. And if something important breaks elsewhere,
Leclerc du Sablon can talk to the ambassador—he doesn't need Boursicot.

Jean is only twenty-eight, but he already moves with the relaxed
good nature of a man who is at ease anywhere in the world. He is
educated, he has family connections. With his generosity and charm he

is very attractive to women, in a foreign correspondent's mildly disheveled way. He also knows something about politics. In the spring of 1967, when the young French leftist Régis Debray was jailed in Bolivia, Jean had been sent to cover the story. Debray had been charged with rebellion for having allegedly carried a message from Fidel Castro to Che Guevara, who was leading rebel forces against the government. Jean was not there simply to get the news. Debray came from an influential French family. His parents feared that without world interest in the case, their son might be killed. Debray's mother had interceded with the head of Agence France-Presse to send a reporter to Bolivia; his father had spoken to de Gaulle. After over three years in jail, Debray was tried and acquitted. In August 1970, Jean arrived in Beijing.

It strikes him as a closed city. Though the book burnings and public harassment of the Cultural Revolution have abated, everyone still seems under the regimentation of the army. The Chinese discourage questions at press conferences. It is difficult to get visas to the provincial cities.

Jean knows that all Chinese who work with foreigners must make reports to their superiors. His own Chinese interpreter, he knows, goes through his desk in the Agence France-Presse bureau every morning. Jean is a sensitive man. He makes certain never to arrive early and embarrass his assistant in the act.

He is also kind to Boursicot. Bernard is a bit impetuous, perhaps at times emotionally unstable, but he is an intelligent man. He is one of the few Europeans who try to explore the city, and Jean admires that. Sometimes on weekends the two go off, and Bernard helps Jean find interesting spots where he can take some unauthorized photos before he is surrounded by the masses.

"Massaged," the journalists call it. A mob surrounds you, the police come and hold you for a while, somebody tries to take away your film. There's a lot of shouting, a lot of fuss.

Bernard doesn't care. He always knows good places for pictures. He is always ready to take on the Chinese.

3

They are like skills: serving two governments, convincing two women each is the only one; and as his first year of espionage comes to an end, Bernard is starting to feel he's pretty good at the double life.

On Christmas Eve, 1970, he goes to a black-tie embassy party and dances until three in the morning. When the guests begin to depart, Bernard returns to his apartment. He changes into jeans and a sweater and overcoat, puts on the surgeon-style face mask the Chinese wear against the biting wind, and bicycles to Pei Pu's. In front of Pei Pu's building, a man stops him and asks him the time in Chinese. Bernard is delighted. His disguise, he thinks, must be excellent. He arrives at Pei Pu's giddy with his talent to deceive. There is no hurried lovemaking this night. Under the blankets his mistress's skin is like silk. He is filled with love for her.

A few days later, Bernard turns his attention to Catherine. He has been ignoring her. Often he doesn't write for weeks, and she grows hurt and anxious.

"Something very grave must have happened to you. Two months without any news," she writes. "If at the end of the week I still have no sign from you, I will go the Quai d'Orsay to get some information."

Other times, like now, she is angry. Bernard doesn't worry about it. The right words, he has found, always bring her around.

"My beautiful angel," he writes, "I have just received your letter reproaching me for not writing. Of course I love you and want to be close to you. You know very well I am here on a contract of three years. When I return in June, we will discuss whether or not I will stay in France permanently. . . .

"My glory, my love, you really have to know what you are for me: My luck, the being with whom I found myself and met myself, the one with whom I can form what is called the couple, the unit. We are faithful lovers, not one to do anything without the other.

"This should not provoke any false jealousy between us. If you think you can love somebody more than you love me, then you have to love, but please always be aware that for me the time is come when I can be closer to you and that if we continue on this path we will always be inseparable. . . .

"If you love me, you have to know that it is not the business of a few minutes. But if you think it is too much, please remember that I love you, I dream of you and your body and your beauty and that makes my sex stand up and call you and straighten out in your direction, so much that I want to scream because this thirst is unsatisfied."

It is a beautiful letter. Writing it, Bernard is so overcome he weeps.

And so the juggling act goes on. And then one evening in April, there is bad news. Bernard senses it when he arrives at Pei Pu's apartment. Her mother, in the little kitchen, looks worried; Pei Pu is tense. Kang and Zhao, in the living room, are sober. Pei Pu goes into the kitchen.

"Bernard," she calls. "Can you come in here a minute and get down a bag of rice?"

He follows her.

"We're leaving Beijing," Bernard remembers her saying. "I have to go to the country, to write a play about the workers. I don't know where."

She looks as if she has been weeping.

"If I am not back in four or five months, you will not see me again," Pei Pu says. "But let's not cry. I know you are a good fighter. Me too. Anyway, you are my best friend."

She tells him she will write to him if she can and that she has worked out a code: "My mother's health is bad" means the political

situation is bad. "My health is improving" will mean she may soon be
returning to Beijing.

The next time Bernard comes to her house, Pei Pu and her mother
are gone.

Bernard is terrified: Thousands of people, Pei Pu has told him,
have been sent to the countryside to be "reeducated" by the peasants.
Most have yet to return.

On his next visit Bernard brings no papers for Kang and Zhao. It is
too difficult this time, he says. He does, however, have a letter he would
like them to pass along to Pei Pu. Bernard brings nothing for three
months. Occasionally, Kang gives him a letter from Pei Pu. Despite the
code, he is unable to learn whether Pei Pu is in difficulty. She does not
even tell him where she is. Bernard burns the letters before returning to
the embassy.

In June, Bernard takes his vacation in France with Catherine. He is
deeply concerned about Pei Pu, he says, and yet he and Catherine have
a wonderful time together. It is so good that rather than fly back to Hong
Kong and make the two-day train trip to Beijing, Bernard changes his
airline ticket, flying direct to Beijing, to get two extra days in Paris with
Catherine.

Returning to Beijing, he says, he drops his luggage at his apartment
and goes to Pei Pu's. His refusal to cooperate with Kang has worked—
Pei Pu and her mother are back.

She looks none the worse for her experience. She is dressed in
military clothes, a green Mao jacket and pants, which is unlike her—Pei
Pu does not care for military people, Bernard knows, unless they are
generals. But her exile sounds like a vacation. She says she had been
living in Kunming with her sister. She doesn't mention having written
anything. She shows Bernard pictures taken with her mother and her
sister in the Stone Forest, the park of limestone hills and caves that is
one of the great natural wonders of China. She also tells Bernard that
their son had been sick and she sent money.

Bernard is delighted to see her. But Pei Pu's return does not prevent him, when he gets an additional ten-day holiday, from making
love with one Italian girl and then another at a resort on the Yellow
Sea.

Why deny yourself? It is so easy, particularly on holiday. You sleep with one, the next morning she asks, "Will I see you tomorrow?"; she sees you with another girl, she cries, and good-bye.

Kang and Zhao, meanwhile, have other concerns. On July 15, 1971, American President Richard Nixon has announced that Henry Kissinger, his assistant for national security affairs, has just returned from a secret visit to Beijing to initiate talks between the United States and China. After years of hostility and distrust, Nixon, the famous hard-line anti-Communist, will be visiting China at the invitation of the government to seek the "normalization of relations" between the two countries. He calls it a journey for peace.

Kang and Zhao are extremely interested in this development. In early July, when Kissinger, U.S. Secretary of State William Rogers, and Vice President Spiro Agnew were traveling through Southeast Asia, Kang had asked Bernard for information. Bernard was unable to furnish news of Kissinger. He was also unable to get information on Agnew's visit to Taiwan, where the French are without an embassy. He did, however, furnish information on Rogers and Agnew's trip to the Philippines. Kissinger's visit to Beijing is news to Bernard—no one, including Ambassador Étienne Manac'h, had known about it, Bernard tells Kang. He is not entirely correct about this. In a trip to Paris two years earlier, Nixon had confided to de Gaulle that he believed U.S. policy on China was absurd and that he had decided to open secret negotiations with the Chinese. De Gaulle had passed the information along to Manac'h. Although the ambassador did not know the exact date Kissinger was arriving in Beijing, he had, he says, been monitoring Kissinger's movements around the Far East very closely, aware that at any moment there might be a meeting.

In September political intrigue grows: There is talk that seventy-eight-year-old Mao is in extremely poor health. It is also rumored that Minister of Defense Lin Biao, Mao's onetime closest ally, who has not been seen for several months, may be out.

Bernard makes a bet with Jean Leclerc du Sablon and Patrice Fava, the French embassy's reference librarian. Not only is Mao failing, he says, but the October 1 National Day parade over which Mao and Lin Biao normally preside is going to be canceled. He'll put twelve bottles of whiskey on it.

The National Day parade is canceled; Bernard collects his whiskey. He had had a safe bet—Pei Pu had told him the parade would be canceled, and to be certain, Bernard had ridden by the workers' stadium where the floats are normally prepared and had seen them being dismantled. A few weeks later, word starts filtering down from the Chinese that Lin Biao and his son Lin Liguo had planned to assassinate Mao and, their plan having been discovered, had fled the country to Russia and died in a plane crash in Mongolia. Photos of unrecognizable bodies, said to be those of Lin Biao and Lin Liguo, are released by the Chinese in January. The diplomats and journalists are skeptical. Lin Biao is quite likely dead, but they doubt he died in a crash.

The National Day bet, says Bernard, gives him a reputation for political savvy. But he comes to regret it. The embassy military attaché, Lieutenant Colonel Henri Eyraud, later asks Bernard in a casual way how he got the information. There is also another incident that makes Bernard nervous. One Sunday afternoon, the embassy screens *Qui Êtes-Vous, Monsieur Sorge?* a 1960 docudrama on Richard Sorge, a German superspy who worked for the Russians in Tokyo for seven years before his arrest in 1941. Bernard watches enthralled. Here, he thinks, is a man who is his spiritual brother, a man who, like himself, put nationalism aside to work for a larger cause. A middle-class idealist who was deeply influenced by the Bolshevik revolution, Sorge became a member of the Communist International in 1925, spying first in China, then in Japan. His work was brilliant. Posing as a Nazi journalist and becoming the confidant of the German ambassador, Sorge learned the date Hitler planned to attack Russia as well as the Japanese plan to attack Pearl Harbor. Well-read and handsome, he was also a great ladies' man. He had a Japanese mistress at the same time he was rumored to be bedding the wife of the German ambassador. After his execution in 1944, his Japanese mistress erected a stone on his grave. "Here lies a hero who sacrificed his life fighting against war and for world peace." It is not a very good movie, and at the end of the screening, says Bernard, only two people remain in the room: He and Lieutenant Colonel Eyraud. The man is onto him, Bernard thinks. No doubt.

Eyraud, some twenty years later, does not remember a conversation with Bernard about the disappearance of Lin Biao. Nor does Eyraud, now a general, remember Bernard being the first at the embassy to break the news regarding the National Day parade. A veteran China watcher, who is fluent in Chinese and had, as a young man, lived on a junk in Hong Kong, Eyraud and his staff had starting making inquiries about Lin Biao in mid-September, shortly after they had observed he was no longer being mentioned in the Chinese press. While the Chinese were floating their official story about the plane crash, Eyraud learned from his contacts at the Russian embassy that the Soviets had recovered the bodies of the victims of the plane crash and made a forensic examination. The Russians had Lin Biao's X-rays because he had once gone to their country for medical treatment. The X-rays of the crash victims did not match Lin Biao's. He was not among the dead.

As for *Qui Êtes-Vous, Monsieur Sorge?* the military attaché's interest had been strictly personal: As a young man, Eyraud had participated in the making of the film and had a bit part in it. He had just wanted to see himself in the movie.

Yet though he is convinced he is suspect at the embassy, Bernard can't keep his mouth shut.

On February 21, 1972, Richard Nixon arrives for a one-week visit to Beijing, Shanghai, and Hangzhou. Pei Pu tells Bernard that a traditional Beijing Opera is being prepared in the event Nixon expresses a desire to see one. Bernard makes a bet with Agence France-Presse China specialist Pierre Comparet: two dozen bottles of Jack Daniel's says that Nixon is going to see a traditional Beijing Opera. Richard Nixon shows no desire to see a Beijing Opera. Bernard pays up—with two dozen miniatures.

The excitement continues. In March the United States lifts its ban on travel to China. In April an American table-tennis team arrives. Bernard leads a happy life of partying and spying, with partying uppermost. One evening—he can't recall at which diplomat's home—he participates in a Best Legs contest. Bernard remembers that night vividly: all the gentleman roll up their trousers and then, as the ladies cheer, they stroll slowly behind a screen, allowing just their calves to show. Pierre Comparet wins the competition, says Bernard, but he comes in second.

Comparet, who was fond of Bernard, remembers it differently.

The men compete not only for the title of Best Legs, he says, but for Worst. Some of the guests are worried that Worst Legs will be awarded to a fat Finnish tenor who is visiting Beijing, which would be rather embarrassing. But Bernard Boursicot is voted Worst Legs. So it is no problem.

In Paris, Catherine is restless about the affair.

Letters to Bernard go unanswered for weeks; plans always remain just that—plans. When Bernard is in France, he has only four weeks and he is always running: to his parents in Brittany, to the Quai d'Orsay. The Big Man aura that fascinated Catherine as a schoolgirl now irritates her. Bernard claims to be a Maoist; he tells her he is doing very important work in China; but when Catherine presses him for details, he is vague.

"I can't speak to you about it, but I am doing very big things," he says.

What things? She knows he smuggled Marxist books into Saudi Arabia years ago, which was very honorable, but he has never mentioned smuggling books to the Chinese. What is he? He speaks so mysteriously. No one in her family is even sure what his job is at the embassy.

"That man is a spy," her grandmother had joked after his last visit.

Catherine is beginning to look at it another way:

She is attached to a theatrical personality. A man who gives the impression of very intense emotion, who lives in a dream of idyllic love, but who is incapable of making a reality of such dreamlike romance and ultimately has to run away. Waiting is what her relationship with Bernard Boursicot is about: short, intense periods of time together and then the waiting. And the dreams. Catherine has never traveled and she had treasured their plans. She would see herself and Bernard walking on the beach in a strange and beautiful land and it never happens. As much as she dreamed, she thinks now, she was deceived, and as much as she was deceived she is bitter. And it was *Bernard* who made her dream. Catherine hadn't asked anything of him; he implanted those dreams and nothing came of them.

He has to have everything his own way, too, she thinks; he doesn't care what anyone else feels. Catherine is a Trotskyite, Bernard a Stalinist. They often argue politics, and after one argument Catherine had given Bernard a book, *Mémoires d'un bolchevique-léniniste,* a collection of underground writing from the Soviet Union. Much of it is critical of

Stalin. Bernard refused to accept it. Catherine was shocked and hurt. It is silly and cruel to refuse a present. Later, she decides it reflects Bernard's closed mind.

Even the sex is not that good.

Bernard is always so quick, so lacking in tender foreplay. He seems at ease with his own sexuality, but he doesn't concern himself with the other person, he isn't *with* her. It is almost like an obligatory act and then—like a windstorm—he is gone.

His letters are beautiful but, finally, they do not sustain her. They are only words. Catherine is tired of words. Perhaps that is why, when she visits her brother, a foreman in a lumber camp in the mountains of Auvergne, in central France, and meets Abdullah, she falls in love so quickly.

Abdullah is a *harki*, an Algerian who fought with the French in the Algerian war for independence. He had enlisted at fifteen after his father, who also fought with the French, had been killed by the National Liberation Front, the group that led the revolution. In 1962, Algeria won its independence and the *harkis*, whose lives were at risk, were brought to France. Abdullah has never been to school. He is illiterate. But he is a very handsome man, tall and dark and gentle. Working in a lumber camp, exiled from his home, without family, he aches for love and stares at this tall, beautiful French girl as if she is a goddess.

The snow, the mountains, the forest make a beautiful environment for love. Catherine goes walking with Abdullah in the woods and he cuts branches from the trees for her to sit on. Just like that, Catherine knows that this is the man with whom she wants to make her life.

She returns to Paris. It will be six months before she sees Abdullah again, but there is not one day when they do not write to each other. He finds people to write his love letters for him. If he wants to, even someone who cannot write, says Catherine, can write.

In the spring, Bernard prepares to leave China. He is not unhappy to go. The spying, after two years is not interesting to him, it is hard to imagine a more exciting time than the one that has been, and Bernard is starting to worry about Catherine. He hasn't heard from her for a long time. He fears there is someone else.

He writes one of his most beautiful letters:

"It seems to me that this time not only millions of kilometers separate us, but also mountains, ravines. Have you given up waiting for me? Why this long uncertain silence, now that in two months I will be flying back to you . . . why, why, why?

"My beautiful angel, I live by waiting with hope of plans and adventures with you. In two months I will be with you, so I may never leave you again. As long as I am away from you, I will find no peace. I smoke cigar after cigar, I drink coffee after coffee. It is really to quiet the pain burning in my heart."

In May he makes his good-byes. Kang tells him it is a pity he has to leave so soon, but if he has any news Bernard can always reach him through Pei Pu. Bernard says he, too, is saddened by having to leave.

"How beautiful it would be if Pei Pu were also in Europe," Bernard says. "We could work together."

"Impossible," says Kang.

Their parting, even so, is affectionate. Kang and Zhao have a farewell gift, two lamps, which are the ugliest things Bernard has ever seen: orange and blue cloisonné bases with garish gold trim and red pagoda shades trimmed with tassels.

"They are too beautiful, I cannot accept," he says, but he does.

When Kang and Zhao leave, Bernard stays far into the night with Pei Pu. Despite his eagerness to get home, he feels wretched. He is leaving China without seeing his child and without keeping his promise to take Pei Pu with him. He is, as he has always known, a failure. Still, he tells himself as he boards the plane home, it is not over. He has met regularly with the Chinese for two years, he has given them so many documents he himself has lost track.

They owe him.

Duet for Reporter and Spy
"WHO DO YOU LOVE?"
Paris, 1989

"Bernard, listen, on one hand you are supposed to be planning the rest of your life with Pei Pu, on the other hand you are talking about the same thing with Catherine. . . ."

"Yeah, when I arrived the first year, particularly when it was very difficult, I wanted to live with Pei Pu. When it became easier, I wanted to live with Catherine. She was so nice with me, preparing the coffee in the morning, bringing it to the bed. She was putting on nice music, a song about the Paris commune. I wanted to marry her and it was for good reason. I told her in a letter, 'I will come to France and we will marry, even if we have less money. . . .' "

"You were saying the same thing to Pei Pu."

"Yeah. At the beginning, '69, '70, '71—but it's hard to live with Pei Pu. . . ."

"Who did you love most?"

"There is not one love. There is love and there is major love, but it is sometimes better not to have major love. Love is tiring, major love."

"You told Pei Pu you would wait for him and marry him?"

"Wait for him. But the meaning was marry him. He was scared I would fall in love with a woman. He used to say, 'One day we will arrive in France, Du Du and I, and you will say, 'I just married last week.' "

"What did you say to him when he said that?"

"Whatever made him happy. 'Never, never. I will wait for you.' "

"Pei Pu is sent off into exile in the spring of 1971, then you go back to Catherine that summer. How can you have a good time with Catherine if you are so worried about Pei Pu?"

"How? It is so easy: You are sleeping alone in your bed in China, the project you are working on is not a success, Pei Pu is not out of China. I was very happy to go back to Paris, to breathe the free air, to be in the arms of Catherine. I remember, we went to the Hôtel de La Harpe in the Latin Quarter, because I did not have the keys to my apartment, and—"

"—You are telling me you were frightened about Pei Pu, you don't know if you'll see each other again, but a few weeks after you come back and find Pei Pu is safe you go off to the seaside and make love to some Italian girl. How can anybody believe that you have any real feeling for Pei Pu when two minutes after you come back you're running around all over China?"

"Joyce, please, don't make me feel American people are asexual. There is nothing strange in this, it is normal. . . . There was also a Finnish girl, I remember. [Kisses his fingers.] Delicious, a bit of *délicatesse*. This girl was not so excited about feeling. It was not a question of love for these girls, it was like taking a yogurt for the health; for them there was no day after. I loved that. For Pei Pu there was always a day after."

"You were excited to find Pei Pu when you returned to China—"

"There was a certain thing which was very exciting, too, it was political: I was also very excited that I was spying with the Chinese, which obliged me to be informed of everything that was happening in China."

"It's hard for me to understand, since at this period you were having sex with a real woman—not just one, but a lot of women—how you didn't see the difference between them and Pei Pu."

"Even for me, it is mysterious. For *me*. Why was I so blind? But it could happen. People are blind."

"Still, you didn't feel anything different when you made love to Pei Pu and made love to Catherine?"

(Pausing to take a Temesta tablet, a tranquilizer, which he takes every three days.) "I wait till the last moment, when I cannot do differently, then I take one. . . ."

"Was the experience with Catherine different from the experience with Pei Pu?"

"Of course, even warmer; the warmth was the big difference. But I was always thinking of Pei Pu, of his problems; he had told me he had taken so many hormones he could not be as natural as he wanted."

"Could you compare them?"

"It's not possible to compare. It's like comparing the Eiffel Tower and a building of two floors. A second-class building of two floors. But I didn't care; we had a lot of things to share, Pei Pu and myself, and I had to save him."

"Did it feel different?"

"Of course. You buy a nice pair of gloves, it's sweeter, but generally I don't spend my life remembering, making comparisons. I accept things the way they are."

"But you were sleeping with Pei Pu. . . ."

"Not really, and each time I was coming back to my building in the diplomatic quarter, the police were noticing, so it was difficult. . . . It is still mysterious to me. Later on, in Mongolia, I had sex with a half-Mongolian half-Russian; beautiful, beautiful, she had two children. When I had sex with her, she was screaming; it was not possible to penetrate her. She was a real girl, with two kids, maybe it was that she wanted to have sex and maybe not, she felt guilty about the husband. It was a disaster. And she was beautiful. She was, really. But it was not an affair."

"And with Pei Pu?"

"Once, that time I told you, it was for Christmas, Pei Pu made me a big favor, told me I could come to his place and we could sleep together and spend the day together. So it was planned. I went to the parties of the diplomats; later on, I came back to my place to change. I put on clothes like the Chinese, a coat that was not typical but like a leader of the Communist party; a mask like a surgeon, against the wind and the cold. When I arrived, Pei Pu was sleeping, and I undressed, we had sex under the covers, and then it was daytime and his mother was there. So he had to put up the mattress and prepare for his mother. It was furtive and there was also the emotional thing; the peasant who asked me the time in Chinese and I did not answer because if I had he would have heard my accent. That was just a short time, with Pei Pu, but it was so emotional. You know what I tell you: 'Six months of fire, forty years of ashes.' That time, I saw only fire. Once more, I saw a spark."

"What position were you in?"

"On his side, facing me. The secret about sex, it is not me who has it, it is Pei Pu. Even now, I don't have the secret. There is a mysterious part. I understand it is not easy to explain, I don't want to be confronted. If people like it, okay, if not, okay. With all this emotion I had with Pei Pu it went easy, you know. I was very healthy, and it worked."

"This was the only time you had intercourse during the second stay in China?"

"I was thinking it was love with my favorite, Pei Pu . . . I was very much obsessed with not hurting him, with acting carefully. 'Let me do it,' 'Now,' 'Go,' 'Back'. And also, I was careful because I did not want to have a baby again. . . ."

"Were you using a condom?"

"No, but he had a handkerchief. It is like *Othello;* there is always a handkerchief running through this story."

"So, how many times did you have intercourse?"

"I got a big favor like this? Very rarely. It was because it was Christmas. Santa Claus present."

"If it was exciting for him, too, if he had gotten an erection, wouldn't that have been difficult to hide? How do you think he dealt with that?"

"I think he did not have an erection. If he decided with his head not to have an erection, he would not have an erection."

"He did not seem excited when you made love?"

"No! 'Stop,' 'Let me drive,' and immediately we dress. It was never relaxing, love with him, except a few times in '65. . . ."

"You said he made love to you with his mouth. Did you ever try to make love to him that way?"

"No, this is not my favorite thing with a woman, anyway."

"Pei Pu wouldn't let you touch him. So when is the first time you did this with a woman?"

"This girl is alive, she is married and respectable, and I do not suppose she would like me to explain this in a story."

"Catherine?"

"It was not my favorite thing, anyway, so it is not important."

"Bernard, gimme a break. I've spoken to her, she talked to me about this stuff, she's a *doctor*. . . ."

"I do not discuss it. If the book depends on it, I do not care, the hell with the book."

"Okay. In general, sexually, '69 to '71, you were having no problems with women?"

"No . . . but after spending a certain time with a woman I was thinking of Pei Pu. Not sexually, but thinking, 'You are betraying your promise.' To save him and the child. It had no form, no shape."

"Bernard, do you think Pei Pu's mother knew Pei Pu was pretending to be a girl with you?"

"Aaah, this is a problem and now it is too late to know, because she died in 1978. Now, when I think about it years later, I think no, because she had moral qualities which were possible to see; I don't think it is possible she would have accepted that situation. Maybe she was like Proust's mother, or the mother of many famous homosexuals, caring for the son until the last breath. Proust used to say, 'The most unhappy thing I can imagine is being separated from my mother.' "

"What was his mother's name, by the way?"

"I don't know."

"You don't know?"

"I was always calling her 'Mama.' "

"Oh. Okay, well, how did you feel she felt about the relationship?"

"She loved it, because Pei Pu was not alone. He had no friends; he is a difficult person, even now. He had one friend, his cousin, who used to see him when he was in Beijing. . . ."

"Did she deal with Pei Pu as a daughter or a son?"

"As a protected person only, like he was always under a sitting hen. She used to obey him, too. Later, he used to say, 'My mother does not like to talk too much because she has a nervous tic.' He said his mother was nervous because of his story and always saying, 'Oh, my poor child.' He was able to fix everything with a story. He made you a story you could weep."

"Did you know enough Chinese to know if the mother referred to him as 'he' or 'she'?"

" 'He' or 'she' is the same word in Chinese: *ta*. That's why Chinese was good for the kind of monkey business we did."

"On this trip to China, you don't see your son. Does the mother mention a son?"

"When Pei Pu's mother was speaking, he was the translator, he could make her say anything he wanted; this is what made everything so easy for him. Generally we used to talk about when we could leave China. She used to say, 'Even me, I want to go.' I used to say, 'With *xiaoer*,' 'With a baby.' She used to say, '*Shi, shi,*' to mean 'Yes.' But I think Pei Pu told her he wanted to adopt a child. If you have a child in China, even if it is not yours, it is happiness. Also, they can look after your grave."

"This was all in Chinese?"

"Yes."

"Sylvie told the cops the mother spoke English."

"She is wrong."

"So you have this family in China and you're thinking about marrying Catherine. Did you ever compare who it was nicer to be with, Catherine or Pei Pu?"

"Oh, it was nicer to live with a woman, but it was more exciting with Pei Pu. Political and daily life with Pei Pu was like in the theater: You hide behind the curtain, you show yourself, you don't show yourself. You are always in danger or in half danger."

"Did you try to extend your stay in China?"

"No. I was missing Catherine. And this was a tiring job, even though I was good actor. . . ."

4

Bernard knows something is wrong the afternoon he arrives in Paris—Catherine is not waiting for him at her house. She's off at an anti–Vietnam War rally at the American embassy, Mme. Lavalier tells Bernard. Bernard stays at the apartment, waiting, an unsettling reversal of roles in this relationship. When Catherine returns, she tells Bernard they are finished. He panics and tries to talk her out of it. When he cannot, he takes off with his cousin on a manic three-week trip to Beirut, sending back desperate poems and letters. In August, still pleading with Catherine to reconsider, Bernard goes to the embassy in Ireland, as archivist and coder. His moods now are fluctuating between manic expansive highs and terrible depressions. He has been rejected by Catherine; he has been advised by Kang it would be safest not to write to Pei Pu. Once or twice he writes anyway, mailing the letters from Ireland, for he fears that the French postal service may be watching him. He does not hear from Pei Pu. Anxious and restless, he lives in three different apartments over five months and tears around the countryside with his learner's license. In November he skids on the ice, makes a terrifying three-hundred-and-sixty-degree turn, and slams into a pole. His new Citroën 2 CV is destroyed. Bernard walks away from the crash with two black eyes, deeply shaken.

By January, bolstered by mood elevators, Bernard is feeling better, and he distracts himself from the tedium of his job with the pursuit of romance. Unlike his experience in China, language is not a problem—Bernard's English is fluent—and he has a zest and a grin, when his moods are high, that make him irresistible. By night he strolls into the park near the grand old Shelbourne Hotel, with its palm court and mahogany bar, and secretly picks up boys. For more public occasions he takes out girls. He enjoys the company of women. They are more indulgent listeners than men. He also likes a stunner on his arm, the kind that will make other men stop and stare, and for the first time in his life, good-looking women flock to him. Bernard believes it is because he does not really care. It may also be that his romanticism, which renders him incapable of domestic love, makes him excel at brief and heady love affairs. Bernard is a great coat-holder, door-opener, bringer-of-flowers. He has an extravagance of emotion that can derail a woman from the realities of life. She mentions a desire for a new handbag and if he has money he will run with her from store to overpriced store until she, laughing and breathless, has five new bags. He gets bored and impulsively suggests running away to a spot the mere name of which is exotic—"Seville," "Paris," "Capri"—and it always must be done *now*. Bernard is a sucker for style. Not quiet style—style with a flourish, style that struts, style that brings a gasp from the crowd. He also requires, as in the movies, a score. These days opera is preferred: Callas in *Medea* or *Madama Butterfly* or *Bohème*. For all his talks with Kang, Bernard will never be a good Communist. Show him a girl in a fur coat and a slouch hat and he's gone.

Valérie is such a girl. Bernard spots her on a flight back from Paris, a plump French blonde, wearing a coat with a luxuriously rich deep fox collar. She looks like the young Simone Signoret. Moving in, Bernard inadvertently spills a cup of tea in her lap. He takes out his handkerchief and slowly dabs at the tea.

"Great stories are begun this way," he tells her. "In this way, de Gaulle met his wife."

Valérie works as a teacher, but Bernard is not one to let work—his or anyone else's—come before fun.

One perfect day in May, after nine months at the embassy, he has an idea.

"It's lovely weather," he tells Valérie. "But don't you think it would be even more beautiful in Capri?"

He arranges to take a week's vacation and convinces Valérie to do the same. A few days later, Bernard and Valérie are in Rome, where they visit Sylvie and her husband at his new post. They go on to Naples and Capri. Capri, with its romantic grottoes and exquisite beaches, is so lovely that Bernard forgets he has a job. He and Valérie stay three weeks. When they return to Paris, Bernard finds a doctor who writes a report to the embassy that Bernard is ill. Bernard lives in the apartment on rue Saint-Denis collecting half-time sick-leave salary. He and Valérie visit the castles of the Loire Valley, Bernard takes Valérie to Vannes to meet his family. But the affair does not outlast the summer. Valérie is a sweet girl, but there is no mystery, no drama, nothing to hold him. Unlike his experience in the break with Catherine, he does not suffer.

Nor does it trouble Bernard when after four months on sick leave Foreign Affairs cancels his three-year contract and requests the return of his diplomatic passport. He collects his ten-franc-a-day unemployment insurance and when necessary dips into his savings. He does not consider returning his diplomatic passport.

Bernard has a pleasant summer. Then in August, his fifty-eight-year-old father, Louis, has a heart attack. Bernard goes home to Vannes, and while he is there Louis suffers a second, more severe attack. He is rushed to Paris by ambulance. Bernard's fifty-eight-year-old mother has recently had hip surgery and cannot go with him. Bernard, then, accompanies his father on the seven-hour drive. A nurse sits beside his father, giving him shots, checking his pulse. It feels very strange to Bernard. His father has always been a powerful figure to him. Now, his face gray, one eye missing from his bicycle accident and the skin over the socket sunken and scarred, Louis Boursicot looks a beaten old pirate on his last voyage. His face is ravaged, his big body flaccid, his breathing comes hard.

It moves Bernard. His father may have yelled sometimes but Louis had always slipped him a few hundred francs before he went on a trip. Wherever Bernard roamed there were always letters—in his father's spidery, old-fashioned hand. And what of his father's life? Bernard thinks of Louis's sorrows: That he was the unloved second son, in a family of farmers, forced to take in the harvest while his older brother was allowed to go to school. That he had to wear his brother's cast-off shoes although they were too small. What does it do to a man to be the unloved son? It makes you hate, Louis said. And here he is now, Bernard Boursicot, the second son of a battered second son, with his own pain.

At the hospital Louis has a third heart attack and is not expected to live. Bernard's mother and brothers come up to Paris, taking turns keeping a vigil in Louis's hospital room. Bernard, without the obligations of a job, is with his father more than the others. He finds himself thinking then of Pei Pu and the son he has never seen. He is a father, too.

In two months Louis recovers. Bernard accompanies his parents back to Vannes. Then he tells his mother he needs a vacation—he is going back to Beijing. He hasn't worked for seven months, but he raises the price of the airline ticket by selling the gold bracelets he had bought years ago in Saudi Arabia. They bring five thousand francs. Getting into China is another matter. The Chinese rarely grant tourist visas to individuals in 1973. One has to travel on official government business or as part of a group. Bernard is not worried about this either. He has a special relationship with the Chinese. He also has a diplomatic passport.

In late October, Bernard arrives in Hong Kong and finds a guest house at the hilltop monastery of Tao Fong Shan. It has an East-West mix Bernard likes. Once Jesuit, now Buddhist, the monastery has a Buddha and a cross side by side on the lawn. A room is five francs a night. The guests, like Bernard, are floating between two cultures. There is an American Vietnam War veteran who can't bring himself to buy the ticket home, a British schoolteacher who has lived in the East for twenty years. There is a feeling of adventure, too. One evening, Bernard finds a poisonous bamboo snake in his bathroom. He kills it with a stick, frightened yet elated. One does not find a poisonous snake in the bathroom of the Hilton Hotel.

On Monday, he goes to the offices of the China Travel Service, which is allied with the China Travel Agency, the official government agency for mainland China. He says he has served as a diplomat and would like a visa now to visit China.

Impossible, the man behind the desk tells him.

Bernard is insistent.

We will send your request to Beijing, he is told finally. Return in two weeks. But be warned; very few visas are being issued.

Bernard returns to the monastery and writes Pei Pu. When he returns to the agency, his visa is waiting.

The train trip from Kowloon to the mainland Chinese border at Shenzhen and then on to Beijing takes nearly two days. Bernard savors it. Old ladies with big hats tied with black silk sell spring rolls at the stops; the early November landscape is poetic and bleak. It evokes for Bernard the scene he loves so much in *Dr. Zhivago:* the young poet Zhivago and his family traveling from revolutionary Moscow across the Ural Mountains; the train overloaded with passengers, each a pawn of history; Zhivago a victim and also a hero of history, as Bernard, with his secret story, is now himself.

At nine A.M. the train arrives in Beijing. Bernard takes a cab to Pei Pu's house. When Pei Pu comes to the door, she is smiling.

"I knew you would come back," she says. "But there is a surprise."

Pei Pu steps away from the door.

"I hope you will be happy," Pei Pu says.

And Bernard sees, shyly peeking out from behind the door, a boy about seven years old bundled up in a sweater and corduroy pants. His features are a mix of Chinese and European. His hair and eyes are brown. He has the same square face and solid body as Bernard.

The boy's Chinese name is Du Du, Pei Pu says, but as Bernard has requested, his French name is Bertrand.

After seven years of waiting, Bernard has found his son.

There are weeks, even months, of a man's life that pass without memory, so that looking back one sees nothing, not even a blur.

But the day Bernard meets his son, November 15, 1973, is a day of which he has total recall, for it is the most wonderful day of his life:

His little boy is at first shy with him, just staring. Then he comes to Bernard and sits on his lap and puts his arms around his neck. Then Pei Pu and her mother entice the boy to sing the special song he has learned for Bernard in French.

"Ni chang, Du Du," says Pei Pu to the boy. "Could you sing for your father?" and Bertrand sings the old children's song.

"Au clair de la lune,
Mon ami Pierrot,

Prête-moi ta plume,
Pour ecrire un mot."

"He is like you," Pei Pu says to Bernard. "He cannot sing well."

Bernard cannot agree. He is enchanted. He poses for pictures with his son and they show a happy man. Bernard holds his little boy exuberantly on his shoulders; he hugs him close. The little boy, solemn and shy, holds himself back from this stranger. Kissing Bernard or raising an arm in what is supposed to be a joyful gesture, he looks stiff, as if following off-camera directions. Pei Pu's mother, posing with Pei Pu and Bertrand and Bernard in one time-delayed shot, does not look enthusiastic either. Her eyes covered by sunglasses, she is not smiling. She does not have the appearance of a woman happy to be reunited with the father of her grandson. She looks suspicious.

"Something is going on here," the look says. "I don't know what it is, but I do know I don't like it."

Bernard, however, does not see this. To him, it is a perfect day. Pei Pu's mother makes a lovely meal, Pei Pu puts on the tapes of the sound track of *Zhivago*, which Bernard has brought her, Bernard plays with Bertrand. He has forgotten a good deal of Chinese, but the important things he knows how to say:

"*Ni shi wode qinaide,*" he says. "You are my darling."

In the afternoon, Bernard lies down for a nap and he and Pei Pu make love. It is an emotional time for Bernard. He is full of tender feeling, but Pei Pu's mother is in the next room and there is also now a little boy in the house. Pei Pu satisfies Bernard in her usual way. Bernard knows better, after all this time, than to try to touch her.

Afterward, Bernard recalls, Pei Pu tells Bernard how she had gotten the boy back.

Her life has been sad since Bernard went away, says Pei Pu. Her poor mother's health is failing. She wanted to see her grandchild one more time before dying. It seemed to Pei Pu it might now be possible. The political climate was more liberal; persons who had been criticized and sent to the countryside were returning home. Mme. Shi, then, takes some of her savings and pays a friend of the family who works in the government to bring Bertrand home from Xinjiang Province. The boy arrived only a few months before Bernard. Pei Pu and her mother go through the motions of adopting the boy so that no one will suspect he is Pei Pu's son. As his features are foreign, and they fear someone might realize Bertrand was conceived during the time Bernard was in Beijing, Pei Pu and her mother also lie about Bertrand's age, telling the authorities he is four, not seven.

"*Feiji Shi Shi*," "The Uncle of the Plane," Bertrand first calls Bernard, but Pei Pu, says Bernard, corrects him.

"He is not your uncle, he is your papa," Pei Pu says.

Bernard feels like a papa. He goes to the Friendship Store and buys Bertrand a soccer ball and a toy plane and car and balloons. He gives him his bath. For the first time in their relationship, he is able to live with Pei Pu, sharing her room.

And yet Pei Pu is not content:

"You are so happy with your child," Bernard remembers Pei Pu saying. "But I am a bit less happy than you, because I cannot tell him who I am."

"One day you'll have to tell him," Bernard said.

"When he turns twenty," says Pei Pu. She makes a reference to a melodramatic story about a man who twenty years later finds his son: "Like in the book by Alexandre Dumas, *Twenty Years After*."

Until then, Pei Pu says, she will have to let the boy believe that she is merely looking after him and that his natural mother is dead.

Bernard sees no one from the French embassy on this visit to Beijing—it is best, he feels, that it be a secret visit.

But he is visited one day by his old friend Kang.

They share a meal. Kang is sympathetic when he hears Bernard is unemployed. He is certain, he says, with all of Bernard's fine qualities something will turn up. He also arranges an extension of Bernard's two-week visa.

Pei Pu introduces the boy to Kang, telling Bertrand to call Kang, who is a great friend of the family, "Papa." It will force Kang to protect Bertrand, Pei Pu tells Bernard later. She has given him the responsibility of family.

After staying in Beijing for a few weeks, Bernard and Pei Pu travel. Sometimes Bertrand accompanies them. Hotel rooms are inexpensive; only twenty yuan—ten American dollars—a night. They go south to the city of Hangzhou, beside the West Lake, where the tenth-century governor Qian Liu, when the city was threatened by tidal waves, placed archers on the riverbanks to shoot at the waves. They visit the neighboring city of Suzhou, famous for its gardens, lakeside teahouses, and temples, where the parks have names like poems: the Garden of the Pavilion of the Waves, Kiosk for Watching the Fish, Pavilion of the Enlightened Way.

"Above there is heaven, below there are Hangzhou and Suzhou," the Chinese say, and indeed they have a lovely time. It is having a son, Bernard feels, that makes it so. In the morning, as the fog rises up from the water, Bernard and Pei Pu go rowing on Suzhou Lake, near which Mao is said to have a home.

And yet, Bernard says, there is little sex between him and Pei Pu. While Bernard wanted Pei Pu upon arriving in Beijing, that was a momentary longing. He is far more interested in his son.

In December, Bernard returns to France. Bernard leaves Pei Pu and Bertrand in the city of Guilin, from where he takes the train to Canton. At the station, he literally strips himself of his valuables, giving Pei Pu his watch, his sunglasses, his Mont Blanc pen. Pei Pu suggests a final picture of him and his son for remembrance. Bernard lifts the boy up on a stone wall so they can pose shoulder to shoulder.

"Wo ai ni," he says to Bertrand. "I love you."

He does not remember what he says to Pei Pu.

5

For years Bernard had been shipping the treasures acquired in his travels back to Vannes for storage. Now Chinese wall hangings, blue and white three-foot-high porcelain vases, the tasseled lamps from Kang crowd his parents' black leatherette living room set with the family pictures of his grandmother in her traditional Breton lace headdress and his cousins' communions. Carpets lie upon carpets in the vestibule of their little house which is growing more cluttered with every foreign post.

The neighbors have a running joke.

"One day he will bring you back a Chinese girl," they tell Mme. Boursicot.

"Why not?" she says.

He is certainly of age. Her son Roland, just a year older than Bernard, has given Mme. Boursicot her first grandchild, Sonia. Mme. Boursicot has met Bernard's girlfriend Valérie and heard mention of Catherine; she knows her son has no problem getting girls.

And yet the truth is that Mme. Boursicot, a hefty woman whose difficult life has made her weary and blunt, feels she knows very little of her son Bernard's life. They write often, but except for his early days in China, when he fretted about not having the right clothes and his inability to eat with chopsticks, there is nothing about whether he is happy and little about work or friends. There is a dry rundown of facts: I went to the movies, I had the opportunity to buy some fabric in Hong Kong, I am going again to Hong Kong with the diplomatic pouch. His life is unlike anyone else's in the family. Bernard's brothers, Roland and Alain, work in a factory in Rennes, one hour from where they grew up; the youngest brother, Lionel, is a house painter in Vannes. But while Bernard likes to brag about his life, at the same time he seems to want to lock the family out. Once Mme. Boursicot asked him directly what he did at the embassy in China.

"It's a secret," he said.

Still, he is her favorite. He always has been. In the early years of her marriage, when she and her husband quarreled, it was Bernard who put himself between her and Louis, taking her into his room, saying, "Come, Mommy, you'll sleep with me." He is the son who looks after her and her husband now. If she mentions having bought a new refrigerator for which they will have to pay in installments, Bernard sends a check by return mail. This past spring, when she and her husband lost their house to their landlady's family, Bernard came down from Paris and found them a condominium and later made the monthly payments. The condominium was near the land where they had been raised. It meant a lot to them. But his habit of dropping names of bigshots and insisting he cannot discuss his work because it is highly sensitive is a sore point in the family. They are also skeptical of the stories he tells: sleeping with Indians on the Amazon River, visiting famous movie people in Paris, dining with ambassadors. "He tells us stories he has read in books as if they are his own," Louis Boursicot had told his wife when Bernard was a teenager. "And he thinks they are true. He introduces himself as the main character in all these stories—"

"Some things are probably true, some are not," Mme. Boursicot would say.

When Bernard is home, there is often an argument with Louis.

"Listen, mister," Louis would say to Bernard after a few bottles of wine. "You think you're so superior, but if we had a dictation contest, I would make fewer mistakes than you. I don't care what you write, I would make fewer mistakes.

"Stop glorifying yourself, stop being such a smartass. You never know what life is going to do to you. You succeed, you do well, but life can change."

Still, Mme. Boursicot is happy when Bernard is home. She mends the clothes he brings back to her—no matter that he is nearly thirty, he still brings home his torn shirts—she bakes him heavy Breton cakes, thick with plums and prunes.

Now Bernard is home from his China vacation. He sits at the dining room table, where she has her sewing machine set up and is patching his jeans.

"You are lucky, Mama," he says. "You came close to never seeing me again. I was in the country in China, away from civilization, and there was a snake in the bathtub. It was a poisonous snake. I killed it with a stick."

Later, he takes two pictures out of his wallet: One is a Chinese boy of about seven, the other is Bernard with the child.

"Don't you think he looks like me?" he says.

Mme. Boursicot has no patience for this today. She has an eight-inch surgical scar on her hip; her husband is in bed with a scar running from his throat to the bottom of his ribs recovering from open-heart surgery; and the boy in the picture looks nothing like her son.

"Not much," Mme. Boursicot says, because she does not want to encourage this nonsense.

Bernard says nothing. He just puts the pictures away.

But the photograph troubles Mme. Boursicot: How could Bernard have had a child of that age and not mention it to her until now? He never even spoke of meeting a woman. It is very strange, speaking of a child without speaking of a woman, and as she thinks about it there are other strange things about this trip, too:

Bernard had said he was going to China for a vacation. He had just been there working for three years. Why would he need to go all the way back to take a rest?

Also, earlier in the day, he had asked her the time.

"Don't you have a nice watch?" she said.

"No," said Bernard. "I gave it away."

Probably, Mme. Boursicot thinks now, he gave the watch to that child.

She brings up the subject of the child with her husband and with her son Lionel, who is now her main confidant. Louis thinks it is ridiculous, just another lie. Lionel, a gentle, stocky man with a striking resemblance to Bernard, does not want to go that far. Lionel adores his older brother; he shared a room with him when they were growing up; Bernard looked after him when their mother was working. Lionel does not like to think Bernard would lie. Bernard has shown Lionel the picture of the little boy, too, and told all his brothers he has a son whom he is unable to get out of China. But finally even Lionel and his mother decide Bernard's story is best put aside. The family doesn't pay much attention to it, Lionel says, or consider it very important.

So Bernard returns to Paris, to the two little tenement apartments on rue Saint-Denis that he and a friend still keep up. He has been out of work for twenty months, but he's not worried. The rent is cheap, he has rugs and porcelain to sell, and while he was away, his unemployment insurance has piled up to eight hundred and ten francs. His only concern is the weather. Paris in January is cold and gloomy. And so Bernard takes off for a week in Venice with Catherine's mother, Cécile Lavalier.

She is glad for his company, for she is getting along badly with Catherine. Mme. Lavalier had been so upset that her beautiful, brilliant girl, the first child in the family to attend a university, became involved with an illiterate man that she refused to speak to her for six months. And Bernard is a good travel companion. He finds the best exchange rate—never at a bank. He has a nose for finding good cheap restaurants and hotels. The two manage their trip for a thousand francs each, quite a feat, even in the off season. They find a hotel on the Piazza San Marco, they tour the cathedrals by day and in the evenings sit at Florian's café, beloved of Proust.

In April, Catherine and Abdullah marry at City Hall. Mme. Lavalier refuses to attend the ceremony. Bernard is not invited. He is not disturbed by the marriage. He has adjusted to the loss.

On an evening in mid-May Bernard is in a particularly happy mood. Some wealthy acquaintances have invited him to dinner at a fancy restaurant on the Left Bank, and as Bernard is not eating so well these days he is pleased to accept. Afterward, he remembers it is his friend Sylvie's birthday. She is still with her husband in Rome. Since it is growing very late in the evening, Bernard makes a stop at Sylvie's family apartment on Boulevard Saint-Germain and uses Sylvie's phone to send her birthday greetings.

It is after midnight and Bernard, dressed up in jacket and tie, is walking home, down a narrow street near the Seine, when he sees him: a slim, tall young man in his early twenties. He wears jeans and has long blond hair and a drooping mustache.

There is a look that passes between two men faster than the look between a man and a woman, for it comes of having to hide. Bernard and the young man exchange that look. A short time later the young man, whose name is Thierry, invites Bernard back to his place, a maid's room on the top floor of an old apartment building on Saint-Germain. Thierry is twenty-three, six years younger than Bernard, delicate and fair. He is very beautiful, Bernard thinks; he also has a marvelous elegance and reserve. He takes it a step further. Thierry is like a British lord. Bernard has never spent the night with a man before, but now he finds he does not want to leave. He kisses Thierry all over, more intimately than he has ever kissed a man, and the excitement is not over with the sexual act. He stays the night and the next two nights as well. The third morning Bernard remembers that the Cannes film festival has begun.

"The weather in Paris is so nice," Bernard says, "but it will be even nicer in Cannes. Why don't you quit your job and come?"

"Okay," says Thierry, who has been working as a Xerox clerk at the American advertising firm of Young & Rubicam, and when they return from Cannes he moves in with Bernard.

For Bernard it is love very quickly. He holds Thierry through the night; he sings him *"si tu t'envas,"* Léo Ferré's melancholy love song.

"Si tu t'en vas un jour, tu m'oublieras
Les rêves d'amour ça ne voyage pas . . ."

Thierry is not so sure.

"He is dressed very stupidly," he thinks when he first sees Bernard in the street. "Very old-fashioned."

Thierry hates suits and ties, the uniform of the French middle class. What captivates him is the flower-power creed of late-sixties America: tune in, turn on, drop out. He's not one for marijuana. Gauloises are his drug—but he plays at being a hippie. He listens only to American music—The Doors, Jimi Hendrix, Pink Floyd—even if his

English isn't good enough for him to understand all the words. He does temporary office work long enough to pay the next month's rent, then quits. Such a lifestyle is common in the early seventies, an unambitious time, in harmony with Thierry's languid soul.

He has always been lazy, Thierry would say. One of five children of a prosperous French colonial family, Thierry had been raised on Mamoutzu, a tiny tropical island in the Comoros island chain, off Madagascar, then a colony of France. The ylang-ylang tree grew there, its large, fragrant white blossoms gathered for their perfume. In harvest time, Mamoutzu was enchanting. The trees were tortured so that the branches were forced down and one walked under a canopy of flowers. Is there an indolence that comes of spending one's childhood under a canopy of flowers, a pleasure in the moment so sweet and absolute that it disallows any concerns of the future? Moving to France in 1960 when Madagascar becomes independent, Thierry is an indifferent student. Like Bernard, he never gets a high school degree.

Thierry is also sometimes melancholy. At nineteen, he is discharged from the French army for taking an overdose of sleeping pills. Thierry underplays the incident. It was not a serious suicide attempt, he says. He was depressed, but not that depressed. It was just a shortsighted way to escape the army. He had gone to Paris for the first time and discovered the openness of the gay life there, and he was eager to be part of it. Thierry has always known he is gay and has no problem with it. He does not discuss it, only because he feels sexuality is a private matter. It also seems to him if a person is known to be homosexual that becomes his most important characteristic to others. It is never "He is clever" or "He is kind" but "He is gay."

In 1970, at twenty, Thierry moves to Paris and finds a cheap apartment in Montparnasse. He has no master plan. He just feels life should be easy. Bernard, when Thierry meets him, is only another adventure: See a man, take him home, spend a night, maybe a month. Thierry does not think for a minute it will last. But Bernard has such energy, such intensity, such a sexual hunger that it is impossible to be indifferent. And he feels comfortable with Bernard from their first meeting. It is like a pair of shoes that feel good from the minute you slip them on. Thierry is an introspective man. He likes to read, he dreams of travel, he has a few close friends, but there is an inertia about him that often keeps him in his room. Bernard approaches the world like a man helping himself to a second bowl of ice cream, and he carries Thierry along.

"The weather is so nice in Cannes," Bernard had said, and after that, "We're going to Ireland" and "Let's go to Venice."

They have very little money, to wash you have to crouch over the kitchen sink, but as far as Thierry is concerned, upon meeting Bernard, it is a wonderful life. Thierry collects unemployment insurance, and he and Bernard refund soft-drink bottles for cigarette money and live on spaghetti. When they want to travel Bernard sells a carpet from Saudi Arabia or Thierry takes a temporary office job.

A few close friends of Thierry's know that Bernard and Thierry are lovers, but most of Bernard's friends do not. Cécile Lavalier, who knew Bernard for years as her daughter's boyfriend, assumes Thierry is Bernard's buddy. She never sees any displays of affection. Bernard's family assumes the same. Bernard's friend Willi, a Viennese refugee from Hitler, who is a high-powered executive, and his American wife never doubt that Bernard is heterosexual. They see him flirting with women too often to have any doubts.

Bernard and Thierry then live together discreetly, and they make a good couple; they balance each other well. While Bernard is impulsive and emotional, Thierry thinks things over before making a decision. While Bernard demands to be heard when in crisis—and feels himself to be in crisis often—Thierry keeps his feelings to himself. While Bernard is theatrical and flamboyant, Thierry is calm, practically *British*, some people say. When Bernard veers too far out of control, when he is shouting so loudly in a room that people stare and Bernard does not even notice, it is Thierry who quiets him down.

"Doucement, Bernard," "Quiet down," he says, but nicely.

Bernard, after the moods and demands of Pei Pu, finds it all wonderfully easy. Thierry never criticizes Bernard and there is no jealousy. If either wants to go to the streets now and then it is no problem—provided, adds Thierry, it is only sex.

So for a time Bernard is happy.

And yet he cannot stop thinking of Pei Pu and Bertrand. It is a monumental story, a tragic story living inside him, he often thinks, and if you have such a story inside you, there is nothing for it but pills or drink. Bernard does not take pills and he does not have the money that summer to drink.

But one night there is a party in the Latin Quarter with a lot of people Bernard knows from China. There is plenty to drink. Bernard does his share. Then he seeks out a girl he knows from Beijing. She remembers a confusing story about a mistress and a son in China. He recalls telling her everything—including the fact that in order to protect his mistress, he has performed "services" for the Chinese. He does not say what these services are, but there is no need. The girl understands and is shocked.

"Why are you telling me this?" the girl asks. "Why me?"

Bernard does not know himself. Because he wants to explain the way he had been when she knew him in China, the nervousness and drinking? Because this girl, having shared the experience of China might understand? Because he likes her? Because the story is devouring him? Because he is drunk? Because he feels guilty?

Or maybe there are other reasons he does not see: Because he needs to show this girl—who happens to be very pretty—that he is a man of importance. Because regardless of his relationship with Thierry it still matters to Bernard to be successful with a pretty girl.

The girl comes home with Bernard to rue Saint-Denis. Bernard sends Thierry to the second apartment on another floor. The experts are not correct when they say alcohol impairs a man's ability to perform, Bernard makes a point of saying; for a while it excites you, and he does very well by this girl. When he tries to continue the relationship, how- ever, she is cool. It has been a mistake to tell her, Bernard decides, just as it had been a mistake years earlier when he told Pei Pu's secret to his friend Daniel. It is too intense a story to impose on another person. It frightens them. They resent it.

Thierry does not have an ounce of sexual jealousy, Bernard insists; he brings home a few girls that summer and Thierry does not care.

Thierry also underplays the incident with the girl from Beijing. It happened only once, he says. It was only sex. As he recalls, Bernard did not bring home any other girls.

As fall comes, Bernard is once again restless. He thinks of the life in the Foreign Service, he thinks of Pei Pu.

"We always go back to our first love," one of the diplomats had said during Bernard's first stay in China, and for all its stuffiness, perhaps this is what the Quai d'Orsay is to Bernard: an object of struggle and love.

He goes back. Despite Bernard's spotty record, he is permitted to take a civil service exam for chancery deputy secretary, a level "C" post.

It is not a prestige job.

"A" level indicates ambassador. "B" includes diplomatic employees from first councillor to press attaché. "C" indicates an office worker, usually a secretary. "D" indicates typist or chauffeur. The *Annuaire Diplomatique*, the annual listing of French diplomats, does not list embassy employees of "C" level or lower. They are not considered diplomats.

It is, however, an important promotion for Bernard. Passing the exam for level "C," Bernard graduates from contract worker to full-time civil servant. He is offered posts in Toronto and New Orleans. He chooses New Orleans. But before departing, he takes one more trip to Venice with Thierry.

In November there are no tourists in Venice, Bernard says. And the weather is beautiful.

6

The plan is for Bernard and Thierry to go to the United States together, but Bernard's departure is delayed, so Thierry flies off alone, says Bernard, and makes a report for him. Arranges things for him like a valet, it is suggested in this rendering, and indeed this is becoming the pattern of their relationship—Bernard earns the money while Thierry handles the domestic chores. Regarding New Orleans, however, Thierry goes on ahead because he is locked into a cheap charter flight.

Bernard's work in the passports section of the consulate on St. Charles Avenue, the main street in New Orleans, holds little interest for him, as usual. An embassy, dealing with diplomatic and political concerns, has a certain level of glamour, playing host to visiting dignitaries and celebrities. A consulate, dealing with visas and birth certificates and records, is a workaday entity.

Still, life in New Orleans is good. Bernard's 5,000 franc salary, with the dollar at four francs, brings him $1,250 a month, and one can rent a floor-through apartment in an antebellum house on Second Street for $250 a month. As a member of the diplomatic community he is exempt from American taxes, and because he works abroad his French taxes are very low. Bernard buys a Mustang, and Thierry, whom he introduces to his colleagues as his chauffeur, drives him to work. They live in five different apartments in two years, because Bernard likes change. They travel often, parlaying casual acquaintanceships into weekend stays. When Mme. Lavalier visits they drive to Houston, and Thierry and Bernard make friends with Mme. Lavalier's friends Paul and Lu Songer, a middle-aged American couple who work at Rockwell and Lockheed.

"Two fun-loving Frenchmen," Lu thinks of Thierry and Bernard. "Know the best food, know the best wine."

The Songers remember the arrivals of Bernard and Thierry, whom they assume to be a gay couple: Thierry at the wheel of the Mustang, Bernard in back sleeping comfortably with a pillow under his head.

Paul would put a rib-eye steak, Bernard's favorite Texas food, on the grill, while Bernard would mix a vodka and Kahlúa and get the Songers' daughters all bent out of shape with his philosophy of life.

"You only have two weeks' vacation a year?" Bernard would say. "But this is awful. Quit your job."

He's a fellow who'll do anything to avoid work, Paul sees. He also cultivates an air of mystery. He has such a wonderful collection of Chinese art in his apartment in New Orleans that Lu wonders if he's been involved in smuggling. One day he gives her a beautiful Chinese bowl. When she asks him about its history, Bernard refuses to tell her.

"It is better you do not know," he said. "Use it for apples."

Bernard and Thierry also become involved in the city's gay life, frequenting the gay bars and bathhouses.

They discover The Club Baths one month after arriving in New Orleans. On the first floor is a bar and saunas, and men are pairing off and going into little rooms. Going there the first time, Bernard and Thierry, stupefied into paralysis, only watch. But soon they are frequent participants. Bernard is delighted with the abundance, the abandonment. He also enjoys, as he had in his spy days, his secret double life.

It is raw.

It seems to Thierry that he and Bernard have a very open relationship. But Bernard, in the early months of 1976, is secretly troubled. The newspapers are again full of news of China.

In January, Premier Zhou Enlai has died. He is a beloved figure who had tried to moderate the excesses of the Cultural Revolution. When the government forbids public mourning it is the beginning of rebellion. In April, during the Qing Ming festival, the time for paying homage to the dead, funeral wreaths in tribute to Zhou and in defiance of the government appear on the gates of the revolutionary heroes on Tiananmen Square. In early April, there is rioting and protest. Poems are written not only in praise of Zhou Enlai but against Jiang Qing, the wife of Chairman Mao.

In early July, another of the old guard, ninety-year-old Marshal Zhu De, cofounder of the People's Liberation Army, dies. And Mao, age eighty-two, has not been seen in public for months.

Bernard, his initial curiosity about America satisfied, finds himself thinking of Pei Pu and his son. Also, he misses the excitement of being a spy.

Bernard has never told Thierry about Pei Pu. But one day in early summer, when they are spending the weekend in Palm Beach, Bernard can't keep his secret any longer. It is a day for dreaming in Palm Beach. The weather is lovely; Bernard and Thierry are at a yacht club, talking about owning a boat and sailing the world.

Then, Thierry remembers, Bernard blurts it all out in a flood of words as he always does when he has something difficult to say: He has a son in China. He needs to go see him. He has to make the trip alone.

Bernard does not at first discuss the boy's mother; he only talks obsessively about the boy.

"I have a son," he keeps saying. "I want to be with my son."

A few days later Bernard tells Thierry the story of the boy's mother, Shi Pei Pu, who has been forced to live her life disguised as a man. He is no longer in love with Pei Pu, he says, but he does not want to separate her from her child. He wants to bring them to Paris and hopes they can all live there together.

The story is so extraordinary that Thierry, looking back years later, finds it easier to remember what he felt than what Bernard tells him. This is perhaps because he does not want to hear this story, he says. He can accept it—it is a strange story, but given what Thierry had read of old China it is a believable story. But as far as Thierry is concerned, it is a story that is over. He prefers that it remain so. He does not say this directly to Bernard. He says that China is still a very closed country and that the likelihood of getting a woman and child out is remote. Bernard responds as if he does not hear him.

"It would be okay with you, then? We can all live together in Paris?"

"Yes," says Thierry, though he does not want to.

Bernard wastes no time. He writes to the home office of Foreign Affairs, requesting a post in the Far East. He also asks a friend at the embassy in Beijing to invite him so that he may more easily obtain a visa on his upcoming vacation.

On September 9 it is announced that Chairman Mao Zedong, mastermind of the great Cultural Revolution, is dead.

A new life is about to begin for him and his Chinese family, Bernard thinks.

Pei Pu had once spoken of the necessity of training Bertrand for a profession in Europe. She had suggested a job where language is not important, such as musician or cook. Bernard now buys a three-hundred-dollar child's violin for his son so he can begin studying. He also buys the most expensive ginseng he can find for Pei Pu and cartons of menthol cigarettes for her mother.

In October 1976, Bernard leaves for Beijing.

Thierry is driving him to the airport when they hear the news: Four high-ranking members of the Chinese politburo, including Jiang Qing, have been arrested and charged with crimes against the state. They are being called "The Gang of Four."

Bernard's response is as solemn as that of a head of state.

"It is good," he says, "I am going to China."

Bernard's second meeting with his son is not very satisfying. Bertrand accepts his violin politely, then puts it aside to go play ball with his friends.

Pei Pu is not very excited about the presents either. She tells Bernard he has brought the wrong ginseng and should have bought Bertrand an adult's violin—if it had to be sold, it would bring a better price.

Pei Pu does say that she believes things are getting better in China. She does not believe Premier Hua Guofeng, who is being called "the clearsighted president," will last. He has taken too much power too soon, Pei Pu says, and in China power must be shared. Also, he has no chin, a sign of weakness. But some of her bosses in the Writers' Association who had been sent to the countryside have returned, and Pei Pu thinks it might soon be safe enough for her to write again.

Despite this, she has her usual complaints. She is educating Bertrand herself, because if she sends him to school he will be made into a Communist, but Bertrand is rebellious, he does not listen, he does not study. It is a difficult job, raising his son, Pei Pu tells Bernard.

She is not happy with the way Bernard has arranged this visit either. He is staying at the Beijing Hotel, so that he will be able to visit Pei Pu and Bertrand without making his friends at the embassy suspicious. He still, however, must spend time with them. Pei Pu doesn't understand this. If Bernard goes to a party at the embassy, Pei Pu complains that he is spending all his time with his French friends. He must come from the party to Pei Pu's and stay until two in the morning. And even then Pei Pu is not satisfied.

"Stay, stay," Pei Pu says.

Bernard does not want to stay. He no longer has any sexual desire for Pei Pu, he says. He makes love with her simply to be polite and because she is the mother of Bertrand.

Kang, at least, is still pleasant. He arrives at Pei Pu's unexpectedly one day, as polite as ever. Bernard explains he is posted in a consulate in the United States, from where, he regrets, he is unable to be of service.

After three weeks, Bernard leaves.

He is relieved, as always, to get away from Pei Pu. And yet at the same time he does not want to stay away. En route to New Orleans, he stops over in Paris and makes a visit to the Foreign Affairs department to see if anything has opened up in the Far East. Surprisingly, something has. In Ulan Bator, Mongolia, France's smallest embassy, there is an opening for a typist, archivist, accountant, and courier—all one person. The staff in Ulan Bator totals three.

Bernard knows Mongolia from his days in Beijing; diplomats consider it to be the most miserable spot on earth. Most of the country is desert, and the population is sparse. In winters the temperature drops to forty degrees below zero. Decent food and drink must be shipped in from Europe. Mongolian yak herders roam the country on horseback, coming into Ulan Bator for an occasional tear. The Russians are the political power, and they are a dreary bunch. Visas are difficult to obtain.

Thierry probably could not stay long if he could get into the country at all. At the same time, the exoticism of the place is something Bernard cannot resist. And there is one other thing. The courier run is Ulan Bator–Beijing. Bernard would be thirty-six hours from his contacts in China. He tells Foreign Affairs he'll take the job. Then he flies back to New Orleans.

"Was your son happy with the violin?" Thierry asks.

"Not at all," says Bernard peevishly. "Next time I'll take him boxing gloves. That's more what he likes."

Thierry does not ask about Bernard's old flame. Their story, Bernard has said, is finished, and from what Thierry sees it is so: Bernard talks constantly about his son but rarely about Pei Pu. There is no reason to look too closely.

Duet for Reporter and Spy
"Let the Record Show"
Paris, 1989

"Bernard, excuse me, there is one thing I just realized that when you were talking had just kind of sailed on by. It's from 1973, your third trip to China, when you go back to China and meet Bertrand. Most of the time, in your relationship with Pei Pu, you were never able to spend more than a night with him. But this time in China you're with him a lot. You spend about two months in China. You never go to the embassy because this is a secret trip. . . ."

". . . Yes."

"So you're staying at Pei Pu's house?"

"Yes."

"Where do you sleep?"

"We share the bedroom."

"For two months?"

"Yes."

"Well, how can you share a bedroom with somebody for two months and not notice he's a man?"

"We have already answered this, Joyce."

"No, we haven't."

"Look, imagine sharing a room just like this [twelve feet by eight feet]. There is Bertrand in the house so you cannot close the door. There are two beds in Pei Pu's room, divided by a table—"

"I thought Pei Pu just had one bed in his room."

"He put the bed of Bertrand in his room."

"Where did Bertrand sleep?"

"He was sleeping mainly with his grandmother. Sometimes Pei Pu's cousin was there, too."

"Five people in a two-room apartment?"

"This is China, Joyce, it is not the Holiday Inn."

"So, you're sharing a bedroom with Pei Pu. . . ."

"I am sharing everything, the air, the cooking, the kitchen—"

"—but—"

"—you asked me why I didn't see his thing. Because he is very smart, he can hide it."

"You said you were no longer interested in Pei Pu. If you were no longer interested, why did you go off on a trip alone with him?"

"Because he was a fantastic guide, all over China. He is fantastic for this even now. There is a love story with China you should also fix in your head. If he showed me anything in China, he had a story to complete it. He always made scenarios that did not exist in daily life. We would go to Si Hou, which means Lake of the West, in the morning when everything was quiet and there was fog all around and I was rowing. . . ."

"Was Pei Pu romantic?"

"Of course, very romantic. Because it was tragic that we had to separate again. So it was romantic."

"If it was romantic, didn't you want to make love to him?"

"You always imagine this. You make me crazy on this. I was in China, Joyce, people watch themselves. Pei Pu and I are like mature people now, we talk about our son, we are making plans for him. . . ."

"All this is very nice, Bernard, but . . ."

"We had no opportunity for having sex so much."

"Why? You were in the same room at night, you were on vacation together."

"We had already been living together three years between '69 and '72, we were used already to—how do you say people who are . . ." [Consults dictionary.] "It is mundane. And there are other things. Pei Pu did not close his door at night because his mother was sick, and if she was crying out, he had to go to her several times in the night. That is why Shi was not undressing. Shi was giving her shots, painkillers, he knew how to do this. Bertrand was coming in to say, 'Nana is sick.' The cousin was there."

"I understand. But suppose you are reading a love story and a man comes back to a distant place and sees the person who is the mother of his child, and sees his child for the first time. It makes sense that the man would be full of love for the woman and want to make love to her."

"He wants to be polite to the woman. If she does not want to make love he will not be aggressive with her."

"Didn't Pei Pu want to make love on this trip?"

"At that time it was not possible in the hotels; we were thinking there might be microphones in the rooms. Maybe at home it happened a few times."

"Why would you care if there were microphones? You were working for the Chinese."

"Yeah, but Shi and I were always saying unpopular things."

"This is still difficult for people to understand: How could you spend two months in the company of another man—"

"It was not another man. It was my wife. At that time, I was so sure of it, my poor desperate wife. And I had to go back and live with them and if I could not get them out maybe die with them in China."

"Okay, okay. One other thing I want to clear up: after years of fighting it, when did you decide it was okay to be homosexual?"

"Mentally? In Saudi Arabia with the help of my Marxist friend who told me, 'If I was homosexual, I would not hide it.' He explained this, but he was not homosexual, so he did not have to hide or show anything. At the time I decided I could be a homosexual if I wanted, but I was not having a homosexual life. He explained to me that when the world becomes completely Marxist, each one will have his own freedom. We were systematically destroying the taboos. It was just talk. It did not change my daily life. After this, I had this story with Catherine and the other story with Shi Pei Pu which I was believing was a story between two women, and with which was I going to live? So I decided to live with both, as long as it was possible."

"This decision about homosexuality in Saudi Arabia sounds like an intellectual one. In your heart of hearts, what did you think you were, homosexual or heterosexual?"

"I had not done analysis at the time."

"What were you thinking?"

"I was thinking I was very normal, very ordinary, having a few homosexual experiences like most people have, even if they say 'No.' Particularly if they say 'Never.' "

"The girl in Saudi Arabia who came to your room and you just kissed, was that sexually satisfying?"

"That's why I met a boy, because I was thinking I was on the way to being satisfied. Starting to open my sexuality to the truth or part of the truth, anyway. But it was a long time before it happened in Saudi Arabia. I was feeling I should not do it. And also, it's like you have walked in the desert a long time, you are very thirsty, but you are feeling you should not drink everything you see."

"Just on the basis of the sex itself, which did you prefer, men or women?"

"It is like you ask me which scent of which flower is the best. Each one has its own odor."

"You're saying it depends on the person?"

"Exactly."

"So in 1974, when you meet Thierry, have you been seeing more men or more women?"

"Maybe once a month I pick up a boy, plus a few times a girl."

"You've talked about being sometimes with women prostitutes. You said most of the time they liked to keep the lights on?"

"Right."

"Do they usually take off their clothes?"

"Mmm. Depends. The meter, how you like to say, is working. In Paris sometimes yes, sometimes no. They are fast. In Egypt, they work well. In Thailand, they give you gonorrhea for the same price. In Brazil, they like sex."

"When you do it with a prostitute do you have oral sex—make love to them that way?"

"Who do you believe I am? Where everybody fucks I will put my mouth?"

"Penetrate them with your fingers?"

"Nothing like this."

"It's a normal part of sex play."

"No, not with a prostitute. You have to be a masochist to do this with a prostitute. They have to do the job and you do nothing."

"Sometimes it excites a man."

"I am not heterosexual enough to do this with a prostitute. You pay a person to work, why do the work? She has to make you excited, not the reverse, unless you like so much girls, and if I had liked so much girls, this story would not have happened to me. I did not want to have sex with boys and I was just doing it with girls hygienically—not with pleasure, not with big excitement, just like something that had to be done. Like you go to work, without being excited, but you do it because it is supposed to be normal, standard. You have to understand, Joyce, that until the age of thirty I was a man who was doing not what I wanted, but what I thought should be done. . . . The first boy I slept the whole night long with was Thierry. This was not until 1974."

"You were thirty?"

"Going to be thirty in August."

"Bernard, how many sexual partners would you say you had in your life—before you were arrested?"

"How could I say?"

"Some guys do."

"They lie."

"Give me a figure, roughly."

"Not so many, no more than one hundred. Not much."

7

There are many things that the French find unacceptable about Mongolia:

The cuisine, which in their opinion consists primarily of mutton. The winters, which are so miserable that between January and April the French—to the amusement of the British—close down shop and go home. The head of state, Yumzhagyn Tsedenbal, a strutting little Russian puppet whom the Mongolians call "The Khan of Stagnation" for his economic policies and who's been known to inspect the troops wearing a diamond-studded army cap and several rows of medals.

What disturbs the French most of all, however, is their embassy: They do not have one. Though France established diplomatic relations with Mongolia in 1966, in 1977 they are still working out of the Ulan Bator Hotel—a particularly irritating state of affairs since the British, who opened their embassy only three years earlier, have a lovely two-story residence with guest house and tennis court. The French have to wire Paris every few months for money to pay the bills. Working in hotel rooms, they have little security. As of 1977 the ambassador, Georges de Bouteiller, does not even have a secure place to store confidential documents. There is a safe, but the lock is broken. Bernard Boursicot, once and future spy, will arrive before a new safe will.

He flies into Beijing in April 1977, and his first concern is espionage. He makes a quick visit to Pei Pu, telling her to have Kang meet him at her house in two weeks—he has scheduled a civil service secretarial exam at the Beijing embassy to get an extra visit. Then he boards the Trans-Siberian Railway, which links Beijing and Moscow, for the thirty-six-hour trip across the Gobi Desert and up into the snow-dusted plateaus and Ulan Bator.

It is, he decides, one of the ugliest cities he's ever seen. Expanded for two decades with Russian money, it is as utilitarian as a newly built boom town and just as lovely. Street crosses dreary perpendicular street. The city's finest hotel, the Ulan Bator, where the French both live and work, is a boxy seven-story building heralded by a statue of Lenin. The tallest building is the nine-story Russian embassy. Russian soldiers who have come to town for a little adventure walk the streets in their heavy leather boots alongside taciturn Mongolian herders on horseback, rifles in their saddlebags. No question about who is in charge here, Bernard thinks, looking at the soldiers. He also picks up on something else: the energizing and exciting scent of illicit fiscal opportunity—though perhaps it should be added, in 1977 illegal enterprise is so widespread in Ulan Bator as to constitute a national sport.

Bernard's first day is not unpleasant. He has drinks with Ambassador de Bouteiller, sixty-four years old, who with his stocky build, metal frame eyeglasses, and gruff manner resembles Lyndon Johnson. He has dinner with Emmanuel, the twenty-seven-year-old third secretary, and a pretty young woman who is a professor of languages at Ulan Bator University. Later, they go to see a Charlie Chaplin movie at the Lenin Cultural Center—*The Little Tramp* is always popular in Communist countries, Bernard finds. After the film, Bernard says, he takes the professor of languages home. She is living at the city's second-best hotel, which has a statue of Stalin in front. Bernard claims he spends the night. The lady, years later, denies the affair. She hates to sound vain, she says, but her lovers are of a higher caliber than Bernard Boursicot.

The next day, Bernard begins work. His hopes are high. He has served under Ambassador de Bouteiller in Saudi Arabia and considers him a serious man. Born to the upper class, he studied at Saint-Cyr, the French West Point, and still bears the stamp of the career military man: brisk, buttoned up, by the book. He has served in Russia. He speaks Russian, the language of power here, and has been in the country two years, so Bernard feels he should know his way around. And what he knows, Bernard knows. For since he is the only one at the embassy who can type, Bernard, in addition to being accountant and mail clerk, is also the ambassador's secretary.

Security is minimal. Important papers are locked in office cabinets. Cabinet keys are locked in the desks, and staffers are instructed to carry their desk keys. Office keys, however, are left each evening with the concierge, so the rooms can be cleaned. Once inside the offices, it seems to Bernard, anyone could easily pick the locks.

Getting material will be no problem. But glancing over the documents he has typed in his first two weeks Bernard sees only administrative notes: a request from the ambassador for ten humidifiers and a cheese tray; an advisory that the Mongolians plan to stage *Carmen* and would like photos of costumes and scenery. Bernard won't make his name as a spy handing over requests for cheese trays. He goes to the spy-handlers empty-handed.

Zhao is gone but Kang has adjusted to the arrest of the Gang of Four with the dexterity of an acrobat.

China is in good hands now, he says. Those criminals—he and his colleagues had no idea of their activities. But now all is well, and Bernard can once again help the Chinese people who are still threatened by Soviet revisionism. The Russian-Chinese border is one thousand kilometers. Between fifteen and twenty Russian army divisions and thirty-five thousand Russian economic development and technical advisers are estimated to be in Mongolia. They need to know what the Russians are doing—particularly in the area of troop movements.

Bernard promises to do what he can. Meanwhile, he counts on Kang to look after Bertrand.

"Remember, he calls you 'Papa,' " he says.

"I remember," says Kang. "He calls you 'Papa,' too."

Then Bernard heads back to Ulan Bator and gets himself established. He asks the ambassador to request a visa for Thierry—"Cousin" Thierry is how his lover is described—for with approximately two dozen visas issued to French citizens a year, high-ranking intervention is needed. Bernard commandeers a regular table, with a miniature French flag, at the hotel dining room, where he and Emmanuel entertain the members of the European community. It is not a large group. The French and the British are the only Western European nations with representation. The French community numbers six. He spends his evenings at the Ulan Bator Opera House, where the ballet corps, from generations of life on horseback, is bowlegged. Or he hangs out at the Ulan Bator Hotel nightclub. The jukebox features Bulgarian, German, and Russian folk songs and a few selections from *Aïda*. No Mongolians except high-ranking Communist party members are allowed. It is, however, a great place to make deals, and it takes Bernard but an evening to isolate the desired commodity.

"When you come, bring dollars," Bernard writes Thierry.

Bernard also sets up a court of young women students, including Rodika, a Romanian girl, and a twenty-year-old French student, Marie-Dominique. They are crazy about him. Student life at Ulan Bator University is rough: Kitchen and bath are one large room, with a line of sinks and a few stoves, where the girls wash their clothes, brush their teeth, cook their meals. Students are permitted one shower a week, overseen by a hefty matron who shuts off the water after three minutes. Food, the foreign students think, is awful. Mutton two meals a day, no fruit, no vegetables but cabbage. Ulan Bator is a great city, Marie-Dominique thinks, if you like cabbage.

But when Bernard arrives, food is suddenly no problem. He has the best tomatoes and cucumbers you can find in Ulan Bator. He has milk. He has French champagne. He has fruit. And he does not just share food, he gives it away. When students come to his hotel room, he opens his refrigerator and tells them to take whatever they want; if they are shy he stuffs it into a sack himself. He tells the girls to use his bathroom whenever they like. A half dozen damp-haired girls are always in and out of Bernard's hotel room, lounging in a hot tub, bundling themselves in his robe, drinking champagne. There is nothing sexual in his invitation, the girls find; Bernard just needs to have people about.

He seems to have, a good friend notes, mood swings. One day he is happy, the next day he bursts into tears. The professor of languages, who quickly comes to dislike Bernard, feels he has a mean streak, too. He invites everyone in a small group back to his room for drinks—pointedly excluding her. He drinks to the beautiful women of Ulan Bator—they are all exquisite, he says, except one.

Bernard disputes this. He was never discourteous to the woman, he says indignantly—she tells stories about him because he rejected her. Nor did he have severe mood swings. He may have been a bit depressed when he first arrived, he says, because he missed Thierry, but that mood quickly evaporated.

One reason is a beautiful Mongolian-Russian woman who soon caught his eye.

She is married to a foreign technical adviser and hangs out at the nightclub with a web of international drinking partners—the sort of woman, Bernard says with pleasure, whom everyone suspects of being a spy. Everyone wants her, but not everyone, Bernard hastens to say, gets to sleep with her. You have to be a diplomat and bring her a present besides. An English friend wants her, too, so it becomes very important to Bernard to have the girl first.

It is not difficult. He has a formula for married women: You invite the woman to lunch, which is a respectable meal. Then you invite her back to your apartment for coffee, which is merely polite. There you play the bittersweet love songs of Jacques Brel and sit beside her on the sofa and take her in your arms. When she says no you ignore her because she means yes. By six she is returned to her husband.

So it goes: Bernard takes the woman to his hotel room. She is lovely, but sexually she is very cold. Just like Pei Pu, he thinks.

He gives up on the girl and devotes himself to enjoying life in Ulan Bator. He becomes rather famous for his stock of caviar, which he buys in Beijing. Chinese caviar is good and cheap, but oily. Bernard builds a special colander and vanquishes the oiliness by rinsing the caviar in Chinese beer. He parties nightly, saluting the statue of Lenin in front of his hotel in the morning and relieving himself, after an evening of drinking, on either Lenin or Stalin at night. Stalin, lighted less aggressively, is his preferred spot. Emmanuel and Bernard take turns making the courier run to Beijing every three weeks, and Bernard finds great entertainment value in the British couriers: Her Majesty's Messengers, they are called, former army officers who travel in pairs. One has a large mustache and carries a shooting stick; they are often escorted to the train station by their young ambassador, Julian Hartland-Swann. Gentlemen, Bernard laughs to himself, must always accompany gentlemen. Their manners are perfect, their bearing upright, their accent—which

Bernard loves mimicking—is clipped and, to Bernard, absolutely hilarious. They never leave the diplomatic pouch unattended. When one goes to the dining car, the other remains behind, and they are always pressed and starched. Bernard, in his jeans, is a hitchhiker compared to them.

In June, Thierry arrives on a three-month tourist visa, with two thousand dollars hidden in his boots.

"My cousin," Bernard introduces him to the diplomatic community.

Bernard takes cousin Thierry all over. He makes a nice profit on the dollars, charging seven tugriks for each dollar on the black market instead of the official rate of three. He arranges for cousin Thierry and his friends Marie-Dominique and Rodika to accompany him to Beijing with the diplomatic pouch. For security reasons, the Ambassador insists the couriers rent all four seats in the compartment. Bernard's friends travel to Beijing for free.

In August, Thierry returns to France and Bernard's real cousin, Dominique Hamard, arrives.

"My friend," says Bernard.

Then there is his real work—spying.

It is not easy. Though it is part of Bernard's job to make copies of the ambassador's reports, most of the dispatches continue to be administrative, revealing the embassy's position as the poor boy of the Foreign Service.

Communiqué No. 154: The French scholarship exchange students have arrived with no return air tickets. Tickets should be sent. The embassy is unable to cover the funds for them in case of emergency.

Communiqué No. 168: Thanks for sending a new typewriter. The old one cannot be sold; it is in bad shape and has a French keyboard.

Communiqué No. 149: Accounting in Paris has not held back from the de Bouteiller account the amount slated for deposit in a mutual fund.

Communiqué No. 158: There is the possibility of importing sheep intestines directly to France.

Communiqué No. 141: The Bulgarian embassy will be available at the end of the year; the Mongolians have offered it to the French.

Communiqué No. 52: Request for authorization to purchase a color TV.

Communiqué No. 53: Request for a refrigerator.

Nor are there many interesting papers from abroad. Because security in the hotel is poor, confidential reports are rarely sent, Foreign Affairs spokesmen will say years later, after they've learned of the presence of a spy. When an ambassador receives a confidential document, it is customary in this post to destroy it. Making the courier run back from Beijing, Bernard is sometimes given papers from the Hong Kong consulate or the Beijing embassy at the last minute. Often they are not sealed, and when there is time he takes the papers to Kang. But it happens only rarely and he does not recall anything interesting.

It is six weeks before Bernard has something to bring to the Chinese: a report entitled "Cooperation Between the German Democratic Republic and the Economic Development of Mongolia."

It says that East Germany ranks third, after Czechoslovakia and Russia, in economic development programs; that a recent economic agreement plan, signed in East Berlin by Mongolian President Tsedenbal and East German Secretary General Honecker, marks twenty years of cooperation between the two countries.

It details that cooperation:

"One of the natural resources of Mongolia is cows and sheep. The East Germans built in Ulan Bator a meat processing plant, which according to the local press should be the largest of its kind in Asia. It takes the animal on foot to a tin of 'corned beef' (they are also printing the labels). The factory employs 2,000 people. . . .

"Mongolia also possesses a great many wool-bearing animals (sheep, goats, and camels). East Germany has created in the capital a very modern carpet factory, which works now without the help of East German technicians. We have been allowed to visit the factories with a French firm, which signed a contract last November for some supplementary machines not built in Germany."

It is hardly classified material, and the Chinese, with an embassy in Ulan Bator, certainly have access to the same newspaper reports as the French. But it is the best Bernard can do.

On June 2, there is a more interesting report: "Relations of the United States with Mongolia, Activities of the Chase Manhattan Bank."

It indicates that while the Mongolians are cool to the U.S., the Russians are not only dealing with their capitalist nemesis, they may be playing fast and loose with funds belonging to the Mongolians.

"Mongolia and the United States do not have diplomatic relations," the report reads in part. "Nevertheless, the absence of diplomatic relations between the two countries does not at all forbid the Americans from coming to Mongolia. Last year, two American diplomats came here to spend a few days in Ulan Bator. One was part of the commercial representation of the United States in the Soviet capital. Traveling on a private trip, these two had the benefit of special attention of the Ministry of Foreign Affairs. (A car was placed at their disposal.)

"More interesting is the stay from May 20 to 22 of the vice president of Chase Manhattan Bank in Moscow. He was received by the ambassador of Great Britain, who organized a lunch in his honor at which several Mongolian personalities participated. (I have the feeling that the British embassy in Ulan Bator is unofficially involved with the affairs of the Americans in Mongolia.)

"My British colleague has confided in me that the American bank had obtained an agreement (maybe with the Russians acting as intermediaries) that the proceeds from the sale of furs in Mongolia on the London market would be put in an account at the Chase Manhattan Bank. As the ambassador told me, [the Chase vice president] 'has come to see his new clients.'

"It now appears that Chase Manhattan Bank has deposited in the U.S.A. the dollars which are the proceeds of the Mongolian fur sales. I would not be surprised that the accounts of the People's Republic of Mongolia would be at the disposal of the U.S.S.R., which supports this country and makes 80 percent of what is realized here in several sectors of the economy. . . ."

The poor Mongolians, Bernard thinks; they have the furs, the Russians get the money.

But Bernard still has nothing on the Soviet military presence in Mongolia. And the only time classified reports arrive is when some overreaching diplomat in a forgotten outpost has an urge to bolster his own importance by using the SECRET stamp. It is not the spying career Bernard envisioned back in New Orleans. He makes a mental accommodation. Waiting is part of the political game, he decides. The embassy in Ulan Bator is a sleeping embassy, waiting until the moment cool and knowing diplomatic intervention is needed. So it is with him. He is a *sleeping* spy.

He steals the best material he can find, running off copies and carrying them to Kang at Pei Pu's. The visits are always rushed: Bernard never has more than thirty-six hours in Beijing. He usually arrives Monday evenings. He delivers the pouch and socializes with friends at the embassy. The next day he runs over to the Friendship Store to pick up supplies for the girls back in Ulan Bator and also for Pei Pu. Then he runs to Pei Pu's and delivers the papers to Kang. He is as appalled by Mongolian food as are the French.

"It is very bad for you in that country; every day you are eating sheep," he says.

Bernard has little time to spend with Pei Pu and Bertrand.

Bertrand, now eleven, has no interest in Bernard; he would rather be out playing with his friends—he is, Bernard proudly notices, much larger than the Chinese boys of his age. His Breton blood, no doubt.

Pei Pu, as in the old days, complains about how little she sees him and adds complaints about Bertrand:

"He shouts like you."

"He doesn't care about the same things you don't care about, like money. You were an accountant, and yet you do not know about money. It goes from father to son. It is your fault."

"Of course," Bernard thinks. "Anything that is bad is always my fault."

And then he feels guilty. Pei Pu talks about how empty her life is when he is away, but Bernard's life is not empty. He is strong and healthy. Pei Pu's health has been ruined with hormones. Bernard feels no sexual attraction to her either. Pei Pu doesn't look very pretty these days; she's plucked a good deal of hair from the front of her head to look more masculine. And if Bernard wants sex he has Thierry, an exceptional lover, and when Thierry is not there, women who are much more accommodating than Pei Pu. Also, with all his running around during these visits, he is exhausted. But Pei Pu, Bernard claims, still wants him, and she is the mother of his son. It is not right to refuse her. So they fall into a routine:

Bernard arrives with his packages from the Friendship Store, the duck, the chicken, the oil. He delivers his papers to Kang and pays his respects to Pei Pu's mother, who is increasingly frail. He pats his son on the back. Then Pei Pu tells Bertrand to go outside and play. And Bernard goes with Pei Pu to her room and leans back on the bed, half dozing, his eyes covered with an Air France sleep mask. And thus blinded, Bernard gives himself up to Pei Pu.

In late December, there is a nice bit of material for Bernard to give the Chinese: Ambassador de Bouteiller's end-of-mission report, the summation of his three years in Mongolia. It is not classified; indeed, Bernard is instructed to send it to three dozen persons in the Foreign Affairs department. There seems nothing new in the ambassador's assessment of Mongolia as a pawn of the U.S.S.R. But at thirty pages, at least it has bulk.

"The U.S.S.R. would find it difficult to find someone in Mongolia more pro-Soviet than Mr. Tsedenbal. In all his political speeches, no matter what the circumstance, the Mongolian head of state never misses making laudatory remarks about 'the grand Soviet Union' which provides 'generous and disinterested aid' to Mongolia. This is part of the official oratory, even though I believe that Mr. Tsedenbal is convinced of what he says. But what is the opinion of the Mongolian population in all this? . . . It is difficult to respond to this question, as much as it is to know the real opinion of the Tadzhiks and the Uzbeks in regard to 'big brother Russia.' In different circumstances, I have tried to broach this delicate subject. The French students, who live at Ulan Bator University, in immediate contact with the Mongolians, have also tried. Nothing could ever pull from those being questioned a disagreeable remark with regard to the Soviets, never more than an embarrassed silence or a half smile."

And there is another piece of good news: the arrival of an interesting new girl at the university whom we shall call Basia; she is a Polish linguist who speaks English. And she is the talk of the dormitory because she walks around the halls wearing nothing but a towel.

She is pretty, too. Pale perfect skin, a full figure. Her manner is so direct it is practically an assault. The chin is perpetually up as if challenging one to a fight. It is an Eastern-bloc toughness, born of meat rationing and fuel shortages, one that suggests that other nationalities—

the French in particular—are lazy and spoiled and not deserving of what they have. Regarding men, however, Basia is not very tough. She is a woman, one feels, who will invariably make the wrong choice. Also, she is away from her family at Christmas and secretly she is sad.

Bernard takes her to the nightclub. Everyone is there—Bulgarian diplomats, Russian "advisers," Mongolian government people, British embassy staff—and they are in a holiday mood: drinking vodka, singing, dancing. Bernard never takes his eyes off Basia. When they leave the club, it takes her a few minutes to realize they are walking toward his hotel.

"I want to go to my dormitory," she says.

He is wearing a heavy Chinese coat with a fur lining and a fur hat that makes him look six inches taller.

"Aren't you a big enough girl to come back to my place?" he says.

He has a technique for single girls: Ask them back to your place in the evening, offer them a brandy, which is only polite, put on the intoxicating music of *La Traviata,* sit down on the sofa with your arm around the girl. When she says no, kiss her again because she means yes.

So it goes. At his place, he runs her a bath as if he knows there has been no hot water in the dormitory for three months. While she bathes, Basia hears *Traviata,* and when she comes out, damp and contented, they kiss.

Is she in love? She would have to say yes. It is such a carefree time; she has only a few classes a week; she is in the snow-covered landscape of Mongolia, cut off from the world; she suddenly has Bernard. He has two fur-lined gabardine greatcoats that reach nearly to the floor. He bundles her up in one and she is ready for anything: a picnic on the ice, a night at the opera. They see what Basia, in her Polish-accented English, calls *The Lake of the Swan* at the Opera House. It is not bad, but all the dancers have the bow legs, and you could *die of loffing.* As a lover Bernard is enthusiastic; she has no complaints. But of course, she barely gets to know him: It is a very intense love affair, but it lasts only a few weeks. Then it is the first of January and the French are closing the embassy and Bernard is gone.

There is a saying in Foreign Affairs:

"Every newcomer follows an imbecile and precedes an *arriviste*."

Returning to Mongolia in April, and reading the first reports of the new ambassador, whom we shall call Aristide, there is no doubt in Bernard's mind the next ambassador is going to be a newcomer. For Aristide, Bernard has a terrible feeling, is a fool.

He sighs.

The year, he thinks, had started out so nicely, too.

He had told Pei Pu before returning to France that he was living with a man and she was not distressed. It must be only other women, Bernard decides, that upset her.

"I am so happy for you," he remembers Pei Pu saying. "I feel you are less alone if somebody is with you in that awful country. Perhaps sometime I will be able to meet him."

He had a marvelous time with Thierry, spending two months at the home of a wealthy Moroccan whom he had met in Ulan Bator.

He had even had a pleasant meeting with his new boss, an energetic little bantam in his fifties, divorced, who Bernard recalls had asked him what the women were like in Ulan Bator.

He likes the ladies, Bernard thinks; we'll have some fun. Now, reading the new ambassador's first reports, his spy's heart sinks. The new man, he decides, isn't interested in politics—he wants to write comedy.

"The Mongolian leaders always wear fedoras, which give them the aspect of lieutenants of Al Capone rather than high dignitaries of Asia," Aristide writes of the International Socialist Workers' Day celebrations of May 1. "The 'Internationale' followed the playing of the Mongolian national song, which sounds more like a one-step on the other side of the Atlantic than a national anthem. . . ."

There is a serious note: a mention of a speech by a Mongolian minister regarding possible Chinese aggression, which prompted the Chinese ambassador to walk out. But what seems to interest Aristide, Bernard sees in report after report, is word play. He visits a copper mine and squeezes the names of as many minerals as possible into one phrase:

"The sun was like lead and the horizon was like brass. . . ."

He calls Ulan Bator "The Ghost Embassy" or "The Diplomatic Gulag."

"So we'll make some copies," the ambassador says. "Even if it is not interesting for the government, my friends will have a laugh," and Bernard runs off a few dozen to be sent to embassies and consulates around the world.

The ambassador, unlike his predecessor, is not fluent in Russian. His part-time translator—in what Bernard considers a typical Foreign Affairs lapse in security—works mornings at the French embassy and afternoons in the Mongolian Foreign Office.

Nor are Aristide's serious reports compelling. A six-page report, "Mongolian External Policy in the Context of Sino-Soviet Antagonism," is little more than a rehash of information already noted in the press.

Even dispatches marked CONFIDENTIAL are not, in Bernard's opinion, very interesting.

A confidential report entitled "American Representation in Mongolia," which Bernard is instructed to dispatch to sixty-one persons, deals largely with information already dispatched by Ambassador de Bouteiller.

A four-page confidential report on the visit of Soviet defense minister N. V. Ogarkov in June contains little hard information. Ogarkov's trip has been reported in the newspapers, and the ambassador's analysis of the Soviet military presence contains little the Chinese diplomats in Mongolia cannot see for themselves.

"It is difficult to give an exact idea of the impact of the Soviet armed forces in this country, because of the secrecy which surrounds the movements of troops," the report reads in part. "It is always obvious, even for the tourist, that the Soviet military presence is everywhere and that the number of soldiers seems, according to visitors who have come back after a year, to have noticeably grown. Yesterday morning's Moscow train again was taken by assault by numerous men on leave, the majority of whom were officers, but also a number of enlisted men. . . .

"Has the Soviet army recently received reinforcements? It is not only possible, but very probable. According to certain information that I can't verify, a supplementary tank division was in Mongolia for some time, which makes it a minimum of three divisions. According to other sources, maybe exaggerated, there were at least five combat divisions, without counting, obviously, the missile launchers, some of which are around Ulan Bator, and the air power composed of many hundreds of planes of all models, including the most recent."

And much of the time, Aristide is sending off lighthearted wires. Or a dispatch complaining about "the precarious situation" of operating out of a hotel and the tiny staff.

"The situation created is ridiculous and obvious to anyone in the diplomatic corps . . . that the French do not even have one secretary who can type. . . . It is impossible to fill a form for a visa, to answer any letter or any telegram, and naturally to have a place card at the table in case of an invitation at the last hour. . . ."

How can Bernard give this to the Chinese? They will think he is a mole in a circus.

When Aristide presents his credentials to President Tsedenbal, he appears—perhaps having heard of Tsedenbal's penchant for medals—with a row of decorations across his chest. Tsedenbal, this time, has none. He is always poking his head in Bernard's room when the girls are there. The ambassador says he's checking security; to Bernard, he's dying for an invitation.

Bernard does not care much for the number-two man, whom we'll call Jérome, either. Age thirty, he is a thin, serious fellow who, in Bernard's opinion, wants too much to be boss.

Bernard gives him his own nickname: "The First Communicant."

Ambassador Aristide is not happy.

From the moment he arrives in Mongolia, Bernard is impossible. They are in a hotel, there is no security, Aristide and Jérome read incoming dispatches immediately and destroy them or lock them in the cabinet in Jérome's office. Bernard Boursicot goes off for a beer and leaves his office door open and papers scattered about. There are sometimes foreigners from Eastern-bloc countries, Poles and Romanians, around when Bernard is typing the ambassador's papers, though the ambassador repeatedly forbids it. Bernard denies he acted carelessly.

It drives Aristide crazy. He is not sending back anything of great importance his first few months; he is just getting his feet wet; but there is the principle of the thing. Also, things are difficult enough in a Communist country where one is hard pressed to get any information but the official party line and the secret police are on your back. Aristide knows that sometimes he is being followed. He also suspects Russian agents are trying to get into the rooms of the embassy. But he is vigilant: He sometimes gets up in the middle of the night and patrols the halls just to let them know the French are on guard.

Meanwhile, almost every evening there are people in Boursicot's room attending his parties. All those women! But the good times and late nights don't seem to affect Bernard's work. He is always on time in the morning. He is also very strong. He can hoist an enormous bag with no difficulty and he is very fond, for some reason, of the trips to Beijing.

It is hard being with a guy, thinks Basia. They promise you a lot at the beginning because they want to make love to you, and then when you fall in love they are not interested and you suffer. Worse, she is always stupidly in love with men she should not be seeing in the first place. She does have her types: athletes, because they are always in great shape; musicians, because they have a good fantasy life. The first man she sleeps with, as a student in London, is a musician, black, from Trinidad.

Her family would have hated him because they are bigoted, but Basia does not care. Musicians have imagination; they are wild men. She cannot bear middle-class men with their dreary little salaries who spend their money fearfully and grudgingly. The routine of that life would kill her. She has had, she must say, some very smart boyfriends. Several diplomats, one ambassador, one councillor, a minister—all very pleasant, though being high-ranking representatives of their countries, they can't be seen in public with her. They are married men.

In Mongolia she chooses Bernard Boursicot, who is single.

And now, only a few months into the affair, *he* is trouble.

He hints of a life together—they could make a good team, he suggests. But he always stops short of making a commitment.

"I am ninety-nine percent certain I love you," he says. "I think I might love you."

They are seldom alone. She likes looking after a man, cooking and cleaning, but there is always a group of French parasites around, and when they see Basia cooking and cleaning the bathroom, they do not bother helping.

He can also be terribly cruel.

"I need some fresh flesh," he says one spring evening when Basia arrives at his room, and he goes off to the nightclub alone.

In June, when his cousin Thierry arrives, Bernard ignores her. It upsets her so much she goes to his room and pounds on the door, crying. He still will not let her in. He is a selfish man, he doesn't care about anyone else, she decides.

His cousin, Thierry, however, is just the opposite. A few days later, when Bernard has invited her over—for he runs hot and cold; you never know what mood he will be in—Basia meets Thierry. He is a good listener, thinks about what she says; he is gentle. In a few weeks, Basia has fallen in love with Thierry.

An emotional girl, Basia, Bernard thinks. One day crying and saying she does not want to see him again, the next day laughing and acting as if nothing had happened. "Let's dance, without shirt and pants," Bernard hears her yell at parties. She is very efficient and a hard worker, too—a diplomat could do worse than have such a woman as a wife. What

Bernard does not like is her possessive streak. He sees her a bit more than other people, but that does not mean she is his girlfriend. Nor does he feel an obligation, when Thierry arrives, to tell her about their relationship. He does not owe her anything.

Pei Pu can drive him crazy, too.

"I know you aren't interested in me any longer," Pei Pu says when he comes to town. "Your heart is good, but it is like a porcelain: When it is broken, it is never possible to make it like it was before. I know something is broken between us. But I know you will not leave Du Du."

"It's not true, Pei Pu," Bernard says, though it is. "I love you very much."

At the embassy Jérome keeps trying to throw his weight around as if rank matters out here. Bernard gets even. He has the key to the office supplies. When Jérome really irritates him, Bernard cuts off his pencils.

In mid-July the embassy closes down for the summer holidays. Thierry returns to France. His leaving is painful to Basia. She goes to his room and tells him she loves him.

"It is quite impossible," he says.

She assumes he is in love with another woman.

"Nothing is impossible," she says.

Jérome and Bernard leave for Beijing, to be put at the disposal of the embassy.

Bernard has promised Pei Pu he will come see her as soon as he arrives. Her mother, he knows, is failing. But when he arrives in Beijing he finds some old friends waiting for him at the train station. It is three days before he gets around to visiting Pei Pu. When he does, he feels the pain in the house.

"Now we are alone," Pei Pu says. "My mother has died. She was waiting for you. She wanted to see you. She died two days ago."

"I'm sorry," says Bernard. "I wanted to come, but it was not possible. I had friends waiting."

"So you prefer your friends to us," Pei Pu says.

Bernard tries to make it up to her. He spends much of his free time in August with Pei Pu and Bertrand. Bernard receives condolences from Kang, who is kind, telling Bernard how sad he is about Pei Pu's loss.

He also tells Bernard that when he returns to Ulan Bator, he should not trouble himself about finding additional papers. It is too dangerous for him, he says. If there is any information, Bernard can just tell Kang.

And so, his spy career ended, Bernard turns to other pursuits. He tours with his friends. He travels to Hong Kong to buy several dozen pairs of blue jeans, which are in great demand in Ulan Bator. When Bernard returns to Mongolia in September, he gives the jeans to Basia to sell. He suggests a thousand percent markup, saying they will split the profits. Bernard and Basia also resume their affair. Later, Bernard hears that Basia has been collecting a fifteen hundred percent markup. His admiration for her increases.

Jérome, meanwhile, is not doing well. After what was supposed to have been a month and a half of light duty in Beijing he looks so exhausted that Ambassador Aristide asks what is wrong. The third secretary, according to Aristide, tells him that Bernard Boursicot has been as mean as humanly possible. He now wishes to return to France. Bernard Boursicot, asked about the problem years later, cannot remember anything he did in Beijing. Jérome declines to discuss Mongolia or Bernard Boursicot. Bernard does remember an incident, after he returned to Mongolia, in which Jérome reprimanded him for using the embassy car and driver without his permission. Bernard claims Jérome had wanted to use the car to get some milk. They quarrel. Bernard says he then pins Jérome against the wall.

"Maybe you should drink beer instead of milk," he tells him. "It might make you stronger."

Jérome goes to the ambassador saying Bernard Boursicot has threatened his life and he is placing himself under his protection. He does this twice. Jérome also tells Aristide a Swiss businessman has informed him that Boursicot has been trafficking in dry goods. The ambassador, years later, will say he wanted Foreign Affairs to replace Bernard, but Bernard was leaving shortly and he had to put up with him —there was no one else.

In early October, Thierry arrives for another visit, this time accompanied by Mme. Lavalier.

It is apparent to her that she has walked into a situation of some turmoil. There is a Polish girl named Basia who doesn't know whether she is in love with Bernard or in love with Thierry and is ironing both their shirts. Bernard seems one day to love Basia and the next day to be mooning over a Romanian student named Rodika. The ambassador—the first she has ever met—has to her mind a most unambassadorial style. She also has the impression that Bernard has told people she is his aunt.

At the end of October, Jérome returns to Paris. Aristide tries to be cordial to Boursicot because he is his sole colleague, but it is not easy. Coming home one evening in late winter, he finds Bernard drunk on the steps of the hotel.

"You never wanted to be my friend, Mr. Ambassador," Aristide remembers Bernard wailing.

It is a relief in December when the embassy closes for the winter.

"This friend who is living with me in Mongolia—I told him your story," Bernard tells Pei Pu when he and Thierry arrive in Beijing.

"It is difficult with you," Pei Pu says. "You tell everybody everything."

"But it's better that you should know about each other," says Bernard. "If I was not in Paris when you arrived, I would send Thierry to look after you. What would you do if I was not there? He is in Beijing. You should meet."

Pei Pu is not enthusiastic. Neither is Thierry.

But it is impossible to go against Bernard. And so one evening he and Thierry set out from the diplomatic quarters on bicycles, disguised in big blue Chinese overcoats, with their collars turned up and their visored hats pulled low over their eyes. Thierry has little confidence they will go unnoticed. He is wearing blue jeans and boots and he is certain there aren't many six-foot-two-inch Chinese with blond hair and hazel eyes. Bernard insists they are fine. They pedal to a neighborhood that looks to Thierry like a suburban low-income housing project, then carry their bicycles up the stairs to the apartment so no one will know Pei Pu has visitors. The apartment is dark, filled with an incongruous mix of Chinese furniture and modern electronic equipment. Thierry has never seen so much gear outside an electronics store. There are three or four stereos, a television, camera, radios. He meets Bernard's old mistress, their son, and a tall, silent middle-aged man who is introduced as a cousin of Pei Pu's.

Thierry studies Pei Pu, who is dressed in trousers and a baggy jacket, as carefully as courtesy permits. Her hair is cut like a man's, but he does not doubt she is a woman, because Bernard told him so.

Pei Pu, however, does not look like a woman.

On the other hand, she does not look like a man.

The hands are very thin, the face is beardless and the voice high. Pei Pu also has an Adam's apple. Of course, Bernard has told Thierry that she had been forced to take hormones, so maybe, he thinks, they caused this. She *is* very maternal. Bernard's son, who is quite shy, at one point curls close to Pei Pu with his head on her lap, and Pei Pu pats his head.

Thierry would not like to say it is an unpleasant evening. Pei Pu prepares a lovely meal and does very amusing imitations of Mme. Mao. She seems to understand that Thierry and Bernard are lovers, although nothing specific is said.

And yet Thierry feels like an intruder. This is Bernard's story, not his. Also, he does not trust Pei Pu. She is intelligent—though not, in Thierry's opinion, the brilliant mind Bernard has described—and she is very nice to him. But she is too nice. He senses that she is not saying what she really feels. Thinking about it later he decides it is probably the result of having to hide her true identity for years. She has also, he knows, had to pretend to be sympathetic to the government under Mao. Of course, Thierry thinks, those two things would have an effect. They would make you unable to be direct and straight with people, even in your own mind.

In January, Thierry makes another visit to Pei Pu's with Bernard to deliver some presents Bernard has picked up in Hong Kong. They bring a camera, two or three watches, a few calculators, and three small television sets—Pei Pu can sell them and make money, Bernard says. Thierry finds himself with Pei Pu in front of a large color television set with the first remote-control either has seen.

"I don't know how to use this thing," Pei Pu says. "Do you?"

A lovely meal is again served.

"I know you are Bernard's friend, so you will take care of him," Pei Pu says to Thierry. "I am not able to follow him all over the world—how

I envy you that you can. But I can see how honest you are, I am happy you are with him. Maybe someday I will be able to come to your country also. But as you know, my condition is difficult. . . ."

In mid-February, Thierry takes a charter flight back to France. There is relief at Pei Pu's home.

"Your friend is very nice," Bernard remembers Pei Pu saying. "But Du Du says, 'I do not like this one with the mustache.' I have to explain that he is your friend who is accompanying Papa so he does not have to travel around the world alone."

A few weeks later, Bernard departs, taking the Trans-Siberian Railway to Moscow and then on to Paris. When the train stops in Ulan Bator, Basia and some girls come to meet him, bearing food and wine and flowers—as one does when greeting an arriving hero.

Duet for Reporter and Spy
"My Name Is Not Sorge"
Paris, 1989

"This is pathetic, Bernard. You're telling me Kang didn't want your papers? You were sent to prison on stuff the Chinese didn't even want? When did they tell you this, exactly?"

"Second stay, the end of my second stay. Summer, end of summer, '78."

"You said at the beginning of your stay the Chinese were happy."

"Happy I was in Mongolia, so they had someone who would be well informed. I was convicted for the gesture."

"Of course, it can be argued that betraying your country is betraying your country—like stabbing someone. Should you get a lighter sentence because it ends up being a flesh wound rather than hitting the heart, if you were aiming for the heart?"

"Joyce, I was not sentenced for betraying my country, *please.* I was sentenced because I had relations with and talks with agents of a foreign country, not even an enemy country. It didn't matter what I gave them."

"But didn't you have any qualms, any doubts, about giving the Chinese government documents while you were in Mongolia?"

"Never! Because when winter was arriving, we used to close the embassy, seal the door with wax, and leave for three or four months in Europe. Could you tell me, if the Russians wanted to see what was inside, were they not able to put the wax back on the same way and open regularly the cardboard boxes, the safe? They had four months to do it. Under the control of the Mongolian authorities. Who of course agreed. So what was the secret? I was making equidistance, giving the same service to the Chinese as we were giving to the Russians if they wanted. I was not feeling guilty. I was enjoying it, even. And it only took a few minutes; it didn't take time. It was like stealing staples.''

"Bernard, you told me once if they had caught you earlier, if they had been able to prosecute you for what you did in China, it would have been years in prison, that then you were a really great spy. But you never brought the Chinese anything marked 'secret' or 'top secret'?''

"No.''

"Why?''

"They were not very interesting even if they were secret.''

"Did you read them?''

"No. Later on I saw a few by mistake. When something is marked 'secret' in the French system, it can mean there is a problem with an individual person. I remember one paper about a Chinese in Algeria coming to France who wanted when he arrived to have protection. This was a secret paper.''

"There had to be others.''

"There were no secrets. There were no spies in China acting for the French government.''

"How do you know?''

"I am sure.''

"Well, when somebody says he is a spy, you expect he gets something, some secret recipe for a bomb, the movement of enemy troops. What did you provide?''

"You believe James Bond?''

"What did you turn over that was secret?''

"Whatever we had at the embassy.''

"Your biggest accomplishment as a spy?''

"Hmmm. . . . I would say being able to say to the Chinese, 'This is what Mr. Marshall Green thinks in Washington,' 'These are the thoughts of the one in Moscow. . . .' ''

"What else?''

"I helped China in the political line to stop being isolated and have a better knowledge of what others were thinking. . . .''

"What else?"

"I used to read the reports in the files, and if there was one that was better written, representing the American point of view maybe, I gave them that. For instance, the last report of the Minister Councillor Pierre Cerles, 'China and the Triangular Game,' about the reactions of Moscow and Washington to the events in China. He left in the beginning of '70. It was very helpful for the Chinese, they had no ambassador in Moscow at the time. Cerles was a specialist in Russian questions. I knew him; he had invited me to his apartment."

"Bernard, what does it feel like to be a spy among your own people? What do you feel like at a cocktail party, betraying your country?"

"I was not betraying my country; I was helping China. Even the Chinese told me, 'We do not want to know the secrets of your country. France is a friendly country; we do not want to know about France, but about Russia.' "

"In the beginning, you cared about the revolution in China. Did you still believe in it, during Mongolia?"

"In the beginning, I was caring; at this point, nobody is caring. Kang does not speak of revolution. Everybody is more practical."

"What is Kang speaking about?"

"We don't have much occasion to meet. He used to let me see Pei Pu without him. No more lessons of Mao."

"So if you have a paper for him, how does he get it?"

"I told him that I arrive generally on Monday afternoon in Beijing, so he can meet me Monday evening at Pei Pu's place."

"So if Kang isn't there, and you have a paper for him, do you ever leave it with Pei Pu?"

"No, no, no. It's a present. It's not Inter-Flora, you know. I like to bring myself the flowers. But generally, he is there. He takes the paper, leaves, and later on he comes back, politely, and gives it back. It was a problem for me, getting rid of it. When I arrived home I would burn it and put it in the toilet."

"When you were alone with Pei Pu—"

"—Remember, Joyce, I used to ride thirty hours on the train and spend forty hours in Beijing, and during those forty hours I had to buy food for the whole embassy: for my friends, for the wife of the British ambassador if she needed anything, for my maid. It was normally seven-teen bags full of beer, food, Chinese clothing, shoes. I used to spend a lot of time in the Friendship Store in Beijing. I also used to buy for Pei Pu things I had to carry myself. I had to come back to my place, spending only two nights, in the morning fix the bags in my apartment, confirm my reservations, have meals with the officials at the embassy. I had not so much time with Pei Pu. I used to get on the train in Beijing and fall asleep and wake up in the Gobi Desert. Without Valium. Get-ting the bags. Spying at the same time. Running, running, running. The weather was different between China and Mongolia. I was really tired when I was coming back."

"How many times did you bring papers to the Chinese?"

"I made seventeen round trips, every month or something like this, and in December we close the embassy up, and I go on holiday to Europe for four months. Come back the end of April and paid just the same as if I am working. This is the life. In the winter, when it is very cold, the second stay, we start to make picnics every day. Picnics when it is forty degrees below zero. We ask the driver to come with us to prepare the fire, we eat, we visit shepherds and have tea with them. Start in the morning for a picnic which is more important than anything, finish the bottle of Champagne René Lalou, which is the best, ask more friends to come. The French sentenced me because I had too good a life. Not for spying. Even the prosecutor said, 'Boursicot, like Ulysses, made a trip of twenty years, and now I will explain to you the Odyssey of Boursicot.' It was a poem, this trial. Everybody coming was telling a different poem—"

"—Bernard, your two terms in Mongolia, how often do you have sex with Pei Pu?"

"Maybe two or three times the first stay, maybe the same the second term, but I was so nervous. I had so many things to do, to buy, to carry the diplomatic bag, to fetch, to go from one side to the other. If I had two dinners outside, Pei Pu was sad because there were only two free evenings, but if I was invited I could not refuse, because people would wonder why. . . ."

"The sex?"

"Sex was usually his idea. Always in a hurry, and also Bertrand was older and he was not going to school. I arrive at his house, I am in a hurry with oil. Oil for him, oil for the neighbors—we were able to get the best quality at the Friendship Store. Then he always wanted me to eat at his place and I didn't have the time and he would say, 'Stay more, stay more.' Sometimes I would sit on his bed and he would say, 'Bertrand, go outside and play.' He would sit down and start to rub my legs and put his hands on me. Sometimes I was so tired after arriving in his place I was putting on my sleeping mask from Air France and taking a nap and he would come and do a service for me for which I was not even looking. I was only doing my duty. Like you have to do military service."

"As a man you didn't want to penetrate Pei Pu, make love more fully?"

"Nooooo! Because when I was arriving in Mongolia sometimes there was Thierry, sometimes there were other girls. It was not a problem to not do it with Pei Pu when it was so difficult. I was not excited by Pei Pu. If I wanted a girl who was a real girl, who looked like a real girl, it was so easy in Mongolia. I was always in a hurry. Maybe less, the first week when I arrived. . . ."

"So you did make love when you first arrived in Beijing?"

"It's possible, but I don't remember. After the flowers, you don't remember the ashes. I explained to you about love: 'Six months of fire, forty years of ashes.' The ashes have already burned."

"Well, you know, Bernard, this is difficult. This story is about two things, sex and politics, and—"

(Shouting.) "You are stupid! You are stupid if you think it is only sex and politics! There is also the love of a child. If Pei Pu asks me for oral sex, I do it to be nice to Pei Pu. Sex has no importance, it's like taking a Kir or a bottle of wine. Sex is ended with Pei Pu since I am with Thierry. Most often I talk with Pei Pu about the situation, how soon we will be able to leave. There is no more sex life. I can sleep without thinking of Pei Pu all the time."

"You say this is about the love of a child, but you haven't discussed Bertrand a lot during this stay in Mongolia."

"You have to understand I will need another trip and a lot of luck to help Pei Pu leave China. I had a lot of luck being posted back in China. If Thierry had refused to come with me, I would have accepted anyway. It was my destiny, but sex was no more. We were already talking like an old couple. 'You should have done this,' 'You should have done that,' but he was not sexually my appetite. There was only one thing for us: How could we leave the country? I abandoned everything for Pei Pu. I put everything last and Pei Pu first."

"But you had discussed marriage with Basia—"

"This is when Thierry is not there. If I stay with Thierry, I don't need Basia. If I am with Basia, it's better than being alone. She can fix the parties, like a diplomatic wife; she gets a diplomatic passport, so she can get out of Poland. I get twelve percent more salary. The wedding gift would be the passport, so she can get out of Poland."

"Why not marry Pei Pu if you wanted to help someone get out?"

"Because Pei Pu was not a person to marry. He first had to leave China as a man, then change his identity."

"Why couldn't you have gone to the Chinese and said, 'He's a woman, and I want to marry him'?"

"You have to understand the Chinese mentality. If you know the Chinese mentality, it's worse than a crime. It would be losing face."

"Did it occur to you that if you married Basia it would be harder to get Pei Pu out?"

"Why?"

"Didn't you plan to marry Pei Pu when he got to Paris?"

"We had talked about this several times, but if I was married to Basia, I would not have to tell Pei Pu and we could divorce and Basia would have French nationality. . . ."

"You had also told Pei Pu you were involved with Thierry. I don't see how this is putting Pei Pu first."

"Joyce, I imagine you will laugh, but let me give you an image. Imagine Onassis talking to Callas about Jackie: 'I am going to marry Jackie, Maria, let's accept her, but I am always your personal friend.' And Callas says, 'Of course, it is good for you, she is closer to your age, fresher than me.' This is how it was with Pei Pu. I told Pei Pu I had a friend with me in Mongolia; Pei Pu says, 'I am so happy for you. I feel you are less alone, particularly in this awful country of Mongolia. Go wherever you want, sleep all over the world, I know you will have to leave, but your heart is with me, she who has provided you a child you will always remember.'

"In this way he was smart. According to the feelings I was giving to

Pei Pu it was impossible for me to fly with anyone, boy or woman. There is so little sex in what I am telling you. There was a bid in Pei Pu's mind, which worked:

"'Never with anyone will you have the beautiful story you have with me.'"

Eight hours later, midnight:

"Forgive me, forgive me. How could I call anyone stupid? I was four years in prison, but I am not a criminal. How could I speak to anyone like this? I was a diplomat."

"Bernard, people are starting to tell me that you said you had a *second* child in China."

(No reply.)

"Bernard, did Pei Pu ever mention another child?"

"Yeah. It's like this—this was in the beginning of 1971, when he had to go out of Beijing for several months. But it was, uh, he was contradictory, he was not giving explanations, so it's even difficult for me to say if I believed him or not."

"When Pei Pu had to leave Beijing—you mean when the Chinese sent him away and you stopped giving them papers during the first time you were spying?"

"Yeah. In '71 he had to go out of Beijing, so he came several months after and he told me that during that time he was sick and he had a child after six months. But he never provided a picture and he used to say that he had sold the child to important people. But after, he stopped talking about this."

"How come you never mentioned this to me?"

"He told me, 'I cannot stay in Beijing.' So I was alone with Kang and Zhao, no spying, because I was unhappy Pei Pu was not there. Every week I am asking Kang and Zhao, 'When do you think Pei Pu will be coming back?' It took time and Pei Pu came back. He was supposed to write, but he never wrote anything."

"How do you know?"

"I don't know, but if he had written something he could have been criticized. He was away three or four months, and I had to take my holidays, and when I came back, Pei Pu was there."

"Did Pei Pu tell you what had happened to him?"

"So many lies."

"Just tell me what Shi told you, without saying whether it is a lie or not."

"He gave me so many versions. He told me he went to Kunming. There was a picture with his mother from '71. He told me that he stayed in his sister's place, that he was believing he could not return to Beijing, so he was calling his Writers' Association asking them if he could come back."

"He also told you when he came back that he had had a baby. Had you made love to him earlier? Did the time work out?"

"Yeah, it was Christmas, end of '70, the time I explained to you I went with the mask, after the Christmas party, one of the times I did stay. Beginning of '71, Pei Pu has to leave Beijing, and before leaving we had sex together. I went on holiday and when I came back he was back. He explained to me he had a baby, but afterward he made so many contradictions. He told me he had given the baby to people to care for it and when the child was twenty-one he would try to get it back. But it was not a big problem for me. I was attached to the first one. If the other one is out, it is sad, but—"

"—You hadn't seen a picture of Bertrand yet, at this time?"

"Yes. He showed it to me and immediately hid it, but for the second one he did not show me anything. He was not very serious."

"Even so, when somebody tells you you have a child and they've given it away you must have some feeling about it."

"No. I had feelings for the first one."

"This doesn't sound like you. When we first met you told me when you heard you had a child back in China, you had to go back because you had responsibilities. You said you don't throw away people like McDonald's wrappers."

"If you imagine the situation at the time, if we save one, I don't care."

"Was this second one a boy or a girl?"

"He explained to me it was a boy."

"Name?"

"No name. Lost."

"Did you believe Pei Pu when he told you there was a second baby?"

(Long pause.) "This is a big question. I was hearing what he was saying. I was believing about the first one. For the second one I was hearing, but without investing heart."

"Did you believe him?"

"It doesn't mean I didn't believe, it means I was not very interested in knowing and he immediately told me, 'It is too sad a story. I don't want to complicate your life.' But for the first baby he was always saying, 'Your son will always be with you.' "

"Bernard, did you not think about it, maybe, because you had started to doubt that Pei Pu was a woman and there was a first baby—started to doubt everything?"

"No. It should have been like this, but it was not, unhappily. Anyway, Pei Pu was smart enough to put oil on the fire and take it off. And also, I had told him after my first trip back to France on my holidays, I wanted to separate from him and marry Catherine if I could not get him out of China, and for a week he was so terrible against me. He said, 'Oh, you want to marry and forget me and your child.' Immediately I said, 'Oh, no, I am sorry, it was a joke.' I stopped talking because he made such a difficult time."

"How soon after you told him you were thinking about marrying Catherine did he have to go to the countryside?"

"Short time, maybe eight weeks."

"How often did Pei Pu speak of this second child?"

"Hmmmm. We didn't speak of it after this. He said, 'My life is sad, as you know.' "

"Bernard, you were back in Beijing I don't know how many times after this kid was supposed to be born. When you were posted in New Orleans, all the time in Mongolia, after you saw Bertrand. It's a child; you must have talked about it, pushed Pei Pu on where he was."

(Sighing.) "This is what I would like to talk about with Shi Pei Pu. This is one of the biggest mistakes I made. You don't understand what a snake he was."

"Did you and Thierry talk about this second child?"

"Sometimes. We were thinking if it was necessary, we could take care of two."

"So how come you never got to see him? Where was he supposed to be?"

"Pei Pu was never mentioning this. And as I was so fair, I was never asking questions. He always made a poetic thing about the second child. Something very indefinite. He said, 'It is such a sad story, don't make me cry, you have one son already.' This was the kind of mentality, tyranny, I should say. He would say, 'He has no hope of leaving, he has nothing, he is weak like me. Bertrand is like you, he is strong.' He said he came early, seven months instead of nine, he was weak when he was born. He said, 'He will die soon, but don't think of him—I am always crying when I am thinking of him—but he is beautiful, he is like a jewel, the contrary of Bertrand. The other one is like a porcelain, he is more like me and soon he will die.' "

"Didn't you ask who was taking care of him?"

"No. It was not possible to ask questions as direct as you ask me to Shi Pei Pu. If it was possible, it would have been different since the beginning."

"After you got Pei Pu to Paris did he mention the second child again?"

"Sometimes, once or twice."

"When?"

"Joyce, remember one thing: Pei Pu arrives in October, I am back in November for two weeks and in February for two weeks and in June for two weeks. At each time Pei Pu says, 'I am thinking of Bertrand's brother. He is not here, but one day we will all be happy.' But there is not so much time to talk about it, because in June I am arrested."

9

It would not be correct to say that Bernard approaches his new post, as accountant in the consulate in Jerusalem, with complete indifference. He is very excited to be in Israel. Arriving in the spring of 1979, Bernard races off the ferry at Haifa, leaving Thierry in the car, so that *he* will be the first to set foot on the Holy Land. The two find a wonderful apartment at the Mount of Olives, overlooking the city. And by night, Bernard and Thierry enjoy something that did not exist in Ulan Bator and that Bernard in particular has missed—an open and easy sex life.

Bernard goes walking alone at night in the mysterious ancient city. Concerned about being spotted by a member of the consulate staff, he waits till midnight and then walks Jerusalem's sprawling Independence Gardens. The Israeli people, Bernard thinks, are beautiful. There is one man in particular he remembers: A young Israeli soldier, perhaps twenty-two, wearing shorts, carrying an Uzi in Independence Gardens. The mouth is plump, the skin is Mediterranean; the boy could be Italian. Sal Mineo exactly, Bernard thinks. Bernard, at thirty-five, is not a bad-looking man either. He has a barrel chest and broad shoulders, he is tanned, and he has a smile, when he's feeling good, that makes him irresistible.

He approaches the soldier. What does he say? "Nice night"?

"Alone"? The words don't matter. It's all in reading the way a body speaks.

The soldier and Bernard fall into step and Bernard follows the soldier to a small engine house. They go inside. The soldier puts down his gun. Then he pulls down his shorts. Sal Mineo. In *Exodus*, he was so beautiful, so unapproachable, and fifteen-year-old Bernard had wanted Sal Mineo, wanted him on a level of need that is below knowledge, like a dream that, upon waking, you cannot remember but that fills you, even so, with longing. Now, making love to the soldier, it is like realizing that dream. The sex is good. Thinking about it later will be even better.

But at home, in the realm of real love, there is a problem. Thierry is restless. He loves Bernard, but he has been with him for five years and all that time Bernard has supported him. At nearly twenty-nine Thierry feels it is time to have his own life. He decides to return to France.

Bernard understands. It is good for a couple to spend some time apart, and having bought an apartment in Paris before coming to Israel, Thierry will have a place to stay. It's a nice place, a sunny corner studio on the top floor on Boulevard Port-Royal, a few blocks from rue Montparnasse with a fine view of the Panthéon. If the apartment is a sixth-floor walkup it is still, at a hundred and seventy thousand francs, a very good buy. Bernard, however, does not like the idea of being alone. So he gets an idea: He will marry Basia. Life is easier if you have a wife at home and also, people do not suspect you of prowling the park for boys. Basia will not constrict his movements. It will be as it was with de Gaulle. When de Gaulle appointed a minister, he made him sign an undated letter of resignation. Basia will be a "transit solution."

"Why not?" says Thierry when Bernard discusses the plan with him. It is only a deal. Anyway, he is going back to France.

The only missing piece in this plan is the bride. But Bernard isn't worried about Basia. When he had arrived in Jerusalem there had been a stack of letters awaiting him. Some expressed love, some anger, some self-recrimination. The most recent claimed acceptance. She had been very upset when Bernard left her, Basia had said, but one gets used to that kind of situation. She realizes now she expected too much and that Bernard never loved her. Perhaps that is for the best—now she and

Bernard can go back to being friends. Bernard had been willing. He had written Basia a friendly letter, inviting her to visit.

Now, having a new program in mind, he changes his tone. In late May, Bernard proposes to Basia by telegram—running the words together to save money: MARRIAGEOK PLEASECOME LOVEBERNARD WAITFORYOU.

Basia, receiving the wire in Mongolia, is astonished. In the five months since Bernard left Ulan Bator, she has heard from him rarely. Yet she is willing. She has been in love with Bernard, and though she does not consider herself a snob, she likes the idea of being a diplomat's wife. She sends back a pragmatic letter of acceptance, which is a striking contrast to the agonized letters Bernard has received after leaving her in Mongolia.

Even if she and Bernard have not been entirely devoted to one another in the past, or completely honest, she thinks they understand each other well enough to make a go of this arrangement, Basia says. At any rate, she will try not to disappoint him.

They move ahead with the plan. Bernard requests permission of the Foreign Affairs department to marry a foreign national, as required. Basia plots her escape. She is due to return to Poland in early July and can visit other countries only with her government's approval. Now she decides she will fly to Moscow, then take the train to Romania, as planned—but from there she will go to Israel.

However, at the last minute, Basia has doubts. The year before, her brother fled to the West. If Basia does not return to Poland she will leave her widowed father with only one remaining child in the country. The family is already in political disfavor because of her brother's defection. Basia does not want to make her father's life worse.

Three days before she is due to arrive in Israel, Basia wires Bernard that she is not coming. She will come later, she says.

Bernard is not upset, even though the news comes as Thierry is flying back to France. Perhaps he knows he will not be alone for long, for three months later Thierry returns to Bernard. He is once again accompanied by their friend Mme. Lavalier, and the three take off and go traveling. Perfect companions, Bernard and her mother, Catherine sometimes thinks back in Paris: all the places she never got to go to with Bernard, her mother and Bernard go to now. Catherine has met Thierry and understands that Bernard is now homosexual and explained it to her mother. She is happy in her marriage, pregnant with her second child. And yet, thinking of Bernard, she sometimes has an occasional twinge of sadness and regret. Her old boyfriend still seems to have a magical life.

In Israel, the three friends do have a wonderful trip. They go across the Sinai Peninsula to visit the ancient monastery of St. Catherine at the base of Mount Sinai, where Moses was said to have received the Ten Commandments. They bob like corks in the Dead Sea, so salty one cannot sink. They get together with Bernard's aunt Mimi when she stops in Haifa on a cruise. Mimi had never met Bernard and is intrigued by his legend as the family adventurer. Animated and outgoing, with short, curling brown hair, Mimi worked as a psychiatric nurse in London before her marriage and has a nurse's down-to-earth style. Her teenage daughter teases that she is also a snoop. Mimi ferrets marvelous secrets out of friends and family, and when there are no real people to challenge her gift for detection, she reads the mystery novels of the British writer P. D. James. Mimi's English is fluent, so she does not have to wait for the French translation. This is good because Mimi hates to wait. She likes Bernard very much. He is spirited, generous, and warm, she thinks. His relationship with Thierry eludes Mimi completely. Bernard is so robust and flirtatious she assumes Thierry is just a good friend.

The visit is lovely. But when Mme. Lavalier and his aunt Mimi leave, Bernard finds he is bored. He has spent no more than six months in Jerusalem, but he knows it's time to find himself a doctor.

He selects a psychiatrist, one Dr. Radwan, of Tel Aviv. The terrorist violence is taking a terrible toll, he says on his first visit; he has also been unhappy in love. The psychiatrist prescribes Aminotryptiline, a drug used to combat anxiety and depression. On the second visit, Bernard can report no improvement. On the third visit, the psychiatrist diagnoses depressive syndrome due to exhaustion and writes a letter to Foreign Affairs recommending that he be sent to Paris for treatment.

In January Bernard returns, with Thierry, to Paris. A consulting doctor for the Department of Foreign Affairs concurs with the Israeli doctor.

"It is certain that this man has had a full nervous depression," he writes in his report. "He took his stay in Jerusalem very badly, conditions there are not at all restful, and moreover, the emotional affair that

Bernard's parents, Louis Boursicot and Jeanne Hamard, did not always enjoy the warmth of this 1939 courtship photo. A man who tried many jobs in an attempt to better his life, and yearned to be his own boss, Louis often took out his job frustrations on his wife and four sons. Jeanne, a talented seamstress, helped support the family and took comfort from her children.

Left and below: As a boy, Bernard was his mother's pet. She sewed him a morning suit for his First Communion. *Bottom:* By age fifteen, Bernard was already eager to escape provincial life: he bicycled long distances and hitchhiked to Spain.

Nom BOURSICOT	Valable TROIS ANS à partir du :
Prénoms Bernard	12 avril 1965
Né (e) le 12 août 1944	
à VANNES (Morbihan)	
Nationalité Française	
Profession Agent contractuel	
Adresse Ambassade de France	
est immatriculé (e) San Li Tun - PEKIN	
à PEKIN	
sous le N° 41/65	Signature du Titulaire :
avril 1965	*Bernard Boursicot*
Le Consul-adjoint	Renouvelée pour TROIS ANS à partir du :
Jean COLOMBEL	
	Cachet

At twenty, with charm, nerve, and just a dash of deceit, Bernard—with only a tenth grade education—convinced the privileged gentlemen of the French Foreign Service he was one of their own and landed a job in the newly opened French Embassy in Beijing.

Shi Pei Pu, at the time he and Bernard met, had already enjoyed some success as an actor and librettist, often playing women's roles onstage, as was traditional in Beijing Opera.

AP/Wide World Photos

Pei Pu was twenty-six and Bernard twenty when they posed for a photo in 1965. Bernard declined Pei Pu's suggestion that they stand closer together. "When we separate, it will be easier to tear the picture apart," he teased.

During his second tour in China, from 1969 to 1972, Bernard carried on two simultaneous affairs—with Pei Pu in China and a beautiful young French medical student we shall call Catherine in Paris.

Bernard met Shi Du Du, whom he believed to be his and Shi Pei Pu's son, on a trip to China in 1973. It was, he says, the happiest day of his life. Shi Pei Pu's mother, who spoke no French and could not communicate with Bernard, seems far less excited.

Ten years later, having finally gotten Pei Pu and Du Du to Paris, Bernard proudly presented his son to his mother—refusing to tell her the identity of the boy's mother. Mme. Boursicot, a world away from China, seems as confused about this mysterious affair as was Mme. Shi, mirroring a look that is as old as motherhood: "I don't know what's going on here," the look says, "but whatever it is, I know I don't like it."

The three-person French embassy in Ulan Bator was the laughingstock of the diplomatic world, but Bernard enjoyed Mongolia. Posted there from 1977 to 1979, he explored the country with his friend Thierry *(far right)* and Mme. Cecile Lavalier, the mother of his former girlfriend Catherine. He also continued to spy for the Chinese.

By his mid-thirties the shy kid from Brittany had become a suave, sexy, globe-trotting adventurer. In 1980, vacationing in Venice, both men and women found him irresistible.

Bernard was away from China for years at a time, but Pei Pu often reminded him of the son he left behind. In this photo from China, Du Du holds a postcard recalling the song he sang when he first met Bernard and asks Bernard not to forget him.

Du Du was a teenager when Bernard visited China in 1981.

Bernard, here at the British embassy, partied enthusiastically in posts around the world.

Once in Paris, Shi Pei Pu became the darling of artists, intellectuals, and diplomats, performing and lecturing on Beijing Opera. Eight months after his arrival, he starred in a television show.

Facing page: Pei Pu's French friends believed the delicate artist, here seen in China, to be a man. Meanwhile Shi Du Du, *right,* here celebrating his birthday with Bernard's Aunt Mimi in Brittany, was joyously accepted by the Boursicots as a member of their family.

Off in Belize, Bernard left Thierry in Paris to look after Pei Pu and Du Du when they arrived in 1982. Bernard's two great loves politely shared his Left Bank apartment, but when he returned, smoldering jealousies erupted and Thierry moved out.

© Peter Serling

Above: Du Du, with Pei Pu before a performance, lives with his father and helps to support him. *Right:* Bernard and Thierry, lounging on the bridge where they first met, keep a studio in Paris and travel the world. Pei Pu and Bernard, both living in Paris, are today like a divorced couple who see each other rarely but are bound together, however tenuously, for life.

"I used to fascinate both men and women," fifty-year-old Pei Pu said in 1988, shortly after his release from prison. "What I was and what they were didn't matter."

Agence France-Presse

By the time of their trial for espionage in 1986, Bernard had finally accepted the fact that Pei Pu was not a woman and Du Du was not his son. So painful was the realization that while in prison Bernard attempted suicide, slashing his throat.

Three years into his sentence, Bernard cut a relaxed and confident figure in the prison yard and was able to joke about his career as a spy. His sole payment for spying for the Chinese, he noted, had been a pair of garish lamps so hideous he could not look at them. He gave them to his mother who, unaware of their history, uses them in her apartment in Brittany.

"I lost everything—apartments, cars, a beautiful life," says Bernard. "I am very disappointed. But it's better to be cheated than to cheat. There is no dishonor in being cheated. I do not feel Pei Pu is a bastard. I am just sorry our story was not the one I believed."

he had with a young Polish woman did not lend itself easily to conjugal realization. I think that for the time being he can't leave for a foreign post, but that a break from work of two to three months must be planned and serious therapeutic action undertaken."

Bernard follows the doctor's orders—he takes three months off from work. Then he turns to the unresolved question of his marriage to Basia, discussing it once again with Thierry. Thierry tells Bernard to do what he likes. But he also gives him a warning:

It may be easy to marry Basia, Thierry says, but not so easy to be married. Basia may want more than a marriage of convenience. She may want children and a home.

In February, still undecided, Bernard goes to Poland for a long weekend. The train to Warsaw takes twenty-four hours, and as always, the romance of train travel makes Bernard nostalgic. He recalls that on his first trip to China he stopped at the Warsaw airport. He thinks of the excitement of that trip and the love affair with Pei Pu, which made him a spy and changed the direction of his life. He is fond of Basia and in Jerusalem he felt she would be useful, but she is not his love. Catherine had been his love; that had been real. Pei Pu is also his love, his impossible love, his need to have his child near him. Basia is just a settlement. Bernard sleeps fitfully, and as he does Pei Pu's mother comes to him, weeping, in a dream. Awakening, he knows marriage to Basia would be a mistake.

He does not tell this to Basia. He lies, telling her permission to marry has been denied by the Department of Foreign Affairs but that he is prepared to resign his post and marry her anyway.

Basia says she couldn't possibly allow that.

They spend a pleasant four days together and when the visit is over, Bernard goes on to Morocco, where Thierry is waiting.

When he receives permission from Foreign Affairs a few weeks later to marry a Polish national he does not inform Basia.

It is remarkable the way an illness can linger. Bernard's keeps him from work for months. Meantime, he keeps a keen eye on his interests: He buys the little studio adjoining his apartment for seventeen thousand francs, a steal. He begins therapy with a psychiatrist but only, he says, to back up his story of suffering massive depression. He talks, he claims, of nothing serious—his desire to give up smoking, perhaps, the idiocies of the Foreign Affairs department.

In June, Bernard returns to work. He is assigned a variety of clerical jobs: archivist, librarian, clerk. He makes up diplomatic passports, pasting the photographs on the papers, affixing the seal, and keeping records. He is not highly regarded by the department. His superiors consider him bright but lazy. When he requests a post in the new Shanghai consulate, he is turned down.

No matter. Bernard finds it very pleasant to be back in Paris. He boards the Number 83 bus in front of his apartment at Port-Royal, choosing to ride in the small open-air compartment in back. He savors a cigarette as the bus takes one of the loveliest routes in Paris: down the rue d'Assas past the Luxembourg Gardens; down Boulevard Raspail and bustling Saint-Germain, then along the Seine to the Foreign Affairs offices, on the Quai d'Orsay, across from the Place de la Concorde, the largest and most magnificent square in Paris. He walks past the high wrought-iron gate and the guards. Then when he gets to his office, at least once a week, he steals a diplomatic passport.

Why?

Why not? says Bernard. It is so easy. And if you are a spy, it is like being in the treasure cave of Ali Baba. He makes four for himself, because a diplomatic passport is valid for three years and can be renewed twice, and he figures thirty-six years of diplomatic privilege should be sufficient. He also makes one for Thierry and keeps a few dozen blank passports. He does not tell the psychiatrist about it. Why, he figures, should the psychiatrist know his business?

March 1981 finds Paris gray, wet, and bleak, so Bernard and Thierry drive down to Morocco to celebrate a friend's fiftieth birthday. On the Strait of Gibraltar, leaving the small Spanish colony of Ceuta to enter Morocco they run into a huge traffic jam. It is like a mobile souk: families with their mattresses piled atop the cars, farmers with donkeys, trucks.

Bernard is not in the mood to wait.

Then he realizes they do not have to: He has his special service passport, issued by Foreign Affairs; Thierry has a diplomatic passport, issued by Bernard.

"C'mon," Bernard says. "Use it."

Thierry is a little nervous, but what the hell, he figures. He flashes his passport and they are signaled across the border.

Nice to see, Bernard laughs to himself, they still respect the French in North Africa.

And of course, back in Paris, there are the lesser dramas of the sexual chase. Sometimes Bernard has women prostitutes, more often he goes to the baths. They do exist in Paris; they are just less conspicuous than their American counterparts. It is at the baths that he sees a young Spanish-Frenchman. "Don't look at him, he's mine," another man says to Bernard, so of course Bernard takes him away. He is crazy for the boy. A few days later Bernard brings the boy home, telling Thierry to sleep in the little room down the hall.

The boy is shocked.

"Thierry looks sad," he says. "Maybe you were a little hard on him."

"It doesn't matter," Bernard says.

He is frank with Thierry.

"I have a big appetite for this guy," he says. "I love him."

"Do what you like," says Thierry.

Wonderful Thierry—Bernard is more in love with him, he sometimes thinks, when he is betraying him. Thierry objects to nothing. Bernard tires of the new boy in a few months.

In summer, Basia comes to visit, and Thierry is once again sent to sleep in the studio.

It has been a difficult year for Basia: The man she was seeing in Poland, a student six years younger than herself, committed suicide. He was a very intense guy; he spent hour after hour listening to Pink Floyd's "Another Brick in the Wall," smoking cigarettes. Then one weekend in the mountains with Basia, he put a bullet in his head. Basia took it badly. Every weekend for a year, she drove the four hundred kilometers to visit his grave. When Bernard invites her to Paris, she is delighted. The day after she arrives, Bernard receives a dinner invitation from a friend and leaves Basia at the apartment with Thierry, who is living down the hall.

"Why don't you invite her?" the friend asks, not realizing Basia's French has improved.

"It doesn't matter, she doesn't care," Bernard says.

Basia stays in his apartment for a time, then Bernard loses interest. After a week, he sends Basia down the hall and brings back Thierry. He tells Basia he is afraid of making her pregnant. He hints he has already had such problems.

After five weeks, Basia leaves.

Thierry, as always, is very kind to her. He gives her a box of chocolates at the train station.

When is it that thoughts of Shi Pei Pu and Bertrand start returning? Bernard cannot say. Sometimes he feels they are always on his mind, sometimes it seems he goes for months without thinking of them. In July 1981, when his old friend Sylvie comes to France from South America, where her husband is posted, she has no reason to believe Pei Pu is part of Bernard's life: He never mentions her.

But later that summer, on vacation in Bavaria, Bernard rises at seven to climb a hill leading to the Neuechuanstein Castle. The sun rises over the lakes, and the ground is wet with dew. Bernard thinks what a pleasure it would be to show this to his son. But Bertrand is practically grown and what has Bernard given him? A soccer ball. A pair of roller skates. Bernard cries. Then he returns to the hotel and checks out, his mind made up to return to Beijing.

Bernard cannot afford the trip, but he doesn't care. He borrows three months' salary at his bank and writes to his Ulan Bator friend Emmanuel, now second secretary at the embassy in Beijing, requesting an official invitation. He arrives in September. Beijing is full of old acquaintances. The journalist Jean Leclerc du Sablon is back. Emmanuel Bellefroid, whom Bernard met while in Mongolia, is in the documentation department. Claude Chayet, who served in 1964 as minister councillor and was the unwitting key to Bernard's entry into diplomatic life, is now ambassador.

There has been, all agree, enormous change in China. The Four Modernizations, the program of economic reform begun by Vice Premier Deng Xiaoping in 1978, allows farmers to sell their surplus crops on the open market and has established economic zones to encourage foreign investors. The establishment, in March 1979, of an American embassy in Beijing and a Chinese embassy in Washington, along with joint industrial, research, and cultural programs, has lessened the Chinese paranoia of the West. Chinese are eagerly buying TV sets and Western-style clothes. Making money and enjoying consumer goods are no longer bourgeois crimes.

But one could not call this a liberal time, either. Bellefroid is living at the embassy, in defiance of the Chinese government, with his Chinese fiancée, Li Shuang. Part of a group of young avant-garde artists called The Stars, Li Shuang had fought for the right of artists to display their work without official permission. For a while they seemed to have won. But the government's tolerance of political dissension and nonconformity was a tenuous thing. In August, while awaiting government permission to marry a foreigner, Li Shuang was tipped off that the police had issued a warrant for her arrest. She fled to safety in the diplomatic compound.

In the evening, Bernard goes to Pei Pu. Her boxy apartment seems more cheerful now. The portraits of government leaders are gone; some of the old carpets and wall hangings are again displayed. In Pei Pu's room, a picture of her late mother hangs above a bowl of incense. Pei Pu seems happier. She tells Bernard that she is writing and performing again.

Bertrand, this visit, is a delight. At fifteen, he's a big, tall boy in rolled-up American-style blue jeans. His indifference is gone. Bertrand treats Bernard now as hero and pal, perhaps because while Pei Pu is strict, Bernard is always ready to have fun. Bertrand still has the soccer ball Bernard brought him when they first met in 1973. If they play ball and Bertrand breaks a window, Bernard just laughs. Bernard takes him out for a beer and shares a cigarette. He brings him a Sony Walkman because he knows the boy loves music. When Bernard bicycles back to the French compound where he is staying, Bertrand bicycles beside him part of the way, reluctant to let him go.

It is, in fact, one of the nicest visits Bernard can remember, a reunion with friends. He sees Pei Pu's sister and visits with her cousin. Bernard sees Kang at Pei Pu's home, but, he says, there is no talk of espionage. When he and Pei Pu are alone, they speak of but one thing: escape. It is an old subject, but never before has Bernard seen Pei Pu so intent. The doors of China are open, she says, but our history teaches that the doors always close quickly. She has seen this again and again: In the "Let a Hundred Flowers Bloom" campaign of 1957, when writers and artists were encouraged to express themselves and then imprisoned; at the Democracy Wall in 1979 when citizens were permitted to post criticisms of the government—until their leader was arrested. If the door is opening again, they must make their escape now.

She speaks longingly of Paris, as they used to do: of seeing the palace and flowers of the Luxembourg Gardens; of strolling across the Pont-Neuf from where one can see the grand edifice of the Palais de Justice and the gargoyles of Notre-Dame. She must see that bridge, says Pei Pu, because Zhou Enlai had such fond memories of it from his student days. Maybe she could make a movie in Paris of Zhou's early life in France, Pei Pu says. Or maybe she could get an invitation from abroad to perform. Her plans are vague, and Bernard knows Pei Pu no longer has friends at the French embassy to help her, but sitting with her, Bernard finds himself as optimistic as he has ever been. He gives her the keys to his apartment on Port-Royal.

Meanwhile, Pei Pu tells him, there is something they must do—bury the remains of Pei Pu's mother. Mme. Shi had been cremated as the law required. The government does not wish to waste land, nor to perpetuate the expense of large funerals and the superstitions associated with the worship of the dead.

Pei Pu's mother, however, had wished to be buried beside her husband in the south of China. Pei Pu also wants her mother to rest in a proper grave. And so, a week after Bernard's arrival, Pei Pu and Bernard and Bertrand make their journey to Kunming, "the city of eternal spring."

It is a beautiful city. Flowers bloom year-round, and on a hilltop, in a grove of bamboo trees, there is a monastery that has survived the Communists. Holding the marble box with her mother's ashes, Pei Pu goes with Bernard and Bertrand to the monastery. She gives a monk ten yuan and they all descend stairs leading down to the grottoes, where a thousand little mausoleums are carved into the stone walls. Pei Pu searches for one and slips the marble box into the wall. Then she and Bernard and Bertrand kneel and touch their foreheads to the floor and Pei Pu prays. She weeps. Bernard passes her his handkerchief. She dries her eyes and stands up and they go.

"Now I can leave China," says Pei Pu.

. . .

Bernard returns to the embassy. Things are in an uproar. Li Shuang, though under diplomatic protection, has been arrested. Receiving a call from security guards that a friend had arrived, she went to the gate of the compound to meet her and was suddenly rushed by plainclothes police. Pei Pu is correct: The gates open briefly, then they slam shut again.

A few days later, Bernard, Pei Pu, and Bertrand leave Beijing and travel to Dalian, a modern beach resort on the tip of Liaoning Province, for a five-day holiday. Bernard takes one room for himself and another for Bertrand and Pei Pu. His tall, beautiful boy: They pose for pictures on the beach, Bernard's arm expansively around Bertrand, who stands with his own arms at his sides, shy and stiff. Bernard teaches Bertrand to swim.

Pei Pu cannot, of course, go bathing. She sits on the shore watching Bernard in the water with Bertrand, shouting after Bertrand to be careful, repeating what she said years ago when she watched Bernard swimming in the canals of Beijing:

"How I envy you, you are so free. . . ."

And yet, with all her complaints, the connection between them is still strong. Bernard feels it one overcast Sunday morning, when Bertrand has gone off on his own and he and Pei Pu go walking together in a park next to the hotel. It begins to drizzle, so they take refuge under a little pagoda overlooking the sea.

Now is the time, Pei Pu repeats, to make real the plans for their departure. She relies upon Bernard: He must find a way to get her an official invitation to visit France. She is determined. The next time they meet will be in Paris.

What Pei Pu will do outside China, how she will share a home with Thierry, is not clear. Yet now Bernard feels excited at the idea that finally, after so many years—the hiding, the absences, the reunions—they may at last realize the old dream. He feels the force of their shared memory and the old complicity.

"Remember when we were young," Pei Pu says. "And I was so much in love with you I was running after you in the bus on Changan Avenue. That was so long ago."

She pauses, acknowledging the time gone by.

"Could Romeo and Juliet be fifty, sixty years old?" Pei Pu asks. "When I see a Romeo and Juliet played by a dancer over fifty I am sad."

But she is light and charming as she says it. And she is not yet fifty and neither is Bernard. It sweeps over him again, the old affection, and though he cannot hold Pei Pu because they are in the open air in China he feels the bond between them; not as a tie that binds but as a ribbon spun lightly round a gift; and looking out to sea, he draws nearer to her, his secret mistress, and he laughs.

"You are asking me the same questions as the police. I said, 'I know he studied with Mei Lanfang.' They said, 'Oh, yes, we know he was his little boyfriend.' I think he was really more of an amateur than anything else. He showed me one or two librettos he had written in China, but in China hardly anyone is out of work. You can just come in and collect a paycheck. It's what we call *un bon fromage*, a good cheese. Pei Pu was a distant cousin of Zhou Enlai by his mother, a very, very distant cousin, so of course he got a good job, it is normal. Do you know who could help you? Tsai Chin—she is the daughter of the very famous actor Show Ha Infing. She lives in London; she was the star in *The World of Suzie Wong*. . . . Z-H-O-U X-I-N F-A-N-G. He was beaten up during the Cultural Revolution and people asked Jiang Qing to interfere for him and she did nothing. . . . Yes, Mei Lanfang was married; he had two sons and a daughter. His son was playing female parts, the daughter was playing male parts. I saw the daughter play in the fifties and sixties, but if you read the scandal sheets of the twenties and the thirties, you'll see he liked boys. . . ."

—*Jacques Pimpaneau*

Author of *A Walk in the Pear Garden: A Study of Beijing Opera;* Director of Musée Kwok On of Asian Culture, Paris

"Shi Pei Pu? He may well have been famous, but I left China in 1953 and he is from the north and I am from the south, so if he was just getting famous in the north I wouldn't have necessarily heard of him. My father, Zhou Xin Fang, and Mei Lanfang were the two superstars of Beijing Opera. My father played the male; Mei Lanfang played the female. Their salaries were higher than any of the state leaders'. Mei Lanfang was the only Beijing Opera actor who was and still is internationally known, partly because he went abroad, partly because he was a great actor. He met Stanislavsky, he met Einstein. He is considered the perfect female impersonator of the century. He was very easy to imitate. My father was not easy to imitate. He believed in the modern sense of the theater, he was interested in emotional content, not only form; he wanted to use theater for ideas. Mei Lanfang was only interested in aesthetics. My father was the first purge in Shanghai and he was purged personally by Jiang Qing. This is all in my book. Mei Lanfang was not political. I didn't know him, I was just a tiny little kid at that time. . . . 'The Story of the Butterfly'? It's one of the classic roles; there is a lovely scene in which the girl tries to tell the boy that she is not a man and he doesn't understand and it's quite funny in the Chinese theater. The young man is always quite stupid. It might relate to your story."

—*Tsai Chin*

Author of *Daughter of Shanghai;* portrayed Kang, London production of *M. Butterfly,* 1989; starred in *The World of Suzie Wong,* London, 1959–1961; daughter of Zhou Xin Fang

"That is my uncle and aunt in that picture [a photo of Shi Pei Pu with Mei Lanfang and Mei's son and daughter], but I don't know that other man. I never heard my uncle and aunt talk about that man. I don't think he is famous in China; this is the first time I hear his name. Usually, famous Beijing Opera students, most of my grandfather's students, I know. My aunt, Mei Bow Yu, is very famous in China. She performs men's roles. My uncle is performing ladies' roles. . . . This story, this is really strange. . . . I think it is disgusting."

—*Sherry Mei* (California, 1990)

Granddaughter of Mei Lanfang; daughter of author Mei Tzu Lin

"Shi Pei Pu was not an actor and he was not famous. He was not a student of Mei Lanfang. Mei Lanfang had probably more than one hundred serious students, but he was not a student. . . . Maybe during a party he wanted to have a photo made, but it does not mean he was a real student. . . . I think they just knew each other, that is all. During that time Shi Pei Pu was a very young man and Mei Lanfang was a master, and he would not play with the young people. Maybe Shi played opera for fun [as an amateur]. . . . Yes, I met him, but when I met him he was a man. He worked in the office of the Beijing Opera, he was a student of Jiang Miao-Xiang. Jiang Miao-Xiang played with Mei Lanfang, not Shi Pei Pu. . . . If he was famous, I don't know it; I never read anything by him. He has a very bad reputation in China. You are in a foreign country, you are doing a book, you have to say true things: Shi Pei Pu has nothing to do with the Mei family. We have no relation to him."

—*Mrs. Mei Tzu Lin*

Daughter-in-law of Mei Lanfang (Beijing–Paris phone conversation, May 1990)

"Yes, I know this guy. He was playing the part of the young boy in the opera, he was not playing the young lady. He was not a professional actor, but he is quite well known. There are people who love Beijing Opera and they play also, but they are not professional. During the Cultural Revolution we went to the countryside together, but afterward we did not see him anymore.

". . . He was not a student of Mei Lanfang; all Mei Lanfang's students played ladies. He was a student of another man, Jiang Miao-Xiang, and was working as a writer. . . . It is true he had a lot of talent and is very intelligent, but he was not professional. My father died in 1961. Before that Shi Pei Pu was very young. I don't know exactly how old he is now, I think maybe my age [sixty]. I don't think my father would have the interest to play with young people at that time; he was very famous and very old. [Did Pei Pu have a love relationship with your father?] I don't know exactly, but we were meeting each other some times. . . . I don't remember this photo you are describing with me and my brother, but people were always taking photos with my father; it was normal. . . . Yes, if you send it to me. . . . I do not know exactly what happened to him. I only know he went out of China and is now in France. . . . I don't know his plays. Anyway, I never read his works."

—*Actress Mei Bow Yu*

Daughter of Mei Lanfang (Beijing–Paris phone conversation, May 1990)

[Photo of Shi Pei Pu with Mei Bow Yu, her father, and brother, sent to Mei Bow Yu in May 1990. There is no reply.]

10

There is something Bernard and Pei Pu have in common besides their desire to start a new life in Paris—it is a shared belief in fate.

"To suffer, such is my destiny," Pei Pu writes Bernard. And when Bernard runs into his old friend Daniel in Paris after his return from Beijing, after having had no contact with him for several years, he knows it means just one thing: Daniel is destined to help Pei Pu.

Daniel is a sociologist now at the Centre Nationale de la Recherche Scientifique, the top government organization for scientific studies. Bernard explains that Pei Pu would like to come to France. Can Daniel arrange an invitation, with Pei Pu perhaps lecturing or performing Beijing Opera? Daniel says he'll be glad to try. Although he spent only two afternoons with Pei Pu some sixteen years ago, Daniel remembers him as an intelligent, sensitive man. He never believed Bernard's anguished outburst years ago that Pei Pu is secretly a woman, though he does not tell this now to Bernard. Bernard, for his part, does not tell Daniel that Pei Pu now has a son.

Daniel is as good as his word. He sends Pei Pu an invitation to come to France. Pei Pu responds with excitement and apprehension.

"I have no experience of travel," Pei Pu writes. "I need you to tell me what to do."

She also starts writing regularly to Bernard, for the first time since 1967. For safety's sake, the letters are mailed to Thierry. They are, as in the old days, heavy with melancholy: He is lucky, Pei Pu writes; it is the opposite for her. Unhappiness always accompanies her, she says. Their second child is not a story of Bernard's invention. Pei Pu writes of a little boy, who is often sick. A letter that is signed by Bertrand and translated into French by Pei Pu does the same. Addressing Bernard as his father, Bertrand says he is enjoying the bicycle Bernard brought him, but that these days he rides alone: his younger brother is too weak and sick to ride a bike. Bertrand also says he envies children who can live with their parents. Perhaps next Christmas, writes Bertrand, they will be together —that would make him very happy.

With a plan to get Pei Pu out of China finally under way, it would seem Bernard should remain in France—particularly after Thierry passes a foreign civil service test, which could send him abroad. But Bernard does not feel this way. It could take years for Pei Pu to get out, he thinks; should he stop living his life? Particularly when he hears of an interesting post: The small Central American country of British Honduras has just become independent and the French are opening an embassy in what is now Belize.

Tucked beneath Mexico's Yucatán peninsula with Guatemala to the south, Belize is one hundred and seventy-four miles deep and sixty-eight miles across at its widest point, much of it consisting of uninhabitable swamp and jungle. It is, one might say, the tropical equivalent of Mongolia, but without even that country's strategic importance by proximity to two great powers.

"British Honduras is not on the way from anywhere to anywhere else, it has no strategic value, it is all but uninhabited: If the world has any ends, British Honduras would surely not be one of them," Aldous Huxley wrote in 1934, and by 1982 things have not much changed. A coral reef attracts a few divers, but Belize is equally famous for its mangrove swamps, which have given it the nickname "The Mosquito Coast." Belize City, the major town, has one lovely residential neighborhood with rambling white frame houses, heavy with patios and wicker, but the larger part of town features tin-roofed wooden shanties and canals into which flow open sewers.

It is, in short, a perfect spot for Bernard. He speaks English and

Spanish, the languages of Belize. He likes the newly appointed ambassador, Jean-Pierre Chauvet, who looks like Winston Churchill and has a
literate, easy air. Bernard and Thierry both apply. Bernard gets the post
but Thierry does not. He is dispatched to Oman, the sultanate border-
ing Saudi Arabia. Typical Foreign Affairs, says Bernard: You request the
jungle, they send you to the desert. But no matter; he and Thierry will
probably benefit from some time apart. In February, Bernard leaves for
Belize. Before he does, he has one important piece of business: He goes
to a lawyer and draws up a will. He leaves everything to his son, Bertrand.

Belize does not disappoint him. In Belize City, Bernard sees not
slums and sewers, but the few sweetly decaying plantation manors that
evoke another wide-screen favorite: *Gone With the Wind*. He also, as he
tells it, has the fun of setting up the new embassy—a responsibility
perhaps overstated, as Ambassador and Mme. Chauvet arrive only four
days later. In Bernard's rendering, however, he whips everything into
shape: He hires a maid, a driver, and a pistol-packing butler and secures
an eleven-room mansion for the ambassador's residence.

His salary, as attaché, is three thousand dollars a month, and life in
Belize is cheap. There is also, after the first two months, little work:
Arrive at nine. Turn on the air-conditioning. Do a few accounts.
Sort the mail. Wait for the ambassador to stick his head in the office and
say to Bernard and the vice consul. "Okay, kids, I'm taking you to
lunch." Off to the Château Caribbeana. Into a hammock at home for the
afternoon siesta. Run the pouch every two weeks to Honduras. Take a
weekend in Tegucigalpa or Cancún.

He finds a pleasant two-story house not far from the ocean breezes.
He finds a lover, a Creole hairdresser named Yvonne.

"I do not care for my husband," she tells Bernard one rummed-up
evening on somebody's veranda. "I care for nothing at all."

Bernard knows from Stendhal's *The Red and the Black* that a good
way to turn up the heat with a woman is to feign indifference, but
Yvonne seems hot already. He takes her to bed at once. He also becomes seriously involved in the social life in Belize. It is prodigious:
parties at the cocktail hour, parties on weekends, parties every night.
One evening the music of his wealthy Scottish neighbors is so loud he
cannot sleep.

"I heard the music of your Scottish dancers last night," he later tells the lady of the house.

"Well, why didn't you come? Next time you must," she says.

They are dancing the farandole that evening. Is he at the head of the line or the back? Maybe he has been drinking, for he can't recall, only a line dance, going faster and faster, and a polished mahogany floor and a crazy Caribbean rhythm, and then, as he falls, a pain in his left arm that is so intense he sees stars. At the Belize City Medical Department, where Bernard Boursicot is admitted the night of April 6, the doctors diagnose a broken and dislocated elbow and recommend surgery. Bernard is damned if he will have it in Belize. The gun-toting butler phones the airport and is told the morning flight to New Orleans is full. The butler suggests there will be serious repercussions if no seat is found for M. Boursicot of the Ambassade de France. M. Boursicot is booked. He has his surgery in New Orleans. To facilitate government payment of medical expenses, Bernard tells the doctors it was a work-related accident: He slipped on the stairs of the French embassy.

When a person truly loves, whether a man, a woman, or a plot of earth, time is unimportant. One will wait years to be united with the object of one's love, and so it is with the Italian journalist Tiziano Terzani. At twenty, he became obsessed with China while reading about the Cultural Revolution. "Seen from afar," he would write years later, China "seemed the most creative, innovative place on earth and Mao a genius attempting the greatest experiment of social engineering in the history of mankind . . . a just, humane society."

A great, strapping man with a broad mustache, a warm outgoing style, and a gift for languages, Terzani studied Chinese in preparation for the day he could realize his dream. He even gave himself a Chinese name—Deng Tiannuo. He got a job covering the Far East for the German magazine *Der Spiegel* and published two books on the Vietnam War and another on the genocide in Cambodia. It was not until 1980 that he arrived at last in China. Now married with two children, he tries to break through the barriers the government erects between foreigners and Chinese: He enrolls his son and daughter in a Chinese school, he bicycles through the countryside, enchanted by such old customs as the raising of crickets for the pleasure of their song. Finding a poem on the song of the crickets delights him:

"Sadness and joy I feel as its chirp now pauses, then continues, vibrating yet prolonged, a heavenly voice, a sound appropriate for the man of leisure."

Yet Terzani is often frustrated. Government officials are present at all his interviews—except when he sneaks off to the country, which he does often. A Chinese acquaintance has been told by the Public Security Bureau he may see Terzani again only if he files a report. Terzani is also dismayed to see that his onetime hero Mao has destroyed much of what is beautiful and fine in China.

But on the evening of April 6—the same evening when, midway around the globe, a wild Frenchman is dancing the farandole on a highly waxed floor—Tiziano and his German-born wife Angela are happy, for they feel that they are experiencing a marvelous, unspoiled view of old China.

A Beijing actor named Shi Pei Pu has invited the Terzanis to the opening night of a Beijing Opera he has written. Angela met him some weeks before at a performance of Kunqu Opera, a particularly stylized and balletic form of Beijing Opera, where he made his comeback performance. The audience was small, but it included the president of the Kunqu Opera Association, who said Shi Pei Pu was very good. Later, Mr. Shi heard Angela speaking French and asked to be introduced. Angela was immediately impressed. He is unlike the earnest, sober Communists she has met; he is elegant, charming, and oddly disquieting. His new opera is an adaptation of a scene from the novel *Journey to the West*, in which the Monkey King steals a fan from the gods. Angela finds the play, with its wild acrobatics, marvelous, though sitting beside his guests, Shi Pei Pu is anxious.

"I wrote this opera in a matter of three weeks," Angela recalls Pei Pu saying, in the diary she will later publish as *Chinese Days*. "Not because I am lazy, but because if I were to deal with different or more current subjects, I would almost certainly qualify for criticism and other problems. . . .

"When I was young," Pei Pu continues, "Zhou Enlai protected me, and Mao said, 'In opera learn from Shi!' But then came the Cultural

Revolution and Jiang Qing and I cannot begin to tell you what happened. . . . Maybe I am too cautious, but I cannot help it; I am horribly afraid of them."

Pei Pu speaks of having received permission from his "leaders" before inviting the Terzanis to come to the theater. He tells Angela he has written two letters to another foreign friend, a Frenchman, but received no reply; he fears they were intercepted.

Angela is surprised that he is so open with foreigners he has just met, but she and her husband like Pei Pu.

"Come for dinner," they tell him.

The Terzanis are casual people; dinner is a relaxed affair; but with Pei Pu, they quickly see, everything is complex:

Tiziano must pick him up, but not at home: it must be at the Lama temple, the Palace of Eternal Harmonies, at six precisely. The Lama temple is one of the best preserved in Beijing. At the entrance are two pagodas. Inside is a sixty-five-foot Buddha carved from a single sandalwood tree. The sun is going down as Tiziano arrives in his little red car, and he is struck by the fact that this setting is highly romantic—if not in the sense of love, certainly in the sense of an important friendship. Terzani's got to hand it to him; the guy has a flair for the dramatic.

As they get better acquainted, Pei Pu tells the Terzanis his story: He speaks of a splendid career as actor and writer in the Beijing Opera before the Cultural Revolution. He says he was the only playwright admitted to the Beijing Writers' Association. At the apartment where he lives with his teenage son, Shi Du Du, he shows the Terzanis pictures of himself as a young man with Mei Lanfang and Zhou Enlai. He also had friends, before the Cultural Revolution, among the French community, Pei Pu says. He mentions several, but never Bernard Boursicot. Pei Pu lost his house and many valuable artworks during the Cultural Revolution, he says, but was never sent to a labor camp. He survived by becoming invisible: He criticized no one and was therefore never criticized. To the Terzanis, Pei Pu is intriguing: His son, at first glance, looks to be of mixed blood. It is also obvious to the Terzanis that Pei Pu is homosexual, but he suggests otherwise. He was married to a Frenchwoman, Pei Pu says, but she returned to her country. She left behind their son, Shi Du Du.

Shi Pei Pu, Tiziano feels, does not belong in today's world. The way he dresses, the way he carries himself, his distinctive pallor make him like a man who has stepped out of an ancient painting, an archaeological treasure who is alive and coming over for dinner. His stories are marvelous—though as Tiziano starts to test those stories he realizes that often they are not exactly true. Tiziano is a reporter; it is important for him to know whether something occurred on April 16 or April 25 and, he soon sees, he cannot get that from Pei Pu. The stories change, they are so heavily detailed one becomes confused and entangled, they often do not check out. Pei Pu, Terzani decides, compulsively hides—probably he had to in order to survive the Cultural Revolution or because of his homosexuality. When you added his actor's ability to play roles and his bent for fantasy, it could make you dizzy. Literally. Pei Pu's home is one of the few places in China one can smell incense; sometimes when Pei Pu is telling stories, with the incense, and the maze of characters, Tiziano falls asleep on the floor.

Angela, who is a more patient listener, feels the same: Shi Pei Pu has an ability to sense what people want of him and to change personalities accordingly. She does not know if Pei Pu studied with Mei Lanfang —she has the feeling he was more of a companion. She does not know the name of the play for which he was allegedly complimented by Mao. But Pei Pu is so full of the history of China, so generous with his introductions, she does not care if his stories are true to the letter of the word. Angela also sees, as the Terzanis grow to know him, a lonely man.

"You are rich," Pei Pu tells them one day. "You don't know what it means to be hungry, hungry also for affection."

Pei Pu also reveals to them that Du Du, as they have suspected, is adopted. He did not want to marry, Pei Pu explains, and so to protect him from unwanted matches, his late mother made up the story about the French wife. Then as proof of the union, Pei Pu's mother bought an orphan from the western province of Xinjiang, near the Russian border. That province, Tiziano knows, is the home of many races, including the Uigurs, who are of Turkish origin. They speak their own language, a Turkish dialect; they are Muslim; and their features, with their light skin coloring and long straight noses, make them look more European than Oriental. Tiziano believes Du Du is Uigur. It is his impression that the tall, shy boy, who is followed around the apartment by three cats he adores, knows he is adopted. It does not seem to bother him in the least.

The Terzanis introduce Pei Pu to their friend the French journalist Jean Leclerc du Sablon. Like the Terzanis, he finds Pei Pu fascinating. When the Terzanis learn that Pei Pu wants to leave China, they try to help. Pei Pu has been invited to France by a French friend named Daniel he says, but the Chinese government is now demanding an official invitation from a cultural organization. Tiziano passes that information along to Daniel, telling him it is important, in sending an official invitation, not to mention that Shi Pei Pu has solicited it. Pei Pu seems very fearful about the government. To ensure that they do not find out about his request, Pei Pu asks Tiziano to mail the letter from Hong Kong. Tiziano does as he is asked.

A week later, back in Beijing, Tiziano receives a desperate call from Shi Du Du: His father is ill, the boy says. Rushing to Hepingli, the hospital for middle-management workers, the Terzanis find the frail little man lying in bed, bare-chested, in boxer shorts. He is having difficulty speaking. A doctor shows Tiziano the electrocardiograph. Pei Pu has had a heart attack.

A week and a half later, the Terzanis visit again. Physically, Pei Pu is stronger. He is, however, Angela Terzani writes in *Chinese Days*, hurt and depressed that they have stayed away so long.

"Maybe I was wrong to be so open with you," he says. "Maybe you are not real friends after all. . . . Maybe I seem like a little nobody to you. And yet I can help you."

He uses his knowledge of the Cultural Revolution with the foreign journalists as if it is a bartering tool, offering information, then withholding.

"Up to now, you are familiar with my story," Angela remembers Pei Pu saying, like a Sheherazade resuming a tale. "Then, during the Cultural Revolution, all members of the Writers' Association were sent to the countryside. Only I and one other remained in Beijing. I know, therefore, who denounced whom. I know who denounced Lao She, for example, causing him to commit suicide. It was an intellectual whose name I will tell you another time.

"Had I stood by him that day, Lao She would not have killed himself," Pei Pu continues. "He was a real man. A true man. The most treacherous of all have always been the intellectuals. As soon as they have a little power, they use it to get at one another's throats. On their own initiative, the Red Guards would never have destroyed China or killed other Chinese. One day I will introduce you to some really good people, to some old Communists who lived in the cult of Mao, our great Buddha."

He alternates stories—many too complex to follow—with requests: He wants Angela's mother to adopt himself and Du Du; he wants the Terzanis to write letters to French friends he knows from before the Cultural Revolution to see if they will help them.

The requests are unnecessary.

In Paris, Daniel has asked Clemens Heller, deputy director of the Maison des Sciences de l'Homme, a highly reputable social sciences research organization, to invite Pei Pu to France as a lecturer and performer in Beijing Opera. Heller asks a Chinese specialist to look into the matter. Daniel provides a list of plays Pei Pu says he wrote or adapted. None of the Chinese specialist's contacts know Shi Pei Pu, but some of the operas are well known. In early July, when Pei Pu comes home from the hospital, an invitation awaits him to spend three months lecturing and performing in France.

And yet when Angela and Tiziano visit they find Pei Pu, despite the invitation he has coveted so long, melancholy.

The little apartment is festooned for Pei Pu's homecoming. Du Du has hung a piece of calligraphy written by Pei Pu's late mother in praise of Mao on the wall and strung the apartment with colored lights. A tall silent cousin, whom they have met on previous occasions, offers tea and dates. But Pei Pu, who seems particularly frail, is troubled by the fact that the Terzanis are leaving soon for vacation in Italy. Angela understands: He fears he will never see them again. Then, she recalls, Pei Pu's mood changes. As if it is a parting gift, Pei Pu tells the writers a much-promised story:

"Let me tell you about Lao She's death," he starts, as if making a sudden decision. "One day, you must tell the world so that nothing of the kind will ever happen again."

He tells a story, Angela records in her diary, of an urgent meeting called by the Writers' Association in 1966.

"The Red Guard has arrived and wants to burn down the library.

Among its many manuscripts there are some very old and rare ones, even some pages of *The Dream of the Red Chamber* in the handwriting of the author, Cao-Xueqin.

"Lao She speaks out. 'Don't destroy books!. . . . It is only by way of the written character that we Chinese can communicate with each other. I am old: I am not saying this for myself. I am saying it for your sake. This is your country, your civilization, do not destroy it. Take the books, take them away if you like, but do not destroy them!'

"The young people listen and calm down. But then a woman stands up, a writer and translator herself. 'Look at the bourgeois revisionist!' she screams. 'That's the real traitor to the revolution! Beat him! Crush him!' "

Lao She is saved, Pei Pu tells Angela and Tiziano, by another writer, who cleverly appeals to the guards to " 'Keep him alive and show him to the masses as a living example of a counterrevolutionary.' "

But the books are lost. They are loaded, with Lao She, on a truck and driven to the Temple of Confucius, which has become the scene of almost daily book burning. When Lao She sees the books set aflame, he throws himself on them, trying to put out the fire. But Red Guards pull him back and beat him. When he is released, Pei Pu tells Angela and Tiziano, he does not go home. He walks to Taiping Lake and drowns himself.

"I was there," Pei Pu says, "but I did not take up his defense. Sometimes I am ashamed of myself."

A few days later, Angela makes a final visit to Pei Pu before leaving. Watching this little man practice the movements of the Beijing Opera in front of his mirror, dressed in a long green silk robe and thick wedge shoes, she again has the sense of someone out of time. How, she wonders, without a cousin to look after him, without his familiar surroundings, will Pei Pu ever be able to survive in France?

Bernard, in the summer of 1982, is spending almost no time in Belize. He returns to Paris in early June on medical leave and undergoes additional surgery on his elbow, which has healed badly. He also makes an effort to have Thierry leave Oman, unconcerned that his lover has at last a job with a future. "Life is so short; why be separated?" Bernard writes. If he will not resign, he should know that he has five vacation days a month, and there is no rule that forbids him—after three months of work—from taking a holiday in Paris now.

There is, sadly, another reason for Thierry to come to France: His mother is battling cancer. Thierry flies home to be with her. In early July, she dies. She is a relatively young woman, only sixty, and they had been very close. Thierry rarely expresses emotion, but now, Bernard sees, his friend is deeply sad.

"Delay your return to Oman," Bernard tells him. "Go to a psychiatrist."

Thierry does, staying in Paris a month. In August, when the embassy wires him to return, he sends off another medical certificate and takes off for Morocco with Bernard. His career with the Foreign Service ends.

In China, meanwhile, Pei Pu completes the plans for the trip. There is one final, not inconsiderable, problem—Daniel still does not know about Shi Du Du. Pei Pu asks a cousin of Angela Terzani's to break the news to Daniel and a few days later follows it up with a note. There is no explanation of how Pei Pu came to be a parent. Pei Pu speaks only of making the trip with a thirteen-year-old son, Shi Du Du.

Bernard delays his return to Belize as long as possible, but on September 15, he must go back. Thierry wants to go, but the arrival of Pei Pu and Du Du is imminent.

"Stay here," Bernard tells him.

In early October, in Beijing, Pei Pu and Du Du finally receive their visas. Angela and Tiziano, returned from abroad, throw a farewell party. They are struck by the fact that though Pei Pu has lived in Beijing for more than twenty years, he has so few people to tell him good-bye: a sister, a few neighbors, some colleagues from the Writers' Association of Beijing.

They can also see Pei Pu is frightened.

"I am not used to running my own life," Pei Pu tells Angela. "Others have always decided for me. First it was my grandmother, then the party. I have arranged this completely on my own. I am amazed that it has succeeded."

Pei Pu's going-away party is small: three of Pei Pu's bosses from the Writers' Association; his cousin; Shi Du Du; Claude Martin, the thirty-eight-year-old French embassy first councillor who remembers

Pei Pu from 1965, when Martin was a young attaché; and Jean Leclerc du Sablon, who is returning to France soon himself and urges Pei Pu to call.

On October 9, the Terzanis take Pei Pu and Du Du to the airport. They have hoped to make this a private moment, but the government will not let that be. Accompanying them are two of Pei Pu's bosses, who have insisted upon coming along.

"I don't want to leave," Pei Pu whispers to Angela at the last moment. Then he is gone.

In Paris, Daniel alerts Thierry, who in turn calls Bernard in Belize.

"There is news," he says. "They are coming tomorrow."

Bernard marches in to his ambassador.

"My arm needs treatment," he says. "I have to get to Paris right away."

**P**ei Pu and Bertrand arrive at Roissy–Charles de Gaulle airport on Saturday, October 9, 1982, and are greeted by Daniel, who takes them to his mother's home in Sèvres, outside Paris. With Pei Pu's recent heart attack, it is felt that will be better than Bernard's sixth-floor walkup.

Nonetheless, within a few hours Daniel brings Pei Pu and Bertrand to Thierry at Port-Royal. Pei Pu wants to see the apartment and call Bernard. Phoning seems to thrill Pei Pu.

"It is so easy in your country to call the other side of the world," Pei Pu says.

Pei Pu and Bertrand leave. The next day, Thierry receives a call from Pei Pu. Daniel's mother has a beautiful old house, with high ceilings and floors as polished as a convent's, but Pei Pu is not happy.

"I can't stay any longer in this lady's house," Thierry recalls Pei Pu saying. "She is very nice, but she is an old lady. I prefer to come to Bernard's. This evening would be good."

"*Aaaaa, merde,*" thinks Thierry, but he has no choice. Bernard, a year earlier, had bought two more rooms on the floor in anticipation of the moment his Chinese family would arrive, but he has since rented them. So Thierry moves his clothes and books into the tiny studio down the hall. He borrows a vacuum cleaner from Mme. Lavalier, far more powerful than Bernard's, to clean the house for his guests. In the evening, Pei Pu arrives with Bertrand. She begins rearranging the apartment at once, moving furniture, drawing the blinds. When Thierry comes back to fix coffee in the morning—there is no kitchen in the little studio—his airy, sun-filled corner apartment resembles Pei Pu's gloomy box in Beijing, shadowy and closed.

They are an odd pair of roommates, Bernard's two loves. While Thierry is content to sit in the apartment and read for days, Pei Pu likes people and chat. While Thierry savors tranquillity, Pei Pu courts drama. She is certain Bertrand will electrocute himself with his new stereo; she entreats an endless stream of friends for assistance and advice. She conducts herself like a diva lost in a strange country.

Still, Thierry has promised Bernard he will help Pei Pu get established in Paris, and he does. He teaches the boy and his mother how to use the public phones and to save money on the Métro by buying a *carte orange*. He takes them to the twice-weekly neighborhood market for groceries. He is surprised by how quickly Bertrand, who speaks very little French, is able to get around. Pei Pu, on the other hand, requires constant looking after. Thierry accompanies her to the Cultural Center of the People's Republic of China in Issy-les-Moulineaux, which also houses the military attaché's office and the scientific and technical services, where Pei Pu has to register upon arrival. He shows her the lush and romantic Luxembourg Gardens, with the seventeenth-century palace and acres of flower beds, where the weathered statues of medieval queens of France, their crowns and features eroded by time, stand in a semicircle up a flight of stone stairs, surveying the fountain below. He takes Pei Pu to the Kwok On Museum of Asian Culture, where Pei Pu meets museum director Jacques Pimpaneau, perhaps the foremost French expert on Beijing Opera. Pei Pu also asks Thierry to escort her to the homes of old friends from Beijing. Thierry does not meet them; he simply takes Pei Pu to the door. Pei Pu does not want anyone to know she is in Bernard Boursicot's apartment. She is also very shy. When one close friend of Thierry's drops by, Pei Pu and Bertrand retreat quickly to the kitchen, which is not more than five feet square, and refuse to come out until she leaves a half hour later.

"Some friends of Bernard's from Beijing," Thierry says vaguely. He does not know what else to say. Despite years of talking about bringing Pei Pu and Bertrand to France, he and Bernard have never discussed how they would introduce them.

To Thierry, there is nothing about Pei Pu's appearance that betrays her secret. Dressed in corduroy pants and a man's shirt and blazer she could be just another guy strolling around Paris. She is, of course, a very effeminate guy, but that, Thierry feels, will not make anyone suspicious. Chinese men always seem more feminine than Western men.

He is, however, struck by Pei Pu's lack of interest in the arts. Bernard has talked for years of his erudite mistress. Now, one Friday, Thierry turns on "Apostrophes," a popular TV talk show about books. As a writer herself, Pei Pu will surely enjoy it. She watches for fifteen minutes, then shuts it off. Pei Pu asks to see the Louvre, but when Thierry takes her she declines to go inside.

Her health is fragile. One day on the way to the Métro on Boulevard Saint-Michel, Pei Pu becomes so short of breath she has to sit down on the pavement. She fumbles in her pocket and takes some tiny pills and after several minutes she can stand. Yet when Thierry tries to convince her to go to a doctor, she refuses. Thierry thinks he knows why —she is afraid she will have to undress and expose her secret. Thierry explains repeatedly that in France doctors are held to a code of ethics that forbids revealing information without a patient's permission. Finally he calls upon Daniel to help. Daniel makes an appointment with a heart specialist and convinces Pei Pu to go.

Thierry tries to respect Pei Pu's privacy, though this is sometimes difficult. The kitchen they share in the larger studio is separated from the bathroom by only a curtain, and one must walk into the studio to get to the kitchen. Sometimes Thierry sees Pei Pu sleeping, in an undershirt and baggy men's boxer shorts. Once or twice, he comes upon her plucking a stray hair from her face.

They do not get on badly. They often sit together with Bertrand in the big studio and watch television. Once or twice Pei Pu speaks of hiding her pregnancy during the Cultural Revolution and Bertrand's difficult secret birth.

She has no romantic feeling for Bernard. One evening, watching television, Pei Pu suddenly takes Thierry's large hand in her little one and says how happy she is that Bernard has Thierry in his life. Their

own relationship is long over and now Bernard is like a little brother to
her, she says. But at times, as they both know, he can be a foolish little
brother, so it is good he has someone to look after him.

Bernard can sleep anywhere, anytime, but as he flies back to Paris three
weeks after Pei Pu's arrival, the gift fails him. Though he has been
traveling for twenty-four hours, with an overnight layover in New York,
he has been too excited to get much rest.

Waiting at the airport on a cold, rainy Sunday with Thierry and
Bertrand, Pei Pu is excited, too.

But as Bernard kisses her formally on both cheeks, he feels something is not quite right. The reunion he has dreamed of for seventeen
years is not as he imagined it. Bernard knows Pei Pu has had a heart
attack and he is sorry, but the truth is that Pei Pu, decked out in a
double-breasted gray gabardine man's suit, is hardly a dream girl. Bernard is coming from the tropics, tanned and healthy. Pei Pu is plump
and looks much older. When she kisses him, it is not pleasant. Pei Pu is
like most Chinese, Bernard thinks; they are not used to kissing and do it
badly, particularly in public. He studies her, trying to figure out how she
could have aged so rapidly, and has a realization. The suit she is wearing
is made of the gray gabardine he brought her from Hong Kong in 1965,
shortly after they became lovers. But the weight of that time, which
held him so sweetly to Pei Pu when they stood together near the sea a
year ago, sits on him now like a burial stone. He feels the awful desola-
tion one has when beginning a date with a woman one suddenly realizes
one cannot bear. And this date, Pei Pu is telling him with her eyes, is
going to last for life.

Bertrand, on the other hand, has never looked better, but Bernard
is unable to get next to him. When they go to the car, Pei Pu follows
Bernard to the back seat and Bertrand sits beside Thierry. Pei Pu takes
Bernard's hand at once. As soon as possible, Bernard removes it. Pei Pu
chatters on. Thierry has been so nice, he insists on sleeping in the little
studio though she has told him she and the boy can sleep just as easily
there. Her mention of Thierry makes Bernard uneasy. He changes the
subject, asking if she is happy in Paris.

"Of course," Pei Pu begins, "but . . ."

There is a "but" that has something to do with changing apartments; there is a "but" that has to do with Bertrand. Bernard does not pay careful attention.

"One minute it is 'I am so happy,' the next minute, 'We should change apartments,' " he thinks. "I know this person."

He is tired when they arrive at Port-Royal, but he doesn't consider sleep. Instead, he calls his mother.

"You remember what I told you a long time ago?" Bernard says. "It has happened. Your grandson has arrived."

"I'm coming," his mother says.

Then they all go out so Bernard can begin to introduce his son to his friends. He would prefer to leave Pei Pu at home. How can he show them this person, he thinks, who is not a man, who is not a woman? Pei Pu wears men's clothing, but she is not handsome and the cheeks are not those of a man—yet the face is not quite that of a woman. The hairline, which she has taken such pains to change, leaves her forehead far too exposed, and her thin black hair is heavily pomaded.

There is another problem, too. If Bernard tells people Pei Pu is his old mistress and the mother of Bertrand, that is a very long story, and he and Pei Pu have not yet decided it is time for her secret to be revealed. If Bernard suggests she is a boyfriend, she is neither handsome nor young enough. His friends, says Bernard, are used to seeing him with either very beautiful girls or very beautiful boys. Usually, he adds, girls. There is nothing to do but continue Pei Pu's charade. They head out to a grand apartment overlooking the Eiffel Tower owned by his friend Willi and his wife. Pei Pu proudly brings a video of his recent performances, Bernard proudly brings Bertrand.

"My son, Bertrand," Bernard announces. "And his uncle, Shi Pei Pu."

He puts an arm around Bertrand.

"He looks just like me, doesn't he?" he asks.

His friends are astonished. They have known Bernard for ten years now and he has never mentioned a son. What is equally surprising is that when Willi's wife later in the evening, asks him about the boy's mother, he refuses to discuss her.

"We don't speak about that," he says.

"You know what I think," Willi's wife says after they leave. "I think he's protecting some girl."

Back at Boulevard Port-Royal, Bernard tells Pei Pu and Bertrand good night and heads down the hall to the little room and Thierry. It is one in the morning and Bernard hasn't slept for twenty-four hours; the exhaustion is finally catching up with him. He collapses beside Thierry on their bed, a mattress on the floor. There is a knock on the door. A very strong knock. Bernard knows exactly who it is: the fat little flower of the East. He has a strong desire to get up and slug her. Instead, as he steps into the hall, he is exceedingly polite.

"I am tired, Pei Pu," he says. "I haven't slept for over a day."

"I need to talk to you," says Pei Pu.

"I am exhausted," says Bernard.

"No," says Pei Pu. "I have been waiting so long for this day and I have things I have to talk to you about."

"Tomorrow we will talk. I promise," says Bernard.

At sunrise she is back, pounding on the door. Bernard walks wearily into the studio. The wailing begins at once.

"I have been waiting all this time to be with you," says Pei Pu. "And you do not even stay with me. You are going to be here such a short time, we could have told Bertrand to go and sleep in Thierry's room. It was a mistake to come here. I want to go back to China."

"I was tired, Pei Pu," Bernard says.

"But you could have slept next to me," says Pei Pu, her voice rising. "I waited for you such a long time and this is the way you treat me. I wanted to jump out of the window when you went to his room. I went down in the street, to walk, and I was so sick I could not get back up the stairs. I could have died in the street. You would not have cared. You don't want me here."

It goes on. Thierry had asked Pei Pu and Bertrand if they wanted to go the top of the Eiffel Tower before Bernard's arrival, Pei Pu says, and though they wanted to very much they decided to wait for Bernard. Then Bernard goes and sleeps with his friend instead of his family. Pei Pu knows Bernard is leaving in two weeks, but she and Bernard will *not* go to the Eiffel Tower with Bertrand now. They will wait until Bernard's next visit, when perhaps things will be better.

Wonderful, thinks Bernard. When they were in China during the Cultural Revolution, there were temples that were closed to foreigners. Now that Pei Pu is in a free country, she is closing down France.

As for her complaint that he does not want to be with her, it is true. Bernard is willing to provide for her, but it is Bertrand he wants. If Pei Pu is not happy with this, it is not his problem. In China, Pei Pu said she was glad Bernard had Thierry. He did not know Pei Pu was still in love with him; he had *no idea*. Now that she's here, she can take care of herself. She's much smarter than he is, anyway.

On the other hand, he does feel a little guilty.

"I do care for you very much, Pei Pu," he says. Then he goes wearily back down the hall to Thiérry. There is no need to tell him what has happened. He has heard the shouting.

"I think it will be better if I go to a friend's for a few days," Thierry says.

Bernard agrees. He is still tired. He would like to stay in bed, he is thinking, for about a week. But the next thing you know, Pei Pu is at the door again, saying Daniel wants to see him. They set off through the Luxembourg Gardens to Daniel's offices on Boulevard Raspail. Pei Pu waits downstairs.

It is a short visit. Just some financial matters concerning Pei Pu and Bertrand. Then, says Bernard, just as he is leaving, Daniel says something odd.

"Do you believe Pei Pu is a woman? You told me he is a woman, but I wonder."

"Of *course* Pei Pu is a woman," says Bernard.

He goes downstairs to Pei Pu and they head back through the gardens. It is early November, and the medieval queens stand now under a nest of barren branches, awaiting the winter freeze and damp that will loosen a crumb of stone from a finger or gown. Beyond, on the dusty pony path, fat little Shetlands, chained five across at the neck, trudge back and forth with the starched and prosperous children of normal unions. Bernard and Pei Pu walk slowly up the stone steps toward the promenade that is the queens' domain. Pei Pu selects a bench in the very center of their semicircle, so that they form a court behind her, and sits down dejected.

"I wanted to marry you," Pei Pu says. "And now there is no result. You are going back to Belize without marrying me. I wish we had stayed in China. You have changed, Bernard."

Bernard can never say no to Pei Pu. When he is with her, he thinks, he forgets the word.

"We'll see, later on," he says. "Anyway, I have to go back to Belize."

"But if you go back to Belize and we don't marry, there will be no result," Pei Pu repeats.

"You don't have to worry," says Bernard. "I'll take care of you. I'll send you money every month. Let's go back to the house, now. Bertrand is waiting."

They start back. Pei Pu has never been a fast walker, but now she is going very slowly, as if she suddenly has bound feet. Leaving the garden, on Boulevard Port-Royal, she collapses, falling back against a wall like a drunk.

"Pei Pu, please," says Bernard. "A few more steps and we will be home."

"Why did I come to Paris?" says Pei Pu. "I am sure Bertrand wants to go home."

"Pei Pu, come," says Bernard, leading her into the house.

"I cannot live in this place," says Pei Pu. "I cannot walk six floors."

Bernard half-carries her up the stairs. On the third-floor landing, Pei Pu collapses again. She cannot get up. Bernard runs back to the little studio, hoping Thierry is still there. He is. They race down the stairs. Bernard grabs Pei Pu's arms, Thierry her legs, and they carry her upstairs. Upright, she seems a small, if pudgy, creature; limp, thinks Bernard, she is as heavy as a dead donkey.

"She had to collapse on the third," he thinks as they maneuver up the worn, circular wooden stairway, slippery and precarious in the best of times. "She couldn't do it on the fifth."

But he is scared. He calls Daniel, panicked. Daniel tells Bernard to call SOS Médecins, a twenty-four-hour medical service, and says he is on his way. But when Bernard starts to phone, Pei Pu objects.

"No, no," she says, taking some pills. "In a few minutes it will be okay."

Bernard is frantic. He runs back and forth between the hall and the windows, looking for Daniel.

"You didn't call a doctor?" Daniel says when he comes. "Why not?"

"Pei Pu wouldn't let me," Bernard says.

Daniel is not certain what is going on in the household, but he has a pretty good idea: Pei Pu is probably jealous of Thierry. Daniel tries to restore some calm. He tells Pei Pu they are going to see a heart specialist the next day; he insists upon it. He leaves, followed by Thierry. For the rest of the day, Pei Pu lies on the couch, a pathetic wraith, bundled in a coat. In the evening, Bernard tells Bertrand to sleep in the little room and moves his pallet next to Pei Pu's bed, on the floor.

As he does so, he thinks of Frederick the Great, who, legend had it, was so stingy that he slept with his dogs rather than spend money for coal. This is what Bernard feels like now: Pei Pu's dog. Thirty-six hours ago he arrived from the tropics suntanned and healthy, a proud man in a Burberry coat. Now the man he loves is gone, just as Pei Pu wants, and Bernard is a little dog, saying, "Oh, Pei Pu, what can I do for you?" He cannot find escape in sleep either. Pei Pu talks until four.

She never utters the name "Thierry," whom she could not praise enough at the airport. Now it is "your friend," pronounced with venom. It is not good for Bernard go back to Belize with his friend, he should stay in Paris with Pei Pu, she will find something for him to do. The apartment is too small, his tenants should move out of the other room, Bernard should buy another apartment. In China, Bernard remembers, Pei Pu said she would be happy to stay in one little room, she would gaze out at the gardens and breathe the free air of France. Now, within a month of arriving, she wants Bernard to move. It is not so cheap in Paris. You do not buy apartments like tins of sardines.

As the days go by, relations between them grow worse. They quarrel when Bernard announces he wants to adopt Bertrand and change the boy's name to Boursicot—he has gone so far as to get the papers. They quarrel when, with friends, Bernard ignores Pei Pu while doting on the boy. He introduces them to many. They visit Mary Meerson's apartment where Bernard explains that "Uncle" Pei Pu is a star of the Beijing Opera and Pei Pu sings for Mary's friends. Marie-Dominique, the French student from Mongolia, meets Bertrand and Pei Pu. They are introduced to friends from the Foreign Service. Sometimes Bernard confides that he has a second child, who is still in Beijing. He does not, when his curious aunt Mimi passes through town, say a word to her about his new family. Nor, to her surprise, does he invite her to his apartment. He cannot, however, lie to Mme. Lavalier. He brings Pei Pu and Bertrand to her apartment one evening and introduces them only as friends from China. The next morning he is back alone.

"The boy is my son," he says. "We tell people he is fourteen, because that is the age on his passport, it is what the Chinese government thinks, but he is really seventeen."

"But what about the mother?" Mme. Lavalier manages to get out.

"That's another story," says Bernard. "I'll tell you one day."

A few days later, walking Mme. Lavalier home from a visit at Port-Royal, Bernard tells her the boy's mother is Pei Pu.

Mme. Lavalier stops. She is hearing things, she thinks.

Bernard says it again. Pei Pu is a woman. He tells her the whole story—excepting the espionage. He says that he has another child in China, whom he has never seen.

An extraordinary history, thinks Mme. Lavalier—she has a difficult time believing. Pei Pu does not look like a girl to her—not with that bald head and Adam's apple! Though he is a little precious, he does not strike her as a homosexual, either. Actors *are* a little precious. And if Bernard is homosexual now, she knows that at the time Bertrand was conceived, Bernard was heterosexual. He was, after all, having an affair with her daughter.

The next day, as if sensing Mme. Lavalier's disbelief, Bernard brings Mme. Lavalier pictures of himself and Bertrand, taken when the boy was perhaps five or six years old. None of this seems very clear, nor very healthy. Mme. Lavalier yearns to ask Bernard detailed sexual questions, but she cannot. She accepts, finally, that Pei Pu is a woman in disguise. What reason would Bernard have to lie? But she tries not to think about the subject because it troubles her. Nor does she like Pei Pu. He—or she—has an obsequious nature. And now their relationship is even more awkward, because she does not know if Pei Pu knows she knows the secret. She plays it safe and pretends she has heard nothing.

"Monsieur Shi," she calls Pei Pu.

.   .   .

Something about the call from Bernard makes Mme. Boursicot decide that before giving the whole family the happy news she should go to Paris and have a look at this new grandson herself. She knows her son has a secretive side, but how, she wonders, could he have a child and mention it to her only once, so long ago? Why did he not tell her he was making plans to bring his son home? Still, she remembers the picture of himself and a young Oriental boy Bernard once showed her.

"Maybe it was true all along," she thinks.

And she remembers something else. A letter that arrived from China four or five years ago. She opened it to see if it was urgent enough to send at once to Bernard, who was due home shortly.

"My mother is very ill and you promised to help us and now there are two children," she recalls the letter saying.

She was struck by that phrase, "You promised to help us." It must be some poor person, she thought. When she gave the letter to Bernard he read it quickly and tore it up.

"Do you know this person?" she asked.

"Don't worry about it," he said.

She finds it impossible, however, to remain calm. She has grand-daughters, but this is her first grandson, the child of her favorite boy. She boards the train, bringing in addition to her sewing kit a basket of oysters from the morning market and a traditional Breton breakfast mug with BERTRAND stenciled on the side. Bertrand, waiting at the station with Bernard, spots her as soon as she gets off the train.

"That's Grandma!" he yells.

Mme. Boursicot, walking with her cane, sees a tall teenage boy. He doesn't look entirely Chinese and he certainly doesn't look French. Then he hugs her. So warm—just like Bernard.

At home, Bernard introduces her to a M. Shi, the boy's uncle and a great singing star. He makes a great deal of fuss over her—never, she thinks, has she seen such fancy manners—but she does not pay too much attention to the funny little man because there is something more important on her mind. She brings it up when Bernard takes her to the little studio for a nap.

"It's fine about this guy," she says, "but what about the mother?"

"We'll see about that later," Bernard snaps and slams the door.

Mme. Boursicot does not mention the mother again for the rest of her three-day stay.

She very much enjoys her grandson, though. He hugs her and calls her "Mami"—"Grandma." On November 11, Mme. Boursicot, Bertrand, Bernard, and M. Shi watch the Armistice Day parade on television in the morning and Bertrand fixes an elaborate Chinese meal for her. He speaks only a little French, but he can make himself understood.

"No, Mami," he says when she goes into the tiny kitchen to help. "You sit."

Bertrand goes to great effort, bringing her a series of small dishes filled with peculiar food: Chinese ravioli, bits of meat in broth; and she is touched by the way he and Bernard watch, hoping she likes it.

On the other hand, there seems to be a bit of tension between Bernard and the boy's uncle. When M. Shi gives her chopsticks, Bernard is curt with him.

"My mother can't eat with those things," he says and often snaps at him over little things.

M. Shi, on the other hand, wants very much to be part of the family. When Mme. Boursicot mentions that her son Lionel is getting married in April, M. Shi congratulates her and says she must invite him.

They all pose together, one afternoon, for family photos. Mme. Boursicot sits on the sofa, M. Shi sits beside her, looking a bit guarded and apprehensive. Sitting casually on the floor in front of Mme. Boursicot is Bernard. His chin is tilted up aggressively; he has a tight, almost defiant smile. Mme. Boursicot, in a proper navy dress, with a touch of white at the collar, does not look happy. Her posture is stiff; she touches neither her son nor the man beside her. It is a world away from Beijing in 1973 when Bernard, having met Bertrand for the first time, posed for another family picture, with Bertrand and Pei Pu and her mother. And yet the expression of Bernard's mother and the expression of Pei Pu's mother, were one to put the two pictures side by side, are identical: a maternal universal transcending culture, country, and race.

"Something is going on here and I don't know what it is," the expression says. "But I don't like it."

I n France if one is nicely connected it is said *"Il avait un bon carnet d'adresse,"* and this, as Bernard returns to Belize in November, is quickly becoming the case with Pei Pu.

Arriving in Paris, Pei Pu contacts Jean Leclerc du Sablon, who is now working for the newsweekly *L'Express,* as well as former tutors François and Françoise. Françoise, who in 1964 had taught the children of then Second Councillor Yves Pagniez, invites Pei Pu to dinner at her home with Pagniez, who has just come back to France after serving as Ambassador to Yugoslavia. Leclerc du Sablon introduces Pei Pu to the distinguished Agence France-Presse China specialist Jean Vincent and to Foreign Affairs secretary Jean-Pierre Lafosse, who heard of Pei Pu as actor and writer while second secretary at the embassy in Beijing, a few years prior.

In the fall the Maison des Sciences de l'Homme gives a lunch for Shi Pei Pu. Beijing Opera scholar Jacques Pimpaneau is there, as is Joel Thorval, a cultural attaché at the embassy in Beijing. Thorval, who has heard of Pei Pu as actor and playwright, introduces Pei Pu to Guy Alain Thiollier, who works at the National Institute of Audiovisual Communications, a government-sponsored production company. Thiollier introduces Pei Pu to Jean Michel Meurice, who is in charge of cultural programming at Antenne 2, one of France's three television networks. Meurice, impressed with Pei Pu's background as well as his excellent

French, contacts freelance filmmaker François Ribadeau-Dumas and asks him to do a television show about Beijing Opera and Pei Pu. Pei Pu brings up the idea of doing a series of television shows on China with François, who is now a television producer at Télévision Française 1. Pei Pu also contacts Claude Chayet, now returning from his post as ambassador to China, for help in extending his three-month residence permit. Chayet hasn't seen Pei Pu since the first days of the Cultural Revolution, in 1965; he is at best an acquaintance, but Chayet considers Pei Pu a cultivated man who will be a cultural asset to France. Also, as a foreign affairs veteran, Chayet gets requests like Pei Pu's all the time— so frequently that years later he can't say for certain that he does intercede for Pei Pu, though he believes it likely. In late December 1982, Pei Pu is granted a one-year permit.

Pei Pu also makes contacts in the Chinese community. There are, in many European cities, Beijing Opera clubs where aficionados, usually amateur singers and musicians, gather and play. Pei Pu is introduced to Mrs. Ou Tseng, a native of Shanghai, whose husband manages a small Chinese restaurant, Loo Tou, at 24 rue Saint-Augustin, in the Second Arrondissement, near the Opéra, where a Paris club meets every Sunday. When in early December Pei Pu makes a personal appearance, the regulars are thrilled to meet a student of the great Mei Lanfang.

Of Pei Pu's private life, little is known. Pei Pu tells Mrs. Ou Tseng that Bertrand is the child of a Frenchwoman who died in Beijing during the Cultural Revolution. Now he and the boy live in the home of the boy's uncle, a Foreign Service employee named Bernard Boursicot. Pei Pu never mentions Bernard to French friends. Leclerc du Sablon is not aware that the two know each other. Neither is Claude Chayet. A number of French diplomats are told that Bertrand is Pei Pu's adopted son. Françoise is told by Pei Pu that he had adopted two sons in China. One, the younger, was the grandchild of a German girl and a Chinese man who fled Beijing during the Cultural Revolution. Pei Pu refuses to tell Françoise the story of his elder son, Bertrand. Pei Pu says only that he wishes he had come to France with his second son.

The old air of tantalizing mystery remains. Pei Pu teases Beijing Opera students, promising to one day tell them tales of the great stars. He tells Françoise that she knows the person in whose apartment he is staying and that one day he will reveal who it is, but he never does. He is amusing. He is charming. And with François Mitterrand, the nation's first Socialist president, elected only the year before, there is a certain amount of chic involved in entertaining an artist who has survived the totalitarian horrors of the Cultural Revolution. Pei Pu is a sought-after guest. On New Year's Eve, 1982, Pei Pu goes off to attend a party at the home of Claude Martin, Conseiller in Beijing, who everyone says will one day be ambassador to China. In January, Pei Pu gives a concert in the Paris suburb of Boulogne-Billancourt and a number of diplomats attend.

In February, Pei Pu begins his most ambitious work: the television show. Filmmaker Ribadeau-Dumas knows nothing about Beijing Opera but he has made a number of documentaries on composers and music, including portraits of Lorin Maazel and Pierre Boulez and films on Senegalese music and Japanese Butoh dancers. He thinks of Pei Pu as a messenger from another culture and he wants to bring Pei Pu together with a French composer and see what they can create. The collaboration is a flop. "Professor" Pei Pu, as he insists upon being called, does not seem interested in working with another artist. The film concentrates then on Pei Pu—but the star is very mysterious. He always gives a slightly different age: forty-two, forty-five, forty-seven. Ribadeau-Dumas has no idea what happened to Pei Pu during the Cultural Revolution: in one version he suffered and was exiled to the south, where he studied the music of the minorities; in another he did not suffer at all. He says the boy Du Du is his son, but Ribadeau-Dumas doubts it—it seems to him Pei Pu is homosexual.

Ribadeau-Dumas shoots Pei Pu discussing breathing and voice projection with a French woman opera singer, his own voice soft and musical, his fingers fluttering. He takes Pei Pu to Brittany, shooting him on the cliffs over the sea, costumed as a shepherdess searching for her lost love. He follows Pei Pu Sunday afternoons to the Loo Tou. There, the restaurant closed and the tables pushed to the side, the musicians play their strange and beautiful instruments: the two-stringed second fiddle, which resembles a croquet mallet; the perfectly rounded moon mandolin. Often, they call out to one another to sing.

The show will be called *The Messenger from Beijing*. For dramatic effect, Ribadeau-Dumas restages Pei Pu's arrival in France. He takes Pei Pu, Bertrand, and a few members of the Loo Tou club to the airport, where a woman presses a huge bouquet into Pei Pu's arms as one would honor a master, while the narrator speaks of Shi Pei Pu, a student of the famous Mei Lanfang.

Pei Pu improvises the small talk of a man who has been on a long flight, and he does it wonderfully. He woke up in Karachi, Pei Pu says. It was much hotter than Paris. Then there is talk of the weather in Beijing.

The weather in Belize is also hot. Too damned hot. Or maybe it's Bernard. Pei Pu is driving him crazy. What was it she said back in September?

"Oooh, it is so easy to call in your country! You pick up the phone and you are halfway around the world."

Now, Pei Pu doesn't stop. The calls come sometimes three times a week and it is always, Bernard thinks, he who pays. And though Pei Pu's career is going as splendidly as she dreamed, she is never happy.

"I know the other one is near you," she says.

Or, "My health is not good, I should not be here alone."

Or else Pei Pu pulls out the big gun:

"I think I will take the boy and go back to Beijing."

He sends her four thousand francs a month through Mme. Lavalier, he pays the upkeep on the apartment, and all he gets is complaints. Bertrand is never at school; he is accompanying Pei Pu on concert tours. On his vacation, he works in a Chinese restaurant. When Bernard complains to Pei Pu that he never hears from the boy, he gets a letter so patently fraudulent it infuriates him. The letter simply does not have the tone of a teenage boy. It also deals mostly with Pei Pu, whom Bertrand, following their public charade, refers to as "Ta Ta," or Uncle: Bertrand says that though Pei Pu criticizes him often, he knows Pei Pu is right. He says that Pei Pu is working very hard on the television special and everyone knows how talented Pei Pu is—everyone but Bernard. He asks Bernard to come back to Paris as soon as possible, where they can all live happily. He reminds Bernard the day before was Pei Pu's birthday—which, Bernard realizes, he has once again forgotten. He says he and Pei Pu are sad. It is Christmas and Bernard is far away.

Bernard can't take it.

He walks into his ambassador's office.

"I'm having trouble again with the arm," Bernard says.

In February, he's back in Paris.

The visit starts out nicely: Bernard stays at Port-Royal, sleeping on a mat on the floor in the same room with Pei Pu, who sleeps on the bed. Thierry is not there, so Pei Pu is pleased. She would be more pleased, Bernard senses, if they were to resume their sexual relationship, but he is not interested and she does not press it. They go, happily *en famille*, with Bertrand to the Eiffel Tower. They attend an avant-garde German play with Jacques Pimpaneau which unsettles Pei Pu, whose knowledge of European theater centers on Molière.

"I was afraid for a moment this man was going to become naked," Pei Pu whispers to Bernard. The next minute the man does.

But within a few days Pei Pu gets on Bernard's nerves.

She tells him again his job is not important and that Belize—where Pei Pu has never been—is a country without culture. She is angry when Bernard tells her he wants Bertrand to attend his brother Lionel's spring wedding without her. She tells him she cannot remain in the apartment much longer—the kitchen is too small for her to entertain properly.

Meanwhile, so many of her friends are around Bernard feels as if Pei Pu owns the apartment and *he* is the guest. Other Chinese come to France and work in restaurants, Bernard thinks; five months after coming to France, Pei Pu is starring in a television show. This man Ribadeau-Dumas is always on the phone; Pei Pu is acting as if she is a big star. She prepares a concert for the end of the month at the Conservatory of Paris. She says she has met the famous choreographer Maurice Bejart, and he is eager to work with her—a probable exaggeration, as Bejart will later say he has little to say about Pei Pu, having met Pei Pu only one time. On the Chinese New Year, they go to the Loo Tou, where Pei Pu performs before one hundred and fifty people. The film crew is shooting and people are calling Shi "Professor." The mood is euphoric: even the cook in the kitchen sings. Bernard, says Ribadeau-Dumas, appears quite drunk. He also sees Bernard quarreling with Pei Pu's son. Bernard says the quarrel was with Pei Pu—she was driving him crazy with her capricious moods, ordering him and Bertrand about.

The next day, Bernard takes Bertrand home to Vannes—without Pei Pu. He introduces Bertrand, who he says is fourteen, to everyone in the family. He takes Bertrand to the Boursicot family farm, where his aunt Annik cooks crêpes in the kitchen off the barn—a country custom to keep the house free of smoke—and his uncle André brings out his strong homemade cider. He takes his son to the airy and modern home of his aunt Mimi, where the most frequently used kitchen appliance is the microwave and the den overflows with detective books.

Mimi finds the visit disturbing. Bernard is certainly attractive to women; it is to be expected he has fathered a child; but Mimi, who is a parent herself, believes the boy looks seventeen or eighteen. Mme. Boursicot has never mentioned a grandson and she dotes on Bernard. Also, when Mimi asks Bertrand about his plans and he says he is going back to China, there is a troubling argument.

"Of course you're not going back to China," says Bernard. "You're my son. You're staying here."

"I'm not your son," says Bertrand.

Mme. Boursicot sees something similar to what is troubling Mimi.

"Call me 'Daddy,' " Mme. Boursicot hears Bernard say often, but Bertrand does so only once when Bernard gets into an argument with his father.

Mme. Boursicot and her husband and sons don't know what to make of it. Alone, they try to avoid the subject. Lionel, a stocky, fair-haired house painter who resembles Bernard, has reason to be more confused than anyone: Bernard confides to Lionel that Bertrand's mother is in Paris, but Lionel knows from his mother that the person who accompanied Bertrand from China is a man. Bernard also tells Lionel there is another child.

"I have the mother and son out. It was very difficult," he says. "Maybe next time I'll try to get the boy's brother out as well."

After a three-day visit, Bernard leaves. A day later, Aunt Annik comes to the house.

"Where is the mother?" she asks Mme. Boursicot.

Aunt Mimi follows.

"Where is the mother?" she asks.

Bernard, though this is his first time alone with his son, never quizzes Bertrand about who he believes to be his mother or what he recalls of his early life. Pei Pu long ago said she had told Bertrand his mother was dead, and when he was of age, she would tell him the truth. There is no reason to pry. And yet back in Paris, Bernard finds himself increasingly irritated with Pei Pu. Early one day, says Bernard, going into the bathroom, he surprises her in the bath. Her tiny breasts are exposed, but she has had enough warning to throw a washcloth over her genitals.

All at once Bernard is seized with an urge to tear it off. He cannot say why.

He yanks at the cloth.

"Let me see!" he demands. For her bad health, Pei Pu suddenly has the strength of a bull.

"No!" Pei Pu is yelling. "I prefer to die! You know I am not normal. What do you want from me? You have your son and he is beautiful. Is that not enough?"

And Bernard, who can hoist the largest diplomatic pouch, who has pinned a colleague against the wall with such force that he has put himself under the protection of his ambassador, is unable to pull off the cloth.

In late February, Bernard returns to Belize, depressed.

He has been unable to exert any influence on his son's life or Pei Pu's—her life, indeed, has eclipsed his. He is paying Pei Pu's rent, supporting himself and Thierry, and sending money to his parents, and it is putting a severe strain on his income. There is one thing that cheers him: Taking the Foreign Service exam for chancery secretary for perhaps the seventh time, he manages to get the questions beforehand. He copies the answers from the textbook, sneaks them into the classroom, and—copying them verbatim—ensures, he is certain, success. Back on the job, his behavior grows erratic; at home, his drinking accelerates. Ambassador Chauvet, initially impressed with Bernard's energy and enthusiasm, is now worried. Bernard is spending a good deal of time on medical leave for an arm broken under circumstances that were not clear to him. His conduct is unbecoming. He tells Mme. Chauvet he has an illegitimate child by a Chinese woman. He tells strangers he is an anarchist and a revolutionary. When reprimanded by Chauvet, Bernard bursts into tears. Mme. Chauvet has told her husband she thinks Bernard may be very fragile emotionally, perhaps even unbalanced. Chauvet gives orders to keep Bernard away from the embassy archives.

Bernard is too obsessed with family problems to notice. Though he has told Pei Pu she may *not* attend Lionel's wedding, she is now calling his mother to ask what one wears to a wedding in France. His mother, in turns, calls him.

"If I invite Pei Pu, won't I also have to invite Mme. Lavalier and Thierry?" she asks.

"Pei Pu is *not* coming to the wedding, Mama," he says.

And though she has time to make expensive long-distance calls to Brittany, Pei Pu has not communicated with Bernard since his return to Belize. Writing her in March, Bernard is trembling with rage.

> It's been three weeks since I left and still no news from you [he writes]. If you think I am insensitive to this, you are wrong. If you think I am just a bank and you owe me nothing, you are wrong again. If I want to pay what is necessary for the education of Bertrand, I also demand compensation. First, news: not in the style of the letter at the end of December. Furthermore, I want him to write to his grandmother and grandfather and *I want him to go see them during Easter vacation for a week—alone.* They are old and tired and it will give them pleasure. If I want to help you, I am not stupid enough to give you everything while you ignore the few things I ask you: That Bertrand sends, to his grandparents and me, a letter from time to time, with his photos. I hope that you will understand and not act as if you have heard nothing.
>
> 1. You must do what is necessary to begin the naturalization process for Bertrand so that he becomes French as soon as possible.
>
> 2. You must encourage Bertrand to write to me.
>
> 3. You must tell him to go to Vannes, and pay for his trip, every time he has a vacation, so that he can keep up affectionate relations with his grandparents.
>
> 4. You have to pay attention to him and watch over his responsibilities with attention, even if it doesn't interest you.
>
> You told me in 1965 and again later, "I can raise a child very well and he will listen to me."
>
> Today, I am not so sure you are taking care of him as you should. Instead of serving in Chinese restaurants, he is at the age where he should be studying, *but in order for him to be interested in*

studying, you must help him, not only "control" him. It's your task, which you have begun a bit late, but which you must continue. You mustn't think only of yourself. It's him and his future that counts. He's already very behind at school and if you don't make the necessary efforts he is going to be even more behind, because he only understands a few things at school. The school where he is now is very damaging, especially for his "spirit." If you don't like discipline, with either the Communists or anyone else, this is still not a reason to get Bertrand used to copying you in this way of doing things. He must study and you must help him with his responsibilities, and I must receive his report card every three months.

I work here to feed you and give you a place to live, to be your support, but in exchange I must have some results in the education of our child.

Pei Pu is furious.

I wanted to write to you regularly, but we live and work regularly, too [Pei Pu writes]. I fell ill after the [filming] and was unable to control myself when I suffered a series of attacks. I do not have the strength to answer you point by point.

I still believe I bring up children very well—[Here, Bernard sees, the phrase "unless someone bothers us" is crossed out.] I've had Du Du for more than sixteen years and I never asked anyone for anything, except for very little. . . .

Du Du's teacher says he has made lots of progress. He does not work in the restaurant anymore. . . .

Well, excuse me, I am unable to control myself.

Pei Pu

Mimi has a problem: She cannot stop thinking about Bernard and his son.

There is mystery here—not the murderous bloody sort of P. D. James, to be sure, but something that is not right. A man feels obligated to lie about a boy's age? A man refuses to tell his family the most basic information about his son's mother? Mimi has business in Paris anyway; she knows Pei Pu is living in Bernard's apartment, and when she arrives, she phones. It is clear to her the man doesn't want to meet her.

"Bertrand is not here," he says. "I will have him call you tomorrow."

Bertrand does not call the next day so Mimi calls again. Pei Pu still does not invite her. She forces the door.

"What a pity when I had so wanted to meet you," Mimi says, shaming him into it. "Well, perhaps one day we'll be able to meet in Brittany."

"Perhaps you could join us for something to eat," Pei Pu says.

"I'll be there in an hour," says Mimi.

At Port-Royal she finds a man dressed in black pajamas, wearing a wig that makes him look like Joan of Arc. She cannot quite get a fix on him. He is very effeminate, but after all, he is Chinese. He has very theatrical gestures and talks a good deal, but about nothing that interests her. They have a meal and make small talk, and after a while Mimi gets to it:

"So, where is Bertrand's mother?" she asks.

"You are the first one to ask me this question," he says.

Mimi doubts that—it is a pretty natural question, she thinks. She waits, unspeaking, for his reply.

"Don't talk about the mother," Pei Pu says. "Bertrand does not ask about her."

That stops Mimi. Maybe, she thinks, the mother is dead. Maybe she is not a good woman. Maybe she has married again. Mimi drops the subject.

It is possible Pei Pu *should* advise Bernard about his career—for his own is going splendidly. While Bernard is broke, Pei Pu is making and saving money: There is a four-thousand-franc payment from the Maison des Sciences de l'Homme; eighteen thousand francs for the documentary; and an average fee of three thousand francs for lectures and concerts. In May, Pei Pu confides to a friend, he has saved up sixty thousand francs —roughly ten thousand dollars. Though he tells his French friends he fears his government representatives, Pei Pu makes sure to maintain good relations: Xio Te, the cultural councillor of the People's Republic embassy, is invited to his performances.

His success, for a newcomer, is remarkable. After seven months in the country, Pei Pu, in May, does a live show for channel TF1 and gives a lecture and performance at both Paris's Musée Guimet and the University of Stockholm. His biggest triumph is the May 8 broadcast of *A Messenger from Beijing* on A2-TV.

Le Monde, previewing the show, gives it high praise.

"Shi Pei Pu presents himself not so much as an actor or singer— stating that he does not have the required talent—but more as librettist," writes critic Alain Jacob. "Despite his modesty, we see Shi Pei Pu in three roles, one feminine and two masculine, during a brief story developed from a traditional tale and filmed on the coast of Brittany. Beautiful cinematography . . ."

Even more impressive is the company Pei Pu keeps the night of the show: He sees the program at the home of Ambassador Claude Chayet.

Across town, the Loo Tou opera group is not so impressed. They have, out of courtesy and respect for Pei Pu's passion for opera, worked on the film, but they do not consider him a star. His voice is not professional quality, no one had heard of him before his arrival, and after a few meetings, one musician recalls, Pei Pu more or less confessed that he was more playwright than performer. Another, out of town during the screening of *Messenger,* recalls returning to Paris distressed at having missed the television debut of a man the French newspapers had called a big Beijing Opera star. His friends told him not to worry.

"You didn't miss much," they said.

Bernard has gotten into a habit: He comes home every day after work, has a pitcher of mint juleps, and rants about Pei Pu. She never leaves him in peace. When her career is going well she writes him that she is upset because they have still not dealt with the problem of their second son. In May, after agreeing to send Bertrand to Vannes for the christening of Bernard's niece, she changes her mind and Bernard's brother is left waiting at the train station. A few days later, Bernard receives the most disturbing news of all.

Pei Pu writes that she's returning to China—and soon. Though she
had told Bernard she would wait until the end of May before returning
to China, so that she could see him one more time—perhaps the last
time—now, because Bernard is returning late, that may not be possible.
She is very unhappy; she has not had the chance to build a real family in
Paris with Bernard as she dreamed. She does, however, remember the
good times.

Then she says good-bye.

Bernard is not certain that Pei Pu is leaving, but he is frantic—he's got
to get posted closer to France.

Then Bernard's luck suddenly turns. In June, the Foreign Affairs
office wires Bernard that he has been upgraded to first assistant to the
consul general and posted to Scotland. Ambassador Chauvet apparently
still has some affection for Bernard. When he hears Bernard has no place
to stay in Paris, he offers a studio near the Eiffel Tower.

Bernard leaves Belize. En route, filled with happiness, he stops in
Houston to visit his friends the Songers and whips out a picture of
Bertrand.

"The issue of my first visit to China," Bernard says grandly.

Lu and Paul stare at the picture of a Eurasian boy who looks
nothing like Bernard.

"Yeah, Bernard," Paul says. "We can see the resemblance."

On June 22, Bernard is back in France. He and Thierry do not yet have
the keys to Ambassador Chauvet's apartment, so Thierry goes to his
family in Bordeaux and Bernard stays with Bertrand and Pei Pu at Port-
Royal.

Despite the warnings of imminent departure, Pei Pu is not pack-
ing. There is no need. Pei Pu's residence permit is valid until late fall,
and Pei Pu has also been soliciting assistance among an ever growing
circle of powerful friends. Pei Pu asks Jean-Pierre Lafosse, the secretary
in Foreign Affairs, to help. Lafosse calls a technical adviser on the staff
of Minister of the Interior Gaston Deferre, who is one of President
François Mitterrand's oldest advisers. A few days before Bernard's arrival, Pei Pu also contacts Philippe Orengo, a friend of a French Beijing

Opera aficionado, and an aide to the mayor of Paris. Pei Pu proposes becoming a cultural liaison between Paris and Beijing. Pei Pu also requests a ten-year residence permit.

Now Pei Pu tells Bernard she wants a new apartment. She has the property all lined up: a large studio on Boulevard Saint-Germain owned by a Chinese friend. Bernard can knock down the price, she tells him, by paying with some of his Chinese antiques.

As on his last trip, Bernard and Pei Pu sleep in the same room but in separate beds. Bernard, however, gets little rest. At night Pei Pu lies awake giving Bernard career advice, carrying the implicit weight of her recent triumphs. When after a few days Thierry gets the keys to Ambassador Chauvet's unfurnished studio on rue Duvivier Bernard is relieved. He calls Bertrand; they fetch a large mattress from the little storeroom next to the apartment and carry it down the stairs.

"So you are going with your son and leaving me alone?" Pei Pu asks.

"Right," says Bernard, though Bertrand is merely helping.

It is far nicer this way. Bernard buys Bertrand a bicycle, and his son visits daily. There is no phone in the rue Duvivier apartment, so Pei Pu is unable to bother Bernard. He and Bertrand take long walks around Paris. Bernard takes Bertrand to meet Catherine.

And then Foreign Affairs informs Bernard he has not passed the chancery exam after all. While nothing is said directly, it is clear he is suspected of cheating. Bernard's new job is not in jeopardy, his superiors seem to want to quietly put an awkward matter aside, but Bernard wants the higher rank and salary. He goes to the union. If Foreign Affairs thinks he cheated, let them prove it.

And yet, he is worried. He has had periods of anxiety and depression before, but this is different. He has the feeling that something, somewhere, is very wrong; that the basic structure of his life is in danger. He feels the gnawing, helpless anxiety of imminent and inexorable loss such as a husband feels the week before his wife says she is leaving or a worker feels the days before he is dismissed. He feels the knives are out. He feels people are watching him.

He tries to push the anxiety out of his head and concentrate on the good things: his new Renault 5, the trip he will take to Vannes in a few days with Thierry and Mme. Lavalier. Pei Pu is petulant about being left behind, but Bernard placates her by promising to show her the Saint-Germain apartment.

On June 29, he goes with Thierry and Bertrand to Service Auto d'Ambassades, the auto shop on rue de Monttessuy that caters to Foreign Service people, to have the new car serviced. As it's being driven into the shop, he hears a familiar voice.

"That's my car," a woman says.

"No, Sylvie," Bernard says. "It's mine."

It has been two years since the two old friends, who met so long ago in China, have seen one another.

"Sylvie," Bernard says, "let me introduce you to my son."

Sylvie is stunned. The boy is sixteen, seventeen years old, and all this time Bernard never said one word about a son. But she has no time to talk now; she has an appointment. She and Bernard agree to get together later in the week, and in the car outside where her husband is waiting Sylvie tries to make sense of the news. Bernard must have wanted a child and adopted the boy in Belize, Sylvie decides. He is an Indian—she can tell by the features. It never occurs to her that this may be his son by Pei Pu. Sylvie was in China after Bernard left; she never saw Pei Pu pregnant.

In the evening, Bernard, Thierry, and Bertrand go with Mme. Lavalier for dinner at a place an hour outside of Paris. Returning to Paris, they drop Bertrand off at Port-Royal, then have a nightcap with a friend. At three A.M., Bernard calls Pei Pu—who rarely sleeps nights—from a pay phone near the apartment.

"Did Bertrand have a good time?" he asks.

Pei Pu does not answer. When he asks about things he cares about, Bernard thinks, Pei Pu never answers. He moves on to her favorite subject, the apartment at Saint-Germain, which they have arranged to look at the next afternoon.

"I will meet you, as we discussed," Bernard says.

"And remember," Pei Pu says, "I am always your best friend."

The next morning, Thursday, June 30, Bernard and Thierry sleep late. Around eleven, they get up and leave the house, walking down Champ-de-Mars. As it enters the wide, commercial Avenue Bosquet, they separate. Thierry takes a right, heading to the garage to pick up the car. Bernard goes left, toward the Métro station of École Militaire, to see his physical therapist on the Place d'Italie about his arm.

A minute or two later they are on him, and the badges are out, and the awful fear Bernard has had all week has form and face and the faces are as expected and inevitable as death. They are the faces Bernard has awaited for twelve years, since he slipped a sealed letter from the embassy mailroom in Beijing under his shirt, and cushioned it with cardboard to absorb his sweat, and delivered it to Kang. They are the faces of the agents of the Direction de la Surveillance du Territoire.

"We just want to talk to you," they say. "Only a few questions; it won't take long."

In a way, it is a relief.

You can lie your whole life to one person, but you cannot lie your whole life to everybody, Bernard thinks. If he tells them, it will finally be finished. Pei Pu will not have to go back to China. He will have his boy. They will understand that this was a love story and the documents he gave the Chinese were useless and no harm was done. He doubts he will even go to prison, and if he does, he will not stay long.

My Dear Sylvie,

When, the day before my arrest, I presented to you the product of my old love in China, my son Bertrand, I was one hundred leagues away from knowing what would happen the next day.

My lawyer lives on Boulevard Saint-Germain. He is *Maître* Gérard Even.

My story is the consequence of destiny. Would it be possible for you to go in the evening and tell him how much I loved Pei Pu during that time and that it was following an abortion which happened soon after our return from Beidaihe and which traumatized me so that I did everything I could so that Shi wouldn't stay alone and that "for a woman a child was the completion of everything," as you explained to me.

You can say that you tried to see Shi Pei Pu again but that the violence of the Red Guards prevented all contact. Explain to him about the English journalist who was arrested who had lived just next door. That which becomes complicated.

Explain to him the genesis of my story. Starting from Chayet's house until the coming of her femininity and of my departure December 13, 1965. Explain very well to him the following years which passed in anguish trying to send money to Shi

234

to be able to buy her departure. The rest is written down at the investigating judge's office.

I kiss you affectionately and hope you can do this service for me.

Your friend who is in prison for saving his son who was not able to leave.

—Bernard Boursicot
Prisoner Number 725196
1 Avenue du Général-Leclerc
94261, Fresnes

P.S. You know I wanted to get Shi out and to marry me. The other stories are false. You know the thousand hours that I cried. Remember—for me and my child and his mother.

BOOK III

Knowledge

Thierry is irritated. Bernard was supposed to meet him after his doctor's appointment, near the Place d'Italie. Now it is one-thirty in the afternoon on June 30 and Thierry has been waiting over an hour. He finally goes upstairs, and the doctor tells him Bernard did not keep his appointment and did not call. Thierry goes back to the rue Duvivier studio to see if he is there, then calls Mme. Lavalier. She has not heard from Bernard either. Thierry spends the afternoon going between the apartment and the nearest telephone booth, in case Bernard calls. At around nine in the evening, there is a knock on the door. It is Bertrand. He and Pei Pu waited for Bernard for two hours at Boulevard Saint-Germain, he says; he never showed up. Thierry, frightened, goes to Mme. Lavalier's. They call a half dozen hospitals. Finally, Mme. Lavalier calls the police and tells them a young man is missing.

"How old is he?" the cop asks.

"Thirty-eight," says Mme. Lavalier.

"Maybe he's with a girl," the cop says.

"I don't think so," says Mme. Lavalier.

The next morning, Friday, July 1, Inspectors Jean-Louis Flori and Patrick Lamongie of the D.S.T. arrive at Port-Royal and climb the six flights of stairs in the old building to interview Shi Pei Pu, the Chinese opera singer, who has now been implicated in espionage. A tall teenage boy, half Caucasian, half Oriental, answers the door. The apartment is dark, the curtains are drawn, the walls hung with Chinese calligraphy.

Shi Pei Pu, the police know, is supposedly a woman; the boy who answered the door is her son by Bernard Boursicot. But the pale creature who sits before them now wears a man's shirt and trousers. Pei Pu has an Adam's apple, but the hands are small and delicate. The voice is neither masculine nor feminine; it is high and singsong. The singer, moreover, is not in good health—immediately after the police identify themselves, Pei Pu complains of weakness and a history of heart problems. Nonetheless, Pei Pu does not want the police to call for a doctor.

Flori and Lamongie are not certain how to proceed. They call headquarters and because of Pei Pu's poor health receive permission to question the suspect at home. The boy is sent from the room and they begin:

Pei Pu states profession as "singing artist, writer, and voice professor." Date of birth is given as 1938, in Shandong Province. Pei Pu confirms what Bernard has told them: She is a woman and the mother of his child.

"I was born into a family of mandarins, high-ranking civil servants," Pei Pu says. "I was raised my whole life as a boy and even today, in the eyes of the Chinese authorities, I am of masculine sex. In my youth, I learned to sing in Kunming. After the war, in 1945, I continued my studies at the University of Yunnan with Professor Mei Lanfang. The husband of my mother's sister Ting Hsi Ling was the minister of culture in Beijing, where I went when I was eighteen or twenty years old. I put together a play, wrote poems, and gathered a certain fame. Among the people who appreciated my work and protected me, one of the first was Zhou Enlai.

"In 1964, when China and France established relations, the Chinese authorities were in need of people who spoke French. It was on this occasion, at a French exposition in Beijing, that I met M. Robert Richard, commercial councillor of the embassy of France. Later on, I met M. Chayet, first councillor at the French embassy. During a cocktail party given by M. Chayet during the winter of 1964 I met Bernard Boursicot. We met a number of times and I finally told him I was a woman. Bernard left for France on December 13, 1965, when I was pregnant with his child. Our son, Shi Du Du, was born August 12, 1966. I was able to hide my pregnancy and give birth secretly. My son was raised in the province of Xinjiang by a female friend of my family. For the Chinese authorities, he was born of unknown parents in 1969 and I definitely adopted him in 1973. In 1970, I believe, Bernard came back to Beijing to work at the embassy. I did not know it and I was surprised to see him again. I then admitted to him that we had a child. . . ."

Pei Pu tells the police that Red Guards and the neighborhood *commissaire* discovered he had a relationship with a foreigner when Bernard returned to China on his second tour. Pei Pu speaks of being arrested and reprimanded for seeing a foreigner but quickly released because Pei Pu was "a personality."

"A few days later," Pei Pu tells the police, "a certain Kang who declared himself to be from the Beijing city government came to see me. He explained to me that I could see Bernard twice a week if I were to teach him the thoughts of Chairman Mao. Bernard came back and we pretended to learn the thoughts of the Chairman. A few months later, Kang came back and asked me to introduce him to Bernard. Later on, each time that Bernard came to my home he would meet Kang in the kitchen. I do not know what went on between Bernard and Kang. In April 1971, Kang ordered me to leave Beijing for Kunming. Bernard did not come to see me while I was in Kunming. . . ."

Knowledge of espionage—and even Bernard's work at the embassy in 1969—is denied.

"Were you aware of Bernard Boursicot's functions at the embassy in Beijing?" the police ask.

"Françoise, the tutor of the children of the second councillor at the embassy, M. Pagniez, told me he was 'a little accountant,' " says Pei Pu.

Did Pei Pu ever see Bernard Boursicot give documents to Kang?

"I must tell you that it is I who went to the kitchen with my mother when Bernard met Kang," Pei Pu says, changing the story slightly. "Kang would teach the thoughts of Chairman Mao to Bernard, sometimes with a man named Zhao. I never saw Bernard give printed documents to Zhao or Kang."

Did Bernard Boursicot carry a briefcase with him when he came to Shi's home?

"Sometimes he would bring meat to my mother," says Pei Pu.

The police decide to call for a doctor after all—not because Pei Pu seems to be weakening, but because they have decided they would like to bring the suspect in and are not certain the suspect's health will permit it. They call SOS Médecins. The doctor, José Juhel, confirms that Shi Pei Pu is indeed in poor health. He notes in his report that the patient—whom he refers to as "he"—suffered a stroke a year earlier and is complaining of palpitations.

"His present state dictates either incarceration in a hospital environment or that he undergo an electrocardiogram before the incarceration," the doctor writes.

There is something else the police are wondering about, but their curiosity goes unsatisfied: the doctor is not permitted to examine the genital area.

Dr. Juhel leaves and the police continue their interrogation. They ask Pei Pu about Bernard's Mongolia tour and Pei Pu tells them Kang was never present during Bernard's visits at that time. They ask how Pei Pu was able to leave China and Pei Pu explains that it was through the intervention of the vice secretary of the Beijing Writers' Association, who said an official invitation from a foreign organization was required. Pei Pu arranged to bring the boy, she explains, by telling the Chinese authorities it would be best if Shi Du Du remained in China—the authorities, Pei Pu says, always do the opposite of one's desires. When the interrogation is over, since Pei Pu reads French with great difficulty, the police read the statement. Pei Pu signs all the four pages, insisting on only one change:

There is a section regarding Pei Pu's early meetings with Bernard Boursicot that reads: "We met a number of times and I finally told him I was a woman."

Pei Pu wishes the words "I was a woman" deleted.

The police, apparently, are not certain: Their report of the July 1 interrogation refers to Pei Pu as "he." But by the next day, their minds are made up. When Commissaire Divisionnaire Raymond Nart of the D.S.T. makes a report to the prosecutor, it is clear that the police have not merely accepted the story but that they are rather smug about the secret they are about to reveal:

Shi Pei Pu was raised, right from the start, as a boy by his mother [the report reads in part]. His true nature was hidden from everyone until this day. In 1964, Shi Pei Pu was a writer prodigy of the Beijing Opera, the rave of the artistic and cultural groups of China. It was as such that she was invited to the French embassy in Beijing and that she met Bernard Boursicot. A sincere, loving relationship between the two of them began and was solidified with the secret birth of a son, Shi Du Du, in August of 1966. This son was raised in the province of Xinjiang and was officially declared as a found child. In 1973, while passing through Xinjiang, Shi Pei Pu adopted the boy. Today, Du Du is ignorant of the fact that Shi Pei Pu is a woman and his mother. . . .

Shi Pei Pu says she was not present during the private conversations between Bernard Boursicot and Kang and was ignorant of the fact that Bernard Boursicot was turning over documents to Kang. This is possible.

. . . It must be stated that Shi Pei Pu refused any mention of the fact that she is a woman on the official deposition. The doctor who performed the cardiac examination was not permitted to perform a more intimate examination. In light of the weak health of Shi Pei Pu (a stroke in 1982 with lasting effects), the questioning was performed in her home and she was not incarcerated following the judicial orders. In light of the information given by Shi Pei Pu, no search was made on the home.

Thierry, the day Bernard disappears, spends an awful night. He sleeps poorly, starting at every sound, and arrives at Boulevard Port-Royal on Friday, July 1, soon after the police have left. He is somewhat relieved: Calling Bernard's parents in Vannes that morning, Thierry has learned that Bernard called them the day before. He is with friends outside of Paris, Bernard says, and will come to Vannes at a later date. Pei Pu now tells Thierry she received a similar call at about the same time. It still, however, makes no sense: Bernard had been looking forward very much to this trip. And if he was making calls, why didn't he call Mme. Lavalier and leave a message for Thierry?

Pei Pu is also shaken: The police just left, Pei Pu tells Thierry. They asked her many things. She thinks it looks very serious for Bernard.

Pei Pu does not say what she was asked by the police but Thierry no longer believes a word she says anyway. Pei Pu isn't upset by the police, if they were ever there, Thierry thinks. She is upset because Bernard has disappeared and she is not getting her stinking apartment.

Then he has another idea: Maybe, he thinks, Pei Pu is behind this. Maybe she has kidnapped Bernard, bound and gagged him, and locked him up. In the storeroom.

It is a crazy thought; it makes him feel as if he is losing his mind. And yet he has to act on it. He gets the key to the storeroom from Pei Pu, telling her there is a flashlight in there he needs, then he walks, trembling, down the hall.

Bernard is not in the storeroom.

Thierry is mad with anxiety. He goes from the rue Duvivier studio to the phone booth down the street to Mme. Lavalier's. On Saturday morning Thierry calls up Christiane, his closest woman friend. Thierry has never spoken to her of Bernard's relationship with Pei Pu. Now he tells her only that Bernard has disappeared. They head to the Thirteenth Arrondissement precinct.

"He is a diplomat and he had a Chinese living in his apartment," Christiane says. "Maybe he is having trouble with the D.S.T."

"The D.S.T. is not us," the cop says. "And even if we knew, we could not tell you. The D.S.T. are secret police."

"Why would the D.S.T. be involved?" Thierry asks.

He leaves rue Duvivier and moves back into the apartment at Port-Royal with Pei Pu. Bernard has called there once, Thierry thinks; if he calls again he will be there. They spend Saturday evening and Sunday waiting for a call. On Sunday, they call the morgue.

On Monday, July 4, the phone rings. Thierry picks it up. The man at the other end says he is a journalist from *France-Soir* and he wishes to speak to M. Boursicot.

"Why?" asks Thierry.

"Because of the spy story," the journalist says. "Because of what has happened with M. Boursicot and the police."

Thierry has no idea what he is talking about.

"May we meet?" he says, making an appointment to see the journalist at the apartment.

Then, getting off the phone, he realizes it is stupid to have a journalist come to the house. Particularly a journalist from an afternoon tabloid that pays more attention to its page-three pinup girls than to serious news.

"I'm sorry to have made you climb all the stairs," he says, greeting the man at the door when he arrives, "but I think I'd rather talk in a café."

They go downstairs, to a restaurant in the building.

"You didn't know Bernard Boursicot was arrested by the D.S.T.?" the journalist asks.

"I don't know anything," Thierry says. "Do you know where he is?"

"I thought he was free again," the journalist says.

"I haven't heard a word from him," says Thierry.

Bernard has been arrested for spying, the journalist tells Thierry. The charges date to his posting in Beijing.

"What are you talking about?" asks Thierry. It must be, he thinks, that Bernard has gotten in trouble because he has a Chinese in the house.

"What about this story that he had a child in China—do you know anything about this?" the journalist asks.

"Yes," says Thierry, "he had a child in China."

"But with whom?"

Thierry is not about to tell a journalist the mother is upstairs.

"I don't know about the woman. I think Bernard knew a woman in China, but she disappeared during the Cultural Revolution," he says.

He does not mention Pei Pu's name, and the journalist promises not to use Thierry's, but the man has gotten a lot of information somewhere, because the next day a long story with a bold headline breaks on the front page of *France-Soir:*

"FOREIGN AFFAIRS CLERK CHARGED WITH SPYING," the smaller headline reads, and in much larger type, "THE 'CHINESE GEORGE SAND' HAD GIVEN HIM A CHILD."

> An administrative worker for the Ministry of Foreign Affairs, Bernard Boursicot, 39, arrested last Thursday by the D.S.T., denies having given away confidential or secret documents [the story begins]. He

has, nevertheless, just been indicted on the charge of conspiracy with agents of a foreign power.

In this case the country is China. The documents thus handed over have the power to bring harm to the diplomatic, military or economic interests of France.

Police sources confirm the existence of the case but refuse to make any further comments. It is difficult at this time to evaluate the importance of the act with which this civil servant is being charged. In charge of the diplomatic pouch at the French embassy in Beijing, he allegedly handed over to a Chinese agent dispatches, particularly those dealing with the U.S.S.R., Southeast Asia, and the U.S.A.

Rather tall and with a somewhat athletic stature, Boursicot's resemblance to a spy of the silver screen goes no further. As for the rest, and as is often the case in such circumstances, Bernard Boursicot was more a victim than anything else, manipulated through the use of blackmail. In this case he was being extorted because of his feelings. Bernard Boursicot, who had a child with a Chinese woman while living in Beijing, hoped to bring this child with him to Paris.

He is barely twenty when he discovers China at the beginning of the sixties. It's his first job with the Foreign Ministry, where he is employed as a civil servant on a contractual basis. He is put in charge of the mail. It is most probably during this first stay in Beijing (his child is supposedly sixteen years old) that he encountered a writer: a woman who can be considered the "Chinese George Sand" since many of her readers think she is a man.

Two or three years later, as his profession warrants it, Bernard Boursicot is transferred out of Beijing. He finds himself in Ireland, then Saudi Arabia, and later back in China. In 1972 and 1973, he lives in Paris working for a publisher. . . . Later, he returns to embassy life, first in the United States, then in Mongolia, from where he can frequently return to Beijing. . . .

There are also a number of quotes from Thierry, who is not identified by name.

"The French embassy in Mongolia closes its doors regularly," a friend of Boursicot's says. "He could thus return often to China. It was during one of his trips to Beijing that I went to visit him there. I was aware of the existence of his son and I knew that he very much wanted the child to discover France. On the other hand, he did not speak to me of the boy's mother. . . ."

In Vannes, meanwhile, Lionel Boursicot receives a call from his father-in-law in Paris: He has read a report about Bernard's arrest in an afternoon paper. Lionel knows it is only a matter of time before the story will be in the papers in Vannes. He calls his mother.

"Ma," he begins, "this might hurt. . . ."

Jean Leclerc du Sablon would not say he is surprised when he sees *France-Soir* that afternoon and learns that Bernard Boursicot has been arrested for spying: He is incredulous. His warm, emotional, generous friend from Beijing—it just does not fit. Leclerc has not seen Boursicot since his 1981 visit to China, but now he calls Bernard's home. A man answers the phone. Leclerc introduces himself as a journalist from *L'Express* and a friend of Bernard Boursicot's. The phone is passed to another man, with a higher voice, which sounds familiar. Leclerc introduces himself again.

"So, my friend, you don't recognize me anymore?" the man says.

It is Shi Pei Pu.

Leclerc has seen Pei Pu four or five times since his arrival in France, he has been to dinner at the apartment at Port-Royal, but he does not know the apartment belongs to Bernard Boursicot. He rushes over. Pei Pu has apparently seen the story in *France-Soir*, too.

"Don't go searching for the Chinese George Sand," says Pei Pu. "The Chinese George Sand is me."

Thierry watches Leclerc's face as he hears the secret: His mouth falls open. Exactly, Thierry thinks, like a man in a comic strip.

Leclerc thinks it is a joke. Then he sees Pei Pu is serious. Pei Pu tells Leclerc a complicated and confusing story: about being the daughter of a high official from Yunnan Province, as Leclerc remembers it, about Pei Pu's mother having to hide the fact that he was a girl, because otherwise his father would have taken one of his concubines as his wife. Pei Pu speaks of a friendship with Bernard Boursicot that sounds to Leclerc like a love affair. Pei Pu says he knows nothing about espionage.

Leclerc does not understand a word of the crazy love story. But later, he tells Pei Pu, they will try to understand.

Then Leclerc leaves. He keeps replaying the incoherent love story in his head, trying to make sense of it. He decides, finally, that it is a homosexual friendship, though that is surprising to him—he did not know Bernard was homosexual. Pei Pu has been trying to tell him he had a love affair with Bernard in which Pei Pu played the role of a woman. Leclerc has seen Pei Pu portray a woman onstage, he's very effective. He does not believe Pei Pu is a woman for a moment. But it is a beautiful story, he thinks, and not every story has to be true.

Tuesday evening, following Leclerc's advice, Pei Pu takes Bertrand and goes to the home of a French friend, a middle-aged widow who has accompanied Pei Pu on the Sweden tour.

Wednesday, July 6, Pei Pu's name appears in *France-Soir*. Pei Pu calls Thierry to come and fetch him: His friend no longer wishes Pei Pu and Du Du to remain in her house.

Ten o'clock Thursday morning, July 7, Thierry is awakened by a knock on the door. Two D.S.T. agents are facing him with a warrant for the arrest of Pei Pu. They have been pounding on Pei Pu's door for the last five minutes, they tell Thierry, and nobody answers. Does Thierry have a key?

Thierry lets them in.

Pei Pu, rigid with fear, is sitting on the sofa, in a T-shirt and baggy pants, her hands pressed on her knees and her knees squeezed tightly together.

Despite his feelings about her, Thierry is moved.

"The poor *misérable,*" Thierry thinks, and out loud, "These people want to see you, they have a paper to bring you to the judge."

Pei Pu does not move. "The judge only wants to talk," Thierry says. "It will be only a few hours."

Pei Pu changes clothes. Then she goes with the agents to the Palais de Justice, to the office of Bruno Laroche, the investigating judge. Laroche is in his late thirties, dark eyed, balding. He has seen the court papers in which Bernard Boursicot and Shi Pei Pu affirm that Shi Pei Pu is a woman, but what stands before him now, in a gray double-breasted suit, appears to be a man. A man who, like Laroche, is losing his hair.

Pei Pu is charged with the same crime as Boursicot: delivering information to agents of a foreign power.

Pei Pu denies the charge.

"I was unaware that my friend Bernard Boursicot had given documents to the Chinese authorities and most particularly to an individual named Kang whom he would meet at my home in Beijing outside of my presence and without me knowing about it," says Pei Pu. "He would meet this man who would come to give him lessons about Chairman Mao."

The judge tells Pei Pu he is going to prison. He is also ordering a medical examination to see whether Shi Pei Pu is male or female and to determine whether or not the defendant has had surgery of the genital organs. Pending that decision, and in view of the defendant's poor health, the defendant will be held in the hospital of Fresnes—a men's prison.

Pei Pu's strength wavers.

"I will never be able to stand prison," says Pei Pu.

At Port-Royal, Thierry sits with Bertrand. The poor kid, he thinks —in a strange country less than a year and his mother gets taken away to prison. He knows she won't be returning home soon, not with Bernard still in jail and what he is reading in the newspapers. He has to get him out of here, away from police and reporters. He mustn't upset him, either.

"Pei Pu and Bernard have had a little trouble with the police," Thierry tells Bertrand. "But it is nothing."

Then he calls up Daniel to come and get Bertrand.

By the next day, the story has evolved into a full-blown scandal— the news is full of stories of the arrest of Beijing Opera singer Shi Pei Pu.

"SPY FOR LOVE: A BEIJING OPERA SINGER ARRESTED," reads the headline in *Le Parisien*, a working-class tabloid. "BON BAISERS DE CHINE," "From China with Love," proclaims *Le Matin*, the semiofficial paper of the Socialist party.

The problem is, none of the papers are quite certain whether to use the masculine or feminine when describing Pei Pu.

"IS THE MALE BEIJING OPERA SINGER A WOMAN SPY?" asks *Liberation*, while *Le Matin* reports that there is a "mysterious and ambiguous" element to the arrest:

> A singer of the Beijing Opera, Shi Pei Pu, 45, was arrested yesterday morning at the home she has shared for a year with Bernard Boursicot, a former civil servant in the embassy of France in Beijing, who has been imprisoned in Fresnes since July 2 for supplying intelligence to agents of a foreign power.
>
> . . . According to the D.S.T., there exists a doubt about [Shi Pei Pu's] identity. The male singer may be a woman in reality. "She" would have had a child in 1966 with an employee of the French embassy, who would have brought him to France in 1982. This version completely contradicts what is known by many friends of the singer.

It is hard for Bernard to keep track of time in prison. Probably that has to do with the drugs. He sees a psychiatrist as soon as he arrives who prescribes three ten-milligram tablets of Valium daily. He is also given Rohypnol, a drug used to combat anxiety. A guard comes to his cell and makes Bernard take the drugs in front of him, to make certain he does not hoard them. They make Bernard feel better, though somewhat sleepy and confused. He does remain certain of one thing: As soon as everyone understands that this is a love story, he will be released. Which is good, because prison is horrible.

Arriving at Fresnes the evening of July 2, Bernard is body-searched, fingerprinted, and placed in a cell with five other people. In the night there are rats and Bernard has nightmares. The next morning, a cell mate tells Bernard he is serving a two-month sentence for drugs.

"Thank God I'm not staying that long," says Bernard.

A few days later Bernard is moved to a floor where the inmates are former civil servants. Compared to the first, it is like a three-star hotel. There are three persons to a cell; his cell mates are a former policeman and a former prison guard; they have a radio and a chess set. When Bernard arrives, the former policeman offers him a beer. The men have heard he's a spy and are impressed. Bernard hasn't seen any newspapers, so he isn't sure what's being said about him, but he can tell he is already kind of a famous guy.

He is also a man with a mission. The anger Bernard felt for Pei Pu only days before has evaporated. Pei Pu is once again the woman he loves and must protect. Marriage will prove to the world this is a love story. On July 4, four days after he is brought to Fresnes, Bernard writes Pei Pu a four-page letter and proposes.

"I love you, see you soon, your eternal friend, Bernard," he writes, mailing it to her at Port-Royal.

He also sends a letter to Mme. Lavalier.

"I look to the future with serenity," he writes. "Especially if Pei Pu stays in Paris and marries me, as I hope she will do."

Early Friday morning, July 8, when Bernard thinks he has been in prison about a week, the key man unlocks Bernard's cell and takes him to a little room near the entrance. Bernard is told that the D.S.T. is coming for him. He sits, waiting, and then overhears the key man talking to another guard.

"The other one is here, too," he says, and Bernard realizes they have arrested Pei Pu.

It is very strange to Bernard—Fresnes is a man's prison. Why is Pei Pu here? The only thing he can think of is that Pei Pu refused to be examined or body searched, and assuming she was a man, they brought her here. He wants to reach out to her, to let her know he is there, but he can't figure out how. Then he sees a heating pipe running along the floor. Bernard knocks on the pipe three times. A minute later he hears, along the pipe, three taps in response. A half hour later, the D.S.T. arrive and Bernard is led to the prison yard. Pei Pu is there, in the gray baggy shirt and trousers of the prison uniform. They look like the clothes she wore during the Cultural Revolution, Bernard thinks, and that thought makes him even sadder than the fact that Pei Pu is in prison.

"Ce n'est pas grave," he whispers to her as they put him in one car, Pei Pu in another.

They are taking them, the D.S.T. men say, back to Bernard's apartment to search the premises—it is only a formality. Bernard is not really listening. He keeps looking back over his shoulder to the car following him, to Shi Pei Pu.

They arrive at Port-Royal at nine-thirty and walk upstairs. A man is introduced to Bernard as the judge who will be carrying out the investigation, Bruno Laroche. There are also about a half dozen policeman in the apartment, as well as Thierry. He looks drained.

"Bertrand is at Daniel's place," Thierry tells Bernard. "How are you?"

"I'm fine," says Bernard. "This won't last."

Bernard is relieved. He is back in his home, even if he is surrounded by police officers; the man he loves is beside him; his son is safe. He feels a comforting wave of normalcy and asks one of the police if Thierry can run out and get some beer. Then he sits beside Pei Pu on the sofa. Her face is weary, her skin ashen; it goes, Bernard thinks, with her gray prison clothes. She says nothing as the police begin searching the apartment: the kitchen, the bathroom, the room down the hall. They are still searching when Thierry returns with the beer. Bernard, Thierry, and Pei Pu watch the police taking apart their home, pulling out the drawers in the desk and cabinet, upending cushions. When the police come across a small address book, Pei Pu speaks up and volunteers that it is hers. The police bag it. When they come across the love letter Bernard has written to Pei Pu from Fresnes in the desk drawer, Bernard readily admits it is his. The police bag it as well.

Bernard is still not concerned. This is a love story. He does not understand why it is taking everyone so long to understand that, but with Pei Pu beside him, he can put his proposal directly to her, and it will be finished at last.

"We have to marry now, it will help us if we marry," he says to Pei Pu, loud enough for Thierry to hear him.

"It is too late," says Pei Pu.

A few days later, on Wednesday morning, July 13, a Justice Ministry spokesman announces the medical examination findings regarding accused spy Shi Pei Pu.

Bernard is in his cell, lying on the top bunk, at eight-thirty in the evening, when he hears the news on the radio.

"Hey," one of the guys says, "they're talking about you."

"The Chinese Mata Hari, who was accused of spying, is a man," the announcer says.

Bernard cannot believe what he is hearing.

"No!" he cries. "It's impossible! It's a lie."

"Shut up!" his cell mates holler, but Bernard keeps yelling. "It's a lie! It's a lie!"

That night, his cell mates hear him screaming in his dreams, "No! No!"

Meanwhile, outside prison, Mme. Lavalier is distressed. She reads only *Le Monde*. She has great faith in it. Picking up the paper, seeing *"Le chanteur de l'Opéra de Beijing Shi Pei Pu . . . est bien un homme,"* she cannot believe her eyes.

She calls up Thierry.

"This is unbelievable," she says. "The doctors are saying Pei Pu is a man."

Thierry, who two weeks after Bernard's arrest has still been unable to get into prison to see him, does not know what to tell her.

Maybe, he theorizes with Mme. Lavalier, the papers are running these stories because for some reason the police want them to. Maybe —but can this be possible?—Pei Pu has had some sort of sex change.

"It's unbelievable," Thierry says. "Of course Pei Pu is a woman."

Bernard's lawyer at the time of his arrest is an acquaintance, thirty-one-year-old Gérard Even, the brother of one of his women friends from Mongolia, who most recently has been specializing in business law. Several days later some of Bernard's friends convince Henri Leclerc, one of the country's premier civil liberties lawyers, to take the case.

Even is aware, in his first meeting with Bernard soon after Pei Pu's arrest, that his client believes his codefendant is a woman, though Pei Pu has been taken to a men's jail. In his first conversations with Bernard, however, Even sidesteps the question of Pei Pu's sexual identity and focuses on the documents Bernard has given to the Chinese—the basis of the criminal charge against him.

Now, when Even appears, Bernard confronts him: He has heard that there has been an examination and that Pei Pu is a man, he says. He knows it cannot be true.

Even tells Bernard it is true.

Bernard will not hear of it. He is not emotional; he simply refuses to change his beliefs. He tells Even that he has made love to Pei Pu and has seen her naked and that she is a woman and the mother of his child. He insists the police are lying. They have lied before, he says.

He tells Mme. Lavalier the same thing.

"I have told you a million times Shi Pei Pu is not responsible, that what I did, I did voluntarily and Shi only opened the door. It is I who am responsible, but I never revealed the secret," he writes. "The press, it seems, knows more about this than I do. I don't know how. It's nothing but lies, particularly concerning you know who; it is *Bertrand's mother* and there were no grafts. The exam was not made by a gynecologist and was only 'a priori,' a premade conclusion. A serious examination will prove that Bertrand is indeed my son. I don't despair because I know the light will shine one day on this subject."

The following day, Bernard writes his parents—referring to Pei Pu, whom they know as a man, as "he," but to Bertrand as his son.

"Nobody duped me," he writes. "What I did I did voluntarily, and the reasons are my own. If the Cultural Revolution changed all my plans, that is another thing and that is at the root of the problems I have today. Shi Pei Pu is nothing in this except another victim, just as I am. He is the only person who really suffered and he has done everything for Bertrand."

He also says he is sending Bertrand to them for a visit and asks that they give the boy as much freedom as he desires.

"Bertrand is a bit like me, he likes to move, and I don't want to take that away from him," he writes.

The same day, he writes a loving letter to Bertrand:

> My dear, dear child,
> Bertrand, will you please listen to Daniel who is a close friend of Tata's and Papa's and go to Vannes to see Mami and Papi, as well as Lionel, all of whom are waiting for you.
> Tata and I agree that you should leave now for a week or two. Your Uncle Lionel wants to go for a sail with you. Everyone is waiting for you there—it is vacation time and you need them too.
> Bertrand, we love you with all our hearts and we want you to become a happy and an honest man.
> Tata and I ask you to go quickly to Vannes.

I kiss you, my great love. Tata and I love you and will be with
you very soon.
                        Your father who loves you very much.
                                        Bernard Boursicot

In late July, shortly after he has received Bernard's letter and been
interrogated by the D.S.T., Bertrand goes to Vannes.

July has been a nightmare for the Boursicot family. There have
been stories about Bernard in the newspapers and on television. They
don't seem, to Lionel, to be so much about espionage as about a love
story between Bernard and Bertrand's tutor, Shi Pei Pu. They are so
crazy they make his head spin. First they say, which is incredible, his
brother Bernard is a spy. Then they say Shi Pei Pu is a woman disguised
as a man, which Lionel, strange as it is, has fleetingly suspected himself.
Then they say Pei Pu is a man. Then they say the worst thing of all: that
Lionel's brother Bernard is a homosexual.

They treat it like a big joke. On one television program they like to
have funny stories at noon, and one morning Mme. Boursicot hears
them promoting one about her son.

"We've never heard one like this before," they are saying. "It's a
steamer. The first time in history a man has given birth . . ."

Mme. Boursicot doesn't look at the newspaper articles, because
they hurt her. But she has some idea of what is going on from Lionel
and Mimi. They say the newspapers say that Pei Pu pretended to be a
woman with Bernard. Mme. Boursicot cannot imagine such a thing. It's
pretty easy to tell a woman from a man. The only thing she can imagine
is that maybe Bernard was drunk.

Bertrand is a separate issue: Mme. Boursicot figures his mother is a
Chinese woman who has stayed at home. She knows Bertrand is her
grandson; she has pictures in the house of him dancing with his cousins
at Lionel's wedding. He looks just like Bernard.

Dealing with the outside world, however, is horrible.

"So, how do you feel?" a neighbor asks Mme. Boursicot when she
goes marketing.

"How do you think I feel?" she snaps. "You know what is going
on."

She gets a newspaper story of Bernard's arrest, anonymous

and hateful, in the mail. "Homosexual traitor," someone has written on it.

Her husband is desolate, though he does not talk about the charge. No one in the family really wants to talk about it; they all go back to their little corners.

But in late July, Mme. Boursicot feels better, because her grandson arrives.

She can see he has been affected by all of this. She and her husband have a little dog, and sometimes Mme. Boursicot sees Bertrand from her window, sitting with the dog, lost in thought. He rides his bicycle for great distances. When she wakes him up in the morning, he puts his arms around her neck and kisses her and calls her "Grandma."

"This is a boy who needs affection," Mme. Boursicot thinks.

Sometimes he stays at his aunt Mimi's, where he has his own room and can spend time with Mimi's seventeen-year-old daughter Catherine.

"He is not fourteen, he's at least as old as I am," Catherine tells her mother.

Mimi, who is increasingly curious about Bertrand, agrees.

Playing chess with Bertrand, at two or three in the morning, under the soothing blanket of night, they talk. Mimi shows Bertrand a silk dress and Bertrand tells her it reminds him of the costumes worn by the women in his country, the far west of China, beyond the Pamir Mountains. He lived there, Bertrand tells Mimi, when he was very young. He tells her about the cats he left behind in China. He misses his cats, he says. But he says little more.

But the night of August 11, Bertrand is troubled. He and Mimi are up late, playing chess, but Bertrand's game is off, his thoughts are elsewhere. The next day is his birthday—the same day as Bernard's— and Mme. Boursicot is planning a special dinner. Suddenly, he blurts it out.

"I'm not Bernard's son," Bertrand says.

Bertrand tells Mimi a story. He was born in Xinjiang Province, in the west of China, near the Soviet border, where there are few Han— few people of the Chinese race. His real name is Toul Son Khan and he is not fourteen. He does not know his date of birth, but he knows he is older than fourteen. From his childhood he remembers his mother and father and a brother and sister who are much older than he. He remembers fighting, perhaps a revolution, and not being allowed to go to school, and having to walk in the street with his head bent, maybe because he is not Chinese. One day he goes out on horseback with his father. He remembers sitting behind his father, holding onto him; he thinks they are heading for the Russian border. Suddenly some Chinese soldiers appear. Bertrand is thrown. When he gets up, his father is gone. The soldiers take Bertrand to his mother. Time passes. He never sees his father again. He and his mother have nothing to eat. One day, Bertrand's mother takes him on the train and they travel for three days to Urumqi, the capital of Xinjiang Province. She hands him over to some men.

"My mother didn't do it because she didn't love me; she did it because she couldn't feed me," Bertrand tells Mimi.

The men, Bertrand continues, bring him to Pei Pu and his mother, who speak a language Bertrand does not understand. Soon after, Bertrand meets Bernard. Bertrand is not unhappy with Pei Pu though sometimes Pei Pu is strict: Pei Pu sleeps with one end of a rope tied around his wrist and the other end at the wrist of Bertrand, the boy says, and if he wants something, he pulls on the end of the rope. Still, life in Beijing is not so bad. They have the best of everything: beautiful fruits, first-quality meats. He has his cats. Pei Pu's mother is very kind to him. Now she is dead. He loved her more than anyone. But he is not her grandson, nor Mme. Boursicot's grandson. He is Uigur. Flying from Beijing to Paris, he and Pei Pu stopped in the airport in Karachi and for the first time since he was small Bertrand saw people who looked like him. One day, Bertrand says, he will go back to China. He has buried the identity papers with his real name in a secret place in Beijing, where no one will ever discover them. He will get them and find his mother. This story that Pei Pu is his mother is astonishing to him. He is very surprised that people think Pei Pu is a woman. To him, Pei Pu has never been a woman, though he knows he is supposed to pretend to be Bernard's son.

"But why did you do it?" asks Mimi.

"I was starving," Bertrand says.

But now he is upset.

"How can we tell Bernard's parents that I am not Bernard's son and it is not my birthday?" he says.

So, says Mimi, she and Bertrand and Catherine go to Mme. Boursicot's house the next day, and they say nothing. There is a cake and Mimi gives Bertrand an evening on a party boat and Lionel buys him a white sports jacket and Mme. Boursicot alters a pair of Bernard's black pants. Bertrand looks terrific, Mme. Boursicot thinks—a very good-looking kid.

There are people in the family who are angry at Pei Pu, but Bernard has told Mme. Boursicot that Pei Pu is just another victim, so after Bertrand's birthday, she writes him, telling him about the celebration. Because Bernard has asked for stamps, she encloses some for Pei Pu, too. He sends back a lovely reply: They are not stamps, he writes, but three golden hearts. He will keep them as souvenirs for always.

Soon afterward Bertrand returns to Thierry in Paris and Mimi happens to hear a radio program about China. They talk about Toul Son Khan, a great rebel leader against the Chinese invaders.

It makes Mimi wonder: Has Bertrand given her his real name or a name from Chinese history—or was he named for this hero?

Are there really identity papers hidden in Beijing and did Pei Pu really tie Bertrand to his wrist with a rope?

Or are these stories, so much like something out of a boy's adventure book, a lie, a fable, a dream?

3

If the outside world accepts the fact that Pei Pu is a man as soon as the medical reports are released, and the case disintegrates into a homosexual sex farce, evaporating from the public consciousness as July turns to August and the French devote themselves to the more important concern of vacation, Bernard, confined to Fresnes, does not accept it. He insists, in letters to Mme. Lavalier and to Thierry, that Pei Pu is a woman and Bertrand his son. Leclerc tends to skip over it.

"Ce n'est pas important," he says. "What's important is the documents."

Thierry, when he is finally permitted to begin visiting Bernard one month after his arrest, in late July, does not press Bernard about his relations with Pei Pu either. In his first visit, Thierry and Bernard do not speak at all. They sit across from each other, separated by a shatterproof plastic window, and for the entire half hour they weep.

But Bernard's insistence that Pei Pu is a woman does not mean that Bernard, who is forbidden any contact with Pei Pu, is at peace with his story. His anxiety is increasing; he is unable, despite sedatives, to sleep; he shakes so, at times, one has the impression of a pressure cooker under a high flame, rattling under increasing pressure, as if any moment it will explode. Bernard cannot understand how the doctors can say Pei Pu is a man when he knows she is a woman. Unless, he thinks, he is going crazy.

Desperate, he seeks out a prison psychiatrist, an intern, in his first year of prison work. The psychiatrist says that it is possible that Pei Pu was born a hermaphrodite—a person possessing both male and female genitals. He explains, making sketches, that during gestation the clitoris and penis develop from the same spot. But in rare instances, in the first few months of natal life, two sets of sexual organs may develop. In such cases, one set of sexual organs is often atrophied or may remain inside the body cavity. An endoscopy—an examination through an orifice—or even surgery may be required to determine whether a person has a second set of sexual organs.

Bernard seizes on this information as a drowning man seizes on a lifeline. He keeps the sketches in his cell and looks at them often, using this new information to bolster his conviction that Pei Pu is a woman—probably malformed. Writing to Mme. Lavalier in mid-August, Bernard does not say he believes Pei Pu to be a hermaphrodite, but he does use a word that is new to him—"endoscopy." There is, however, a split that defies logic: While insisting to Mme. Lavalier that Pei Pu is not a man, Bernard refers to Pei Pu as "he."

"Pei Pu, for reasons all of his own, has chosen not to undergo the 'endoscopic' examination," Bernard writes. "Thus, he will be incarcerated according to his known identity, with the men, at the Fresnes prison hospital, in a private room for cardiac patients. . . .

"Letting himself be considered as a 'man' does have a face-saving value to him and I can only imagine that at forty-five years of age to be forced to make a choice, while continuing to live in this 'false' situation but at least adopted by society, must cause quite a lot of problems."

Bernard also insists to Gérard Even that Pei Pu is a woman.

Sometimes, downplaying his homosexual history, he misleads his lawyer: He tells Even that his first sexual experience was with women prostitutes in Algeria, giving him such explicit detail—the nine-franc fee, the heavily kohled eyes of the prostitutes—that Even, who believes prisoners usually lie, does not doubt him. Bernard claims he had no homosexual experience until three years after meeting Pei Pu, when he returns to France. He says it is only with Thierry—ten years after the affair with Pei Pu is begun—that he discovers how deeply he is attracted to men. He makes a point of how much he enjoys women. He talks repeatedly about Pei Pu's body. She has nice little breasts, Even remembers Bernard telling him; her sex organs are normal. Even questions him carefully on this: Did Bernard see her vulva? Did he have oral sex with Pei Pu? Is he certain he had vaginal sex with Pei Pu? Might not it have been anal sex, because if one is inexperienced—even if one is not—one may not be sure. Bernard tells his lawyer he never had anal sex with Pei Pu.

There is, however, as Even recalls it, one thing Bernard brings up about Shi Pei Pu which is definitely not normal:

Sometime in late summer Bernard comes up with a new theory: He tells Even that it is possible that Pei Pu is a hermaphrodite. At times when they made love he saw an odd extra piece of flesh, something resembling a very small penis or a large clitoris. They talk at length about this, Even recalls, Bernard stressing it was not a normal male organ.

Bernard disputes this: He never saw an extra piece of flesh, any atrophied penis or pronounced clitoris, he says. He never had such a discussion with Even.

The interrogations on *L'affaire Boursicot* begin in September, under Investigative Judge Bruno Laroche, who, under the French legal system, will question the defendants and conduct any additional investigation he sees fit in order to determine whether there is sufficient evidence to bring the case to trial. Pei Pu is the first to be interviewed, on September 9, in the judge's office in the Palais de Justice. Confronted by Laroche with the medical reports, Pei Pu readily admits that the statements he made to the police about his sexual identity were false.

"As the experts declare in the report, I am indeed a man and have never been a woman," Pei Pu says. "I will also specify immediately that I am neither the mother nor the father of Shi Du Du."

He follows that, however, with an extraordinary claim: He says he himself, until three months after his affair with Bernard Boursicot had begun at age twenty-seven, did not know what sex he was.

"There was a period of time that *mes attributs masculins* had not descended, so that they did not show, and I did not know whether I had any or not," Pei Pu says. "At the end of 1965, I met a doctor named Ma. He told me I was really a man and, after making me take hormones and carrying out a little operation, brought down my genitals. I have never had feminine sexual attributes."

He tells the judge his love story. It is clear, in his telling, that the Chinese authorities were aware he was meeting with a foreigner from the time he had his second meeting with Bernard—the Beijing Writers' Association had given Pei Pu clearance to receive Bernard at home and give him Chinese lessons. Whether or not the government was aware of Pei Pu's sexual proclivities, or that the teacher-student relationship evolved into a love affair, Pei Pu does not say. But he is frank with the judge about his feelings for Bernard.

"Initially we got along well," says Pei Pu. "Later, we loved each other."

He refuses to take any responsibility, however, for misleading Bernard on the question of his sexual identity.

"I never specifically told Boursicot I was a woman," Pei Pu says. "It is he who believed it under the following circumstances: One day, when we were with François, I told a story about a woman who was able to pass as a man and the truth was not known until the moment of her death. After this, Boursicot told me that he believed I was a woman and that he loved me and felt sorry for me. I answered that I loved him, too. I let him believe that I was a woman, especially since at that time I myself was not sure what I was, since I only found out that I was a man at the end of the year. We then [after the story] had sexual relations.

"As concerns our sexual relations, these always took place in the dark as Boursicot always showed the greatest *delicatesse* toward me. I want to stress that this was my first sexual experience, and according to Boursicot, the same was true for him. Since I did not have a female sexual organ Boursicot could not penetrate me. When I made love, I kept my legs lightly pressed together, so that Boursicot may have had the impression that he was penetrating me, especially since in place of a sexual organ there was a little orifice through which I urinated.

"At about this time, I began to put on weight, to such a point that I thought I was expecting a child. It was at this time that I was examined by Dr. Ma, who lived next door and specialized in delivering babies. This doctor, after examining me and laughing, told me that I was a man and that my sexual organs had not dropped."

Pei Pu is told of Bernard's statement to police that Pei Pu had an abortion in August of 1965.

"At no time did I have an abortion," he says.

Pei Pu is told that Bernard's friend Sylvie, questioned by D.S.T. agents after Bernard's arrest, confirmed Bernard's story. Sylvie has also told police that she saw Pei Pu in bed after her abortion and saw bloodied rags in a pail.

"I don't know why she should say that," says Pei Pu, "because, for one thing, the scene never took place, as I never, as far as I remember, was sick in August 1965, and for another, because I don't know this [person]."

Pei Pu does, however, offer an explanation of his "pregnancy" and the child Shi Du Du.

"When I had sexual relations with Boursicot, that is to say in the fall of 1965, he used condoms. Then, as he did not find them comfortable, he stopped. Later on, I asked him from time to time to use them, even when I knew I was a man. This request was based on the fact that I wanted to have a child of his and that Dr. Ma had explained to me that it was possible to impregnate a woman by saving his sperm.

"In November 1965, following the directions of the doctor, after making love with Boursicot I saved the condom containing the sperm which he had ejaculated. After he left, or rather, right after the ejaculation, I slipped the condom into a special cold box that Dr. Ma had given me. After Boursicot's departure I then carried the box to Dr. Ma.

"I want to stress that at that time I was still fat, so much so that when Boursicot left China in December 1965 he thought I was pregnant. I did nothing to disabuse him. Before leaving Beijing, Boursicot noted in my dictionary that if it was a boy he wanted it named Bertrand Boursicot and if it was a girl, Michele Boursicot.

"At the end of 1968, Dr. Ma gave me a child aged about a month or two. I don't know whether this child was Boursicot's son or not. Between December 1965 and 1968 I inquired several times of Dr. Ma as to whether she had done something. First she replied that she was looking for a woman, then that the woman wanted money. One day Dr. Ma told me that the child was arriving and I must buy the things necessary to receive it. She specified that the child was mine, speaking of the sperm I had given. For all of this, I paid in the neighborhood of three thousand yuan, which was a lot of money at the time. This money was given to me by my mother, who had savings. Since at the time we were living under the Cultural Revolution and the child was an Occidental type, I sent it to the province of Xinjiang, where it was raised by a woman who took care of abandoned children. I only took the child back toward the end of 1973. During this whole period he only came back to Beijing twice, for a week at a time.

"When the child was given to me by Dr. Ma, no formal birth certificate had been made for him in Beijing. His birth was declared later in Xinjiang Province, which explains Shi Du Du's official age."

Pei Pu's version of his 1969 reunion with Bernard differs slightly from what Bernard told the police: Pei Pu says he tells Bernard they have a child not upon Bernard's first, dangerous visit to his home, but only after they have been arrested and released by police.

Pei Pu also insists that he and the twenty-five-year-old embassy clerk do not have sex ever again after Bernard's return to China—and that he tries his best to tell Bernard about the fact that he is *not* Shi Du Du's mother.

"During Boursicot's second stay in Beijing, and later when he returned, I had no sexual relationship at all with Boursicot," he says. "I never told him that I was a man, but on the other hand he could figure that out himself as he had occasion to touch me at the level of my sexual organs."

Why Bernard would have occasion to touch him at the level of his sexual organs if they were not having sex is not explained—but Pei Pu does present a scenario that suggests Bernard is aware that he has a penis.

"He then said to me, 'It doesn't matter, it can be operated on.' "

Despite this, Pei Pu continues, Bernard continued to believe that Shi Du Du was their son.

"I tried several times to explain to him about the child, what I had done to get it," says Pei Pu. "But each time he started shouting, 'That's not true.' "

During the Cultural Revolution, Pei Pu tells the judge, he was persecuted: In 1967 and 1968, after Bernard left China, some members of the Writers' Association claimed Pei Pu was a French spy because of his friendship with members of the French embassy. Pei Pu was forced to participate in self-criticism sessions and told he would be denied medical care. And after Bernard returned to China in 1969 and was discovered in Pei Pu's home, he was arrested and threatened with a long prison sentence, but released after only one night. Later, when Kang tells him he may see Boursicot if he makes a report of their visits, Pei Pu says he refuses "out of fear." It is only after several weeks, Pei Pu says, that he reluctantly begins to teach Bernard the thoughts of Chairman Mao. Then Kang takes over.

Judge Laroche sees something less innocent than the story Pei Pu tells, less innocent even than the story he tries to obscure—that of one lover trying to hold another by staging a pregnancy. He sees an attempt by the Chinese government to entrap a member of the French diplomatic staff. He wonders if Pei Pu has been part of it.

"According to Boursicot, you let him know that you had a child by him before you were arrested by the Red Guard," says Laroche. "Following that, Kang appears, to whom Bernard has said he gave numerous documents from the French embassy. Given that you are a man and thus physically unable to have a child by Boursicot, it is possible to wonder if the story of the child didn't just serve as bait or later force Boursicot to cooperate with the Chinese authorities to obtain documents from the French embassy. Boursicot might have been driven to act this way by the scene of your arrest—which might have been staged, given how long it lasted. What do you say to that?"

Pei Pu is as unyielding with the judge as he has been with the police.

"There were no machinations on my part with the Chinese authorities," he says. "I didn't even know that Boursicot was handing over such documents."

Five days later, accompanied by his lawyers, Bernard is called before the judge and told that Pei Pu had admitted to being a man.

Bernard is as insistent of his ignorance of Pei Pu's sexual identity as Pei Pu has been about espionage. But his language, as it has in his recent letters to his friends, reveals a split. Sometimes he refers to Pei Pu as "he," sometimes as "she"—as if Bernard is now a man with two minds and one believes while the other does not.

"I'm astounded by this declaration," he tells the judge. "I've considered Shi Pei Pu a woman ever since we had sexual relations together, that is to say from May or June 1965. I have never noticed that Shi Pei Pu had masculine organs, even though I have seen him naked on a number of occasions between 1965 and 1978.''

He disputes Pei Pu's statement that they always made love in the dark.

"When we made love, especially in the beginning, he did not have his body covered with a sheet or similar objects," Bernard says. "We would always go through our sexual relations in the same position, that is to say Shi lying down in the classic position. I would lie down on top of her. As for the legs, I would place them either on top of hers or in between or around. During these relations I would penetrate Shi. I thought that I was penetrating a vagina. As a matter of fact, Shi told me that this was something that was making him feel good and he spoke to me at that moment of 'the little door.' He would say that when my sex would penetrate him. I never had sex "against nature" with Pei Pu. When I was inside of him he would say before the penetration, and as he would be guiding me, 'There it's not as good'; 'Here it's good.' His sex was not particularly tight, but maybe more than that of the other women that I have known. During the penetration I would feel that there was some sort of progressive humidification of Shi's sex.''

Bernard is asked about manual contact.

"I never with my hand touched the inside of Shi's sex. He always refused. I thought that this refusal was part of Chinese culture. When I caressed her, I would caress her head, breast, buttocks, thighs. I never practiced cunnilingus. I never saw his sex completely, only the tips of the lips. . . .

"When we had our first sexual relations in May or June of 1965, Shi Pei Pu had told me that she was a virgin. During this first penetration she told me she was in pain. I later noticed that there had been a loss of blood. It was the only time after our sexual relations that I noticed such a thing. . . .''

Asked by the judge about his own sexual experience, Bernard is unable to be frank. He says he had relations with women in Algeria. He says nothing about his early experiences with men.

"During the first sexual relations, I was not a virgin," he says. "In fact, I had had complete sexual relations with girls in Algeria when I was in the French embassy in Algiers, as well as at least once in Hong Kong in May 1965. In Algeria I had relations two or three times with prostitutes and I would ejaculate right away after I penetrated them. This was not the case with Shi."

Bernard also contradicts Pei Pu's statement that Pei Pu never told Bernard he was a woman.

"I told Shi that I had met a man in Beijing who had brought me to a woman with whom I had made love," says Bernard. "I did not penetrate her because I noticed there was a knife. Shi told me that I was not to do this again because it was dangerous. Following this, Shi invited me for the first time to her house. A few days later, Shi told me she was a woman. First of all, she told me a story of a woman who had been considered a man until her death. He then told me that he was in the same situation and that this came from the threat that his paternal grandmother had made to repudiate his mother because his mother had not given birth to a son in the first three children she had brought into the world. So his mother made him pass as a boy, dressing him as a boy. He even had medical treatment."

Bernard talks about the abortion in detail: He says that after their first sexual relations he noticed that Pei Pu had gained weight and become "more feminine." In August 1965, Bernard tells the judge, Pei Pu informed him that she was "about two and a half months pregnant" and that "if I wanted her to abort it would have to be done right away.

"One morning she called me and asked if we were to do it or not," Bernard says. "I answered that we should. He then answered, 'We will do as you wish.' That evening I went to her house and I noticed that she was completely *decomposée*. Physically falling apart. Also I noticed that she was regularly changing a towel which was stained with blood. She told me that she threw out the embryo in the toilet. I never knew how she was able to abort. She told me that she had swallowed certain herbs and potions. I panicked and in the middle of the night I went to look for a friend [Sylvie], who came back with me to Shi's house. It took Shi about two weeks to gain back his strength. I noticed that Shi had thinned down considerably. We did not have sexual relations for three weeks. In the beginning of November 1965, we left together for Tianjin with a colleague. We stayed two days and one night, during which time I made love to Shi Pei Pu without a condom. Shi began to gain weight slightly. Then, after four weeks, Shi told me that it was starting again like the last time—she was pregnant. We swore this time to keep the child. In December 1965 I left Beijing. He had gained some weight and his face had changed and she was not having any more periods. . . ."

He is quizzed by the judge on Pei Pu's "periods."

"I never saw with my own eyes Shi's periods when she was having them," he says. "On the other hand, I had seen paper with bloodstains. Shi never refused to have sex with me because of [having her period], but they were somewhat spaced apart. Sometimes I noticed that Shi was in a bad mood and I would say to her that she must be about to have her period. She'd say, 'How did you notice that? You guessed.' She would also make comments like 'Tomorrow will be better' or 'It's almost over.' "

Bernard tells the judge that Pei Pu believed she was pregnant when he left Beijing in 1965 and that he learned about the birth of his child in a letter dated August 1966. The letter actually arrived in February 1967—but had Pei Pu become pregnant in October or November of 1965, the child would have been born in July or August.

"In this letter Shi told me that he had lots of problems," Bernard tells the judge. "She went into detail. 'I am in the middle of reading and I am thinking of the abandoned child of Victor Hugo. Don't worry about your health.' I understood that a child had been born."

Pei Pu has told the judge he and Bernard did not have sexual relations after December 1965 when Bernard left China. Bernard tells the judge sexual relations continued until 1978—when Bernard, then thirty-four, was posted in Mongolia.

"I had sexual relations with Shi—in a very irregular manner because of the Cultural Revolution—during my second stay in China until 1978," Bernard says. "Shi appeared to me like a normal woman. I must tell you, though, that after 1972 it was not altogether the same. The penetrations became more and more difficult."

Told of Pei Pu's statement that he had a penis, which "descended" a few months after their affair began in 1965, Bernard is disbelieving.

"I don't understand how Shi can actually state that his male organs came down, or descended, in 1965, because I would have noticed, which has never been the case," Bernard tells the judge.

He also disputes Pei Pu's statement that Bernard, seeing his penis, said it "wasn't very serious and could be operated on."

"I said something of that nature, because Shi Pei Pu told me that she might not be completely normal," says Bernard. "I did not think while I was saying it that she had in fact a man's sex, a sex which I never touched."

Bernard testifies that he first saw his son in 1973—the year Pei Pu told the judge the boy came to live with him.

"The child seemed to be seven, but Shi told everybody that he was five, so people would not think he was born out of relations he had had at that time [during the Cultural Revolution] with a foreigner. The child was a mulatto. I must tell you that my parents say he has certain of my traits and attitudes, particularly his walk."

Told Pei Pu's story of Dr. Ma and artificial insemination, Bernard is astonished—it's the first time, he tells the judge, he's heard that story.

Is Bernard certain Pei Pu had an abortion? the judge asks.

Yes, says Bernard, because Pei Pu was so ill that evening. Bernard could not sleep for months afterward, he felt so guilty. If Pei Pu is denying this event, it is probably because Pei Pu feels guilty as well.

"I believed [at the time of the abortion]—contrary to what Shi says —Shi was a woman," says Bernard. "Maybe with some sort of malformations that did not appear when we had sexual relations. I think that after '72, Shi must have had some sort of mutilation. I am convinced that Shi is the mother of my son and that Shi Du Du is my son."

An odd thing happens to Bernard shortly after Judge Laroche first questions him: He loses the feeling in his right foot. There is no physical injury. One day Bernard has difficulty walking and looks down and sees that his right foot is dragging. Even and Thierry see other signs of disintegration as well: Bernard gains and loses ten to fifteen kilos in a two-week period. He has terrible headaches. He has nightmares that upon waking he cannot recall. Earlier, Bernard had hope. He saw himself as the hero of a great love story. He had written Mme. Lavalier asking her to find a "serious" photo for the newspapers; he asked her to chill a bottle of Chardonnay for his release in the fall. Now he sees his future in prison. He writes, as the judicial inquiries continue once a month throughout the fall, that he is being persecuted for an old story. He speaks often, shunning responsibility, of his "fate." He worries about Bertrand, whom he still believes to be his son and who is living now with Thierry.

Three weeks after the judge informs Bernard that Pei Pu has confessed to being a man, Bernard begins psychotherapy. The psychologist is José Rambeau, a man in his mid-thirties whose sympathetic brown eyes and gentle face remind Bernard of the psychologist he saw when he returned to Paris from Jerusalem.

Bernard is a first for Rambeau. He has been working in Fresnes for seven years, and never before has a prisoner come to him. This prisoner, moreover, is in terrible turmoil. The mother of his child, he tells Rambeau, is now said to be a man, but he made love to her and she is a woman. He thinks he is going crazy. Rambeau sees Bernard twice a week. Bernard does not discuss his early homosexual experiences and speaks of his later homosexual experiences and his relationship with Thierry in a vague way. But it is clear to Rambeau that Bernard is a man who is not at all comfortable with himself. He has suffered genuine depressions in the past. He is extremely depressed now.

As the judge continues his investigation, neither Bernard nor Pei Pu make significant changes from their statements to police. Pei Pu insists he knows nothing about espionage, though he admits he knew Kang was responsible for the surveillance of intellectuals during the Cultural Revolution. He also says he did not participate in the discussions between Bernard and Kang "because I thought it would be too dangerous for me." Bernard, in an attempt to remove Pei Pu from involvement, lies, saying he gave documents to Kang *outside* Pei Pu's apartment.

For Bernard's sense of responsibility for Pei Pu—and his love—is growing. Bernard never sees Pei Pu in prison—they are forbidden to communicate—but he plays their story over and over in his head. He sees her suffering under the Cultural Revolution. He curses the stupidity of his police confession, which brought her here.

Then one day, when Bernard is in the second-floor infirmary, he spots Pei Pu in the exercise yard talking with one of the exercise instructors. She cannot see Bernard. He cannot yell to her. It reminds him of the days during the Cultural Revolution when they sat apart from one another on Changan Avenue, unable to speak.

"Take courage!" he wants to yell, but he does not.

Bernard does not have a good deal of money. His friends have taken up a collection to help him pay for his defense; he is selling one of his apartments. Yet when Thierry comes to see him, as he does three times a week, Bernard tells him to send five hundred francs a month pocket money to Pei Pu. Thierry is also to remind Pei Pu that if need be, Bernard will pay for her defense. She is the mother of his child, he says.

When court-appointed psychiatrists question Bernard, he tells them the same thing.

"As long as there has not been an endoscopy," he says, "I will stay convinced that Shi is a woman."

The psychiatrists feel he is sincere.

Gérard Even does not. Love is blind, the young lawyer thinks, but this is becoming a little bit too much. Maybe his colleague Leclerc is smarter—he does not linger on the subject. But Even does. Onetime captain of the Paris lawyers' soccer team, a great success with women, he considers himself an expert in sexual matters. Now, after dozens of interviews with his client, he has developed a theory:

Even believes that Bernard, when first making love to Pei Pu at twenty, did *not* know that Pei Pu was a man—he discovered it later, probably on his second stay in Beijing. Bertrand, Even feels, is a separate issue: He resembles Bernard and possibly is Bernard's child, fathered by artificial insemination.

Even has tried to be very understanding because he feels that Bernard, heavily drugged, is not in a normal state. Nonetheless, as the months pass he grows impatient. Bernard cannot grasp the gravity of the charges he is facing. He tells preposterous stories. He says he made love to Pei Pu with the lights on and that during intercourse Pei Pu's legs were often spread apart. He says he had vaginal intercourse with Pei Pu in Ulan Bator between 1977 and 1979, at which time Bernard was a very experienced thirty-five-year-old man. He insists that Pei Pu was a hermaphrodite who had surgery that removed the female organs—though there are no scars. Bernard is so sincere when he tells Even these stories that Even feels a little badly challenging him.

But eventually he does.

I like fairy tales, Even tells Bernard, but even if what you say is the truth, truth is sometimes more unbelievable than lying. This is the age of reason. The judge will not believe you. To him this is a spy story. Give me something I can work with.

Even tries to convince his client of what he believes to be the truth:

Imagine that Pei Pu didn't tell you what he really was at the beginning. He is a homosexual man but he managed to make you believe he was a woman. You had no experience, you did it in the dark, he was very shy, he forced you to make love only in one position. He plays this comedy of being pregnant—you have a witness, Sylvie, who backs this up. When you see him again it is after you get a letter that makes you believe you are a father. Then you find out he is a man. *This* is believable. I can plead it without being ridiculous. But when you see Pei Pu after the birth of Bertrand it is *not* possible you did not know the truth; you were too experienced not to know the difference.

That isn't the way it happened, says Bernard.

Listen, says Even, exasperated, there are only two ways to look at it: Pei Pu was a hermaphrodite and had a vagina and a penis which was not visible, and, we must suppose, had an operation. *Or* Pei Pu has always been a man. But the doctors have not found evidence of surgery, and based on their report the judge will find against you. The story doesn't hold. Imagine now that Pei Pu told you when you saw him after the birth of Bertrand he was a man—he made you a child as he explained to the judge with artificial insemination because he was in love with you, he wanted to hold you with this child. You have a solution. You go on with sexual relations with Pei Pu because you have discovered you are homosexual or you have no sexual relations with Pei Pu—it is not important. What is important is that you did what you did with the documents to get your son to France. The fact that you discover Pei Pu is not a woman is not important. *That* can be believable.

But Bernard doesn't want Even's version. The harder Even pushes him to admit that he knew Pei Pu was a man, the more details he provides to prove he did not.

He made love to Pei Pu when he was posted in Mongolia, between 1977 and 1979, with the lights on, he tells his lawyer. He knows Pei Pu is a woman.

That is the truth.

The hell with the so-called medical evidence.

For six months, Judge Laroche has interrogated Pei Pu and Bernard separately. Then one morning, at the end of January, getting into the van that will take him to the Palais de Justice for yet another interrogation, Bernard finds Pei Pu. He is desperate to speak with her, but Pei Pu tells him not to. The police can hear, Pei Pu says.

They go before Judge Laroche to repeat their testimony yet again. Bernard listens to Pei Pu relate the story of their meeting at Claude Chayet's Christmas party, telling the judge about the first time they made love in Beijing.

"It is just as he says," Bernard tells the judge.

A few minutes later Pei Pu says the unthinkable: Yes, he says, months earlier, he admitted he was a man.

Then—dizzy from drugs and the hurt of what Pei Pu is saying—Bernard hears Pei Pu lie.

"I never told Bernard I was a woman," Pei Pu is saying. "I only let it be understood that I *could* be a woman. At the time I thought I was a woman, since I did not have any male genital organs. I had a hole—although I must say it did not resemble or was not exactly like one I had seen on an actress once when I was taking off my makeup at the Beijing theater."

Pei Pu goes on. At the end of 1965, he says, his penis would go up and down, descending from inside his body, and Bernard was aware of it. Sometimes Bernard would penetrate his unusual "hole." He says that while he and Bernard did not have "real" sexual relations when Bernard was posted in Ulan Bator, they continued to have sexual contact until Pei Pu left China in 1982: Pei Pu masturbated Bernard and the contact was infrequent.

It is true, as Bernard remembers it, that he and Pei Pu did not have vaginal intercourse when he was in Ulan Bator—he has lied to his lawyer about that. But hearing Pei Pu challenge his version of events, making up things that are not true, makes Bernard crazy. He contradicts Pei Pu, lying, knowing he is lying, to bolster his own story.

"I *did* have normal sexual relations with Shi Pei Pu during my stays in China, as well as Ulan Bator," says Bernard. "I saw Shi Pei Pu nude and he seemed to have normal feminine organs—I could see the lips protruding."

Gérard Even, standing beside his client, suppresses a desire to moan.

"After 1969, I would sometimes see him naked," says Bernard, "but since he was prudish and did not exhibit himself, I never paid much attention to his sex. I am certain he never had a masculine organ. It is true that sometimes Shi would only masturbate me, especially when penetration would not work."

The judge turns to Pei Pu.

"Do you remember your statement of September 9, 1983," he asks, "when you said that Boursicot had seen for himself that you were a man because he came to touch you in the groin area, telling you that it did not matter because 'it could be operated upon'? Do you maintain that statement?"

"It wasn't exactly like that," says Pei Pu. "What actually happened is that when my sex descended, he would sometimes brush his hand against my underwear. Then he told me to take out the handkerchief— during summer I would wear shorts, and I would slip a handkerchief in my shorts so people would think I had a penis. At first I did not answer; later I said, 'And if something came down?' He answered, 'It doesn't matter, it can be operated on.'"

"That's true," says Bernard. "This happened three or four times. When he told me, I thought it was a malformation, like a hermaphrodite. I wanted to see, but he refused to let me."

Pei Pu is asked about Bertrand.

"Shi Du Du is not my son," he says.

He does, however, uphold his previous statement—Bertrand, through the use of artificial insemination, is the son of Bernard.

Is Bernard at last seeing Pei Pu as a man? In the court record, as Bernard describes Pei Pu's female genitalia, he will refer to Pei Pu as "she." Looking back, he does not remember what he thinks. And if in the courtroom Bernard was angry at Pei Pu, after the interrogation he is simply sad. He is taken away to one holding cell, Pei Pu to another. In the ride back to prison they do not speak.

A week later, Bernard and Pei Pu are brought before the judge together again. The judge, as Bernard recalls, is impatient at this meeting with Pei Pu. He has lied in the past, the judge tells him; he has lied about being a woman. Pei Pu doesn't deny it.

"I thought France was a democratic country. Is it important if I am a man or a woman?" Bernard recalls Pei Pu saying.

Bernard is hearing it from Pei Pu for the second time: He is a man. And still, the record shows, rather than get angry, Bernard continues to try to protect Pei Pu. When Laroche asks Bernard if Pei Pu was aware he was handing documents to Kang, he says he does not know.

"I remind you," says the judge, now impatient with Bernard, "that during your hearing October twentieth you said, 'He knew I was giving Kang documents. He even told me to give Kang the smallest amount of documents possible. Shi presented Kang as a tyrant who was leading us, and particularly me, to our end.' What do you say?"

"I don't know," says Bernard.

"Why did you say it?" the judge presses.

"I don't know what to say exactly," says Bernard. "If I said it, it was because Shi knew."

"Did you witness the transactions of documents in your home?" the judge asks Pei Pu.

"No," says Pei Pu. "And anyway, I did not know."

"Did you know why Boursicot and Kang would meet at your house?" the judge asks.

"I thought they had become friends," Pei Pu says.

The interrogation ends. Bernard and Pei Pu are taken downstairs to await transport back to prison. This time they are placed in the same small holding cell.

Face facts, outsiders hearing of loss often say. Face the fact that the person you love has left you, that he lied, that you have been living, quite alone, in a fantasy. Logic is invoked, evidence proffered. Rational, unencumbered by feeling, outsiders await a change: Evidence should bring acceptance. But it does not. The bereaved will not see, will not hear, will not listen to reason. Vision is fogged with longing. It is, outsiders say, as if they are in another world. And they are: in the fearful, chaotic, ungovernable kingdom of emotion.

Bernard has been told by his lawyers and friends for eight months now that Pei Pu is a man. In the last two weeks he has heard it twice from Pei Pu. He has tried to close his eyes, but how long can a man refuse to see? For months, perhaps for years, but there comes a time, finally, when they squeeze you and time runs out, space runs out. And Bernard is standing so close to Pei Pu in this five-foot-square cell it is as if knowledge and space and time are all converging down upon him and he has no choice, he has to see.

"So it's true," Bernard says to Pei Pu, hearing the words come out of his mouth as if a stranger is speaking. "You are a man."

"Of course," says Pei Pu.

"Show me," says Bernard.

And Pei Pu does, as easily as a man at a *pissoir:* He opens his pants and shows himself to Bernard for a few seconds, then closes his pants and starts chattering, as if the act was of no importance at all. He tells Bernard that he will be leaving prison soon and if Bernard is smart, and keeps his mouth shut, and follows his advice, Bernard will be able to leave, too.

He is going on about the future, planning, maneuvering, telling Bernard he will take care of everything and Bernard can't hold him. Bernard is left locked in the present, abandoned.

"But why didn't you tell me?" he asks, as the cell begins to spin.

"There was no time," says Pei Pu.

Twelve days later, Pei Pu is gone. Bernard remains behind, his depression growing. He attends classes in prison, but his only real interest is Bertrand, whom he still believes to be his son by artificial insemination. He berates himself for talking to police. When his friends come he does not curse Pei Pu as they expect. Bernard just weeps.

A month after Pei Pu's release, Bernard's cache of stolen passports is discovered. Bernard, who had never told his lawyers about the passports, faces additional charges. Thierry is in legal trouble as well.

Then, in late spring, Bernard gets the most terrible news of all: Blood tests reveal Bertrand is not Bernard's son—nor the child of Pei Pu.

Bernard becomes more withdrawn. He lies on his bed, staring at the bars on the window. The guards, looking through the small glass window of the cell door, see him immobile.

"He is doing the lizard again," they say.

Bernard has been taking a number of tranquilizers, including Rohypnol and Valium, for over six months. Rohypnol is an addictive drug. It may cause irritability, aggression, and amnesia. Use for more than ten weeks, some doctors feel, is not advisable and it must be discontinued gradually. But in early May, two and a half months after his confrontation with Pei Pu, Bernard's drugs stop for some reason. Perhaps there has been an administrative error, perhaps Bernard has missed an appointment with his psychiatrist. One week later, Bernard begins having terrible nightmares. He dreams Thierry and his friend Daniel have both been arrested. He dreams Pei Pu is back in prison, walking with a gymnastics instructor in the yard. Bernard has always considered gymnastics instructors to be fascists. There is one at prison he particularly hates, who screams at him to move his numb foot as if Bernard is a fake. In Bernard's dream the instructor is screaming at Pei Pu, marching him through the yard. Pei Pu is trying helplessly to protect himself. "I am innocent," Pei Pu says. Bernard wants to save him, to break him out of this place. He can, he knows, if he can just erase his confession of espionage. He goes to the window and hollers, "There are no documents, there are no documents!" The guard doesn't hear.

Then Bernard wakes up.

The dream is so real he has to go to the window and check to see if Pei Pu is in the yard, though the yard is not visible from his cell. One look does not help. Bernard is back and forth between bed and window all night. It is hard to separate wakefulness from sleep. When he lies on his bed he shakes.

The next morning Bernard does not get dressed. He stays on his bed in his underwear, trembling, and when it is time for his three-hour geography class in the afternoon, he does not move. He thinks, instead, how much he hates this class: They are studying the American West, and instead of discussing the beauty of the country, the breadth of America, how one can get in a car and drive all day and see the plains stretching out like the sea, the teacher speaks about corn production. It is so sad. Bernard has traveled; he knows the American West. Now Bernard wonders: Will he ever travel again? And Thierry? Will he be sent to prison also, because of the passports, which are Bernard's fault? What about his good friend Daniel, who helped to bring Pei Pu and Bertrand to France as a kindness and unwittingly became a party to a scandal? Will this affect his future? When the trial is over, will they send Pei Pu to prison or back to China? How will Pei Pu, in China, survive this loss of face?

It would be better for everybody, Bernard decides, if he were dead. If he were dead and he had recanted his statement that he gave papers from the embassy to the Chinese, there would be no case against Pei Pu. Pei Pu cannot be a spy if there are no documents.

Bernard has a small blunt folding knife which the prisoners are issued for meals—three inches in length, because, Bernard has been told, it is too short to reach a man's heart. He has some disposable plastic razors. Now he gets his knife and pries the plastic away from the blade. When the blade is free, he starts cutting his throat. First one side, then, when it becomes too slippery for the blade to cut, the other. Blood is dribbling down the front of his chest, he can feel it wetting his undershirt, but there is no pain. Nor does it disturb him.

He cuts his throat until the blade slips from his fingers. Then, his fingers wet with blood, he writes on the wall his testament. Last words are almost always the truth; it is rare that a man in the last moments of his life spins a tale; but Bernard's last words, written over and over on the walls of his cell in his own blood, are a lie.

"There are no documents," he writes.

5

The trial begins Monday, May 5, 1986, in the high criminal court, *la cour d'assises*, in the Palais de Justice, a short walk from Notre-Dame. Pei Pu and Bernard are charged with "conspiring with agents of a foreign power, in such a manner as to bring harm to the diplomatic situation of France," specifically, providing thirty-five state documents to the Chinese government between 1977 and 1979, when Bernard was posted in Mongolia. A statute of limitations prevents them from being prosecuted for the documents supplied to the Chinese from 1969 to 1972, in the far more important embassy in Beijing. Convicted, they face a maximum prison term of twenty years. The presiding judge, seated in the front of the wood-paneled courtroom, dressed in the traditional black-and-red robe with ermine collar, is Xavier Versini. The jury, seated in a semicircle around him, is, as it is a case of treason, composed not of ordinary citizens but of seven magistrates. Pei Pu, some members of the Paris arts community having rallied behind him as a victim of the Cultural Revolution, is represented by prominent lawyers François Morette and Jacques Péberay. Bernard has decided to let the more experienced Henri Leclerc defend him in court.

They stand together, the two old lovers, in the raised pen of the prisoners' dock, to the left of the judge, two uniformed gendarmes behind them. Pei Pu, in his old gray suit and blue tie, looks wan and resigned. Bernard, in one of his drug-induced weight swings, is jowly, his body fat. His shirt collar hides the thick red scars of his failed suicide. His sports jacket, unfashionably buttoned, gaps over his belly. His fingers are stained with nicotine—he smokes two packs of cigarettes a day. Even now, in this imposing courtroom, with its gold-inlaid ceiling and chandeliers, he seems unable to grasp the gravity of his situation. His eyes dart nervously around the courtroom. From time to time he grins. It is clear to both his friends and the press, when presiding judge Versini opens the proceedings with the investigative judge's report and then begins his questioning of the defendants, that Bernard is on mood elevators.

"Your name is Boursicot and you stand accused of delivering documents to the Chinese," Versini begins. "In 1964 you arrived at the French embassy in Peking. How were you admitted to the Quai d'Orsay?"

"Well, you know, there are two ways of getting into the Quai d'Orsay," says Bernard, making a little pun in French: *"par concours ou par concours de circonstances*—by the front door or by the back. A guy said they needed an accountant in Beijing and I just happened to be there at the time."

"You own your own apartment, do you not?" Versini will later ask.

Bernard, standing in the prisoners' dock, looks about the room like a comic trying to gauge the mood of the crowd.

"In fact the bank owns it," he says.

It has been over two years since his confrontation with Pei Pu, and for both men life has been hard. Though Pei Pu, over the objections of Judge Laroche, has been released from prison on grounds of poor health, he has been dropped by many of his old French friends and is no longer welcome at the Loo Tou restaurant. Bertrand has left school to work in a Chinese restaurant to support himself and Pei Pu. The two have moved from one borrowed apartment to another. Bernard's dream of a family life with Thierry and Pei Pu and Bertrand is finally gone. "Did Bertrand know?" he says to Mme. Lavalier when she comes to see him, and, occasionally, of Pei Pu: "That bastard. He really took me." Sometimes Bernard gets a letter. Pei Pu, writing to Bernard two months after his suicide attempt, says that sad as Bernard's life is, his own is worse. Bertrand writes that he and Pei Pu have been sleeping in the streets, because Pei Pu's friends threw them out. They are eating very badly, Bertrand says, sharing a turkey casserole with a single spoon. They are sleeping on the ground. Bernard must not believe he is the only one who is in pain, Bertrand writes, because there are men who are suffering *because* of Bernard.

Bernard cannot believe Pei Pu's life is worse. After spending nearly three years behind bars, while Pei Pu was imprisoned for less than eight months, Bernard is convinced that the French are bowing to political pressure from the Chinese, while he is being persecuted. He still believes he has done nothing wrong. Asked by the press to be photographed with Pei Pu, he agrees on condition that his handcuffs are removed. When they are, from habit, Bernard clasps his hands behind his back, so the effect is the same. Forcing a smile that is meant to seem jaunty and relaxed, Bernard looks like a self-conscious buffoon. Pei Pu stares abjectly at the floor. They are, for anyone harboring hopes of a dashing, if naive, adventurer and his bewitching and exotic mistress, a sorry sight: two beaten and shamed homosexual lovers, in the unromantic clutch of middle age.

"In the craziest trial of the year, the box for the accused in *la cour d'assises* has been transformed into a *cage aux folles*—a drag queens' box," reports *Le Figaro*, the conservative morning daily, while *France-Soir* runs an old photo of Pei Pu in costume which to European eyes is a comic-book rendering of an Oriental seductress: eyes outlined in heavy black makeup, a gown embroidered with fire-breathing dragons.

The prosecutor, Henry Saludo, calls Pei Pu a "pawn" manipulated by the Party apparatus, and observes his femininity was credible because "he was an actor, a great actor." Saludo is harder on Bernard: "He betrayed his superiors and his country, and he lacked even the most basic honesty." While Saludo concedes that the documents Bernard handed over to the Chinese were not of major importance, nonetheless "every piece of intelligence information is useful and important, if only to corroborate other information."

It is the sexual aspects of this espionage case that seem to fascinate the judge.

"Explain yourself," demands Versini of Bernard, "because we have to understand what happened. Who manipulated whom and how? You swore to the police, after Shi Pei Pu had been arrested by the D.S.T. after arriving in France with your quote unquote son, that you believed absolutely that Shi Pei Pu was a woman. You said you bet your head on it."

Everyone is staring. Bernard repeats the old story.

"Everything happened in an atmosphere of mystery," says Bernard. "First, it was night, everything happened in the dark. It was a secret affair. The authorities did not allow any interaction between the Chinese and French. Since we were so scared of getting caught, we didn't spend that much time together. The only way we could meet was in a public place, across from the post office. . . ."

"You're evading the question," Versini says, impatient. "You've said nothing distinguished her from an ordinary woman. . . ."

Bernard cannot speak for a moment.

"It's true," he says, finally. "I found it no different from being with a woman. I never saw his sex entirely. He was very modest. I thought it was a Chinese custom."

The courtroom breaks out laughing. Bernard laughs with them, though the object of their laughter is himself. He speaks of Pei Pu's abortion, her pregnancy, their son.

"But how could you let yourself be taken for such a ride?" Versini presses.

"I believed it even when the police told me he was a man," says Bernard. "I believed it until the day in the pen Shi Pei Pu showed me. . . ."

He addresses the charges against him, insisting the papers he gave the Chinese from Mongolia were useless and that at least half were press clippings.

"I don't want to hurt anyone's feelings, but Ulan Bator was not a very serious embassy," he says. "We occupied a floor in a hotel and when we left we handed over the keys to the concierge. We did have a safe, but nobody knew to use it. For the reports, the ambassador would ask the advice of his Mongolian interpreter, who worked part-time at the Mongolian Foreign Affairs Ministry. When we'd go to Beijing because of the cold, a seal was put on the door, but the Mongolians could always enter by the window. . . ."

The judge moves on to Pei Pu, whose composure, since he has seen what is merely another aspect of Western theater including the sorry performance of a costar, has returned. Forgoing the woman interpreter the court has provided, Pei Pu speaks, with an actor's finesse, of his family, his early triumphs on the stage, the destruction of Beijing Opera at the hands of Mme. Mao. He denies any knowledge of espionage.

"My passion is the opera, only the opera," he says.

"Did your extraordinary acting talent help you to mislead Bernard Boursicot for all those years?" Versini asks.

Pei Pu requests his interpreter. Blushing, she recounts his story. There was no attempt on his part to mislead, Pei Pu says; he himself did not know for years whether he was a man or a woman. At twelve, he was told he was a malformed girl, but he was raised as a boy "because in China boys are considered better than girls." At twenty-six, when he met Bernard, he thought he *might* be a woman. Later, with hormone treatment and the trauma of the Cultural Revolution, his genitals "descended" and he learned he was a man.

"Before the Cultural Revolution, I was a woman or almost," he says. "After, I became a man."

The press is incredulous.

"Put the blame on Mao," the reporter from *Le Figaro* will write.

The psychiatrists who have examined the men in prison make their reports. There is, as they speak of the two seemingly dissimilar men in the prisoners' dock, a strong similarity. Both are characterized as naive, immature, and fascinated with the imaginary. Neither is said to be at ease with his homosexuality.

"The psychosexual development of Shi, who stayed a bachelor, was marked by certain inhibitions and ambiguities," one report reads in part. "His father, who was a teacher, died in 1945, and his mother, who was a professor, brought him up. Shi does not have any memories of his father, but speaks of his mother with great emotion. . . . There is, one suspects, a certain complacency in histrionics and mythomania, which is partly cultural, a tendency to make things up . . . a personality that is rich, but very immature on the emotional level, ambivalent in its identifications, emotional, apparently inhibited regarding everything that is outside the theater. He is conformist, suggestible, sensitive. . . . In his affair with Boursicot, emotional feelings were more dominant than sexual."

Contradictions, in Pei Pu's talks with psychiatrists, are many. While

Pei Pu insists he never told Bernard he was a woman and that Bernard
had seen his male sexual organs, he also said he believed, soon after
their affair was begun, that he was pregnant with Bernard's child.

"I grew fat, I was young, I believed," Pei Pu said. "He was very
young; me, it was the first time, I did not know how to do it, I don't
especially like sensuality. He wanted to sleep with me, I am very weak,
I said nothing. I love him like a little brother. I can make love with men,
women, in China and Paris, but I do not search. . . . I slept with him, I
never said I was a woman."

Learning he was not pregnant and "wishing very strongly to have a
child with his friend," according to psychiatrists, Pei Pu said he gave
Bernard's sperm to a doctor, later receiving a baby. Pei Pu told psychiatrists he believed that child was Bernard's son—though a few months
earlier, he had told the interrogating judge he was uncertain. Shi also
says that he never suggested to Bernard he was the mother of the boy.

The psychiatrists see no sign of nervous disorders or psychosis.
They are not certain if Pei Pu is telling them the truth as he believes it,
somehow accepting the apparent contradictions.

Had Pei Pu been so eager to deny his homosexuality that he believed he was of ambiguous sex or that physically he mirrored the
femininity he or Bernard craved? Was a lie less painful to him than the
loss of face in admitting a forbidden act?

"With this actor of great talent, one can't exclude a certain tendency to imagine and create," a psychiatrist says.

Bernard is said to have "a personality which is badly identified,
ambivalent, emotional, open to suggestion, credulous and showing traits
of nervousness with sensitivity and a fascination for the imaginary."

And if Bernard seemed to have accepted his bisexuality at thirty,
living with a male lover, indulging himself in the gay bathhouses of
New Orleans, apparently on a deeper level he has not.

He did not see psychiatrists in Tel Aviv and Paris in 1980 and 1981
merely to expedite a transfer back to France. According to the psychiatrists, Bernard told them he sought help because he was "tormented"
by his homosexuality.

"Recognizing himself as a bisexual, he uneasily assumed his homosexual tendencies, which gave him a feeling of guilt."

When this guilt-ridden young man meets an acutely sensitive actor, says psychiatrist Bernard Defer, "one enters an obscure and enigmatic universe, difficult to grasp," and an extraordinary, unspoken contract is begun: As Bernard Boursicot requires that the love of his life be a woman, Shi Pei Pu, so adept at accommodating himself to other people's needs, becomes that woman.

"While he was in Peking, Boursicot was convinced that Shi was a woman who gave birth to a son after his departure," Defer says. "This conviction projected his own sexual ambivalence and the imaginative and passionate disposition of Boursicot's personality. The relationship situated itself in a psychological context very probably skillfully instilled by Shi, virtuoso of the theater and of the game of seduction. By passing documents to a Chinese functionary, documents of little importance, Boursicot justified his conduct with worry over the safety of Shi and their hypothetical child."

It is a tidy psychological explanation. But it does not address the question uppermost in the minds of the courtroom crowd: How did Shi Pei Pu physically dupe Bernard Boursicot?

And so at last Dr. Jean-Pierre Campana, one of the many physicians who have examined Shi Pei Pu, takes the stand. A dignified man of middle age, he seems disturbed by the laughter in the courtroom and tries to lend some dignity to the proceedings with a professorial approach. The defendant's claims of his testicles descending in his mid-twenties, after he had begun his affair with Boursicot, of his penis retracting into his body, are simply not, he explains, supported by the physical evidence—nor by science. Pei Pu, he says, is a perfectly normal male.

As for how Pei Pu managed to hide his genitals from another man during a relationship that spanned eighteen years, the doctor seems determined to be purposefully vague.

"Shi Pei Pu hid his penis within the folds of his scrotum, which if the thighs are squeezed tightly together can be confusing because of the hair," the doctor tells the court. "Of course, this allows only a fleeting and superficial penetration and requires a very credulous partner."

None of the spectators has any idea what he is talking about.

The defense makes its closing arguments.

"This is the story of two beings, both of whom are psychologically fragile and exalted, who entered into the same dream where each will believe what the other is saying because they both want to believe it," says François Morette, Pei Pu's lawyer. "It is within this context that Shi Pei Pu was able to invent a child in order to complete the story. . . . The intelligence services are offering no proof of a setup in this case. If Shi was the awesome agent that they claim, he would have taken advantage of his temporary freedom to escape to China."

"If this case is anything," Henri Leclerc argues, "it is a crime of passion. The psychiatrists and the police and the investigative judge who has made a study of the proceeding for two years agree that Bernard genuinely believed Pei Pu to be a woman and the mother of his child. But is it truly a crime? Bernard Boursicot has been accused of supplying intelligence to agents of a foreign power and in doing so having done damage to the diplomatic service of France."

The lawyer picks up a few of the papers to which Bernard is alleged to have had access and reads some sections to the court: requests to the home office for a rearview mirror and a cheese tray; excerpts from the dispatches of Ambassador Aristide.

"The yak, to the Mongolians, is what the automobile is to the Americans," Aristide has reported.

Leclerc puts the papers down on his desk.

"Is this the stuff of espionage?" he asks. "Do you really think what we have here hurt the diplomatic interests of France? This case is absolutely at the bottom of the ladder in the spying world."

The jury retires to consider the charges. One hour later, Bernard and Pei Pu are each sentenced to six years in jail.

There was, of course, another covenant between Bernard and Pei Pu that existed beyond the sexual. If Bernard Boursicot was a man who needed to be a hero in one of the legendary stories that had colored his boyhood—larger than life, more thrilling than life—if he had sat through *Dr. Zhivago* a dozen times, he had found in Shi Pei Pu the perfect mate: a librettist whose profession it was to create drama and who could write him a script custom-made for his soul. Ever changing and embroidered with exotic lore to avoid the boredom to which he was prone. Rich with new dangers and obstacles that Bernard might vanquish. Including, as required in an adventure story, a great secret that could be revealed only at great risk. Bernard Boursicot had been a romantic and that was his undoing. He had ended up, finally, a victim of romance.

He and Pei Pu are sent back to Fresnes. Bertrand goes to work as a stable boy on an estate outside Paris, hitchhiking into town once a week to see Pei Pu and Bernard, sleeping in the street when he cannot get a ride back home. Thierry takes a job as a receptionist in a Left Bank hotel, arranging his hours around his prison visits. There is a flurry of interest shortly after the trial, when a guest writer on *Apostrophes* speaks out against the length of the sentence, but the interest passes. A number of persons in the diplomatic community also privately consider the sentence somewhat harsh: Under the law, what Bernard Boursicot did was certainly wrong, believes Ambassador Chayet, who has a degree in law and has served as a legal adviser to the Foreign Affairs department for seventeen years, but it is difficult to place very much value on the Mongolian documents. As for Pei Pu, Ambassador and Mme. Chayet believe he is too much the artist to have any interest in politics. The Chinese may have used him, but they certainly would never have depended upon him. Unless, Mme. Chayet jokes, Pei Pu's appearance as a self-absorbed actor was merely a cover. In that case, the Chinese were brilliant.

So Bernard and Pei Pu remain in prison. And then one day; perhaps six or seven months after the trial, journalist Jean Leclerc du Sablon, who has been corresponding with both men, dines with Régis Debray, for whom he had served as journalistic watchdog when Debray was imprisoned in Bolivia long ago. Debray is now a powerful man. He is adviser on international affairs to President François Mitterrand. He is also thinking of making a film in China and has enlisted Leclerc du Sablon's aid. Leclerc du Sablon has a favor of his own to ask.

"I have this friend in jail. You know what it is to be in jail," Leclerc du Sablon says.

He asks Debray to intercede with Mitterrand in the release of Shi Pei Pu. He does not mention Bernard. Pei Pu, with his history of heart disease, seems in more urgent need, and because he is a foreign national, the case may fall within Debray's domain. Leclerc du Sablon also believes Bernard already has people working on his behalf. He has never considered either man a villain. Spying in China? During the Cultural Revolution all Chinese citizens who had contact with foreigners were obliged to report to their work unit chief. And as Leclerc du Sablon had said repeatedly: There were no secrets to be had in the embassy of France in Beijing.

Debray promises to look into it and checks with D.S.T. He then brings the matter up to Mitterrand, who is not very well informed about the case. Some time later, on a trip to China, Debray has lunch at the French embassy with the Chinese minister of foreign affairs. The minister takes Debray aside and insists "very strongly" that the French liberate Shi Pei Pu. It's strange to Debray that the Chinese are making such a big deal about this case. It seems to him they are embarrassed to have an agent, or an occasional agent, in jail. It is also obvious to Debray that the Chinese, though they do not say so outright, want Shi Pei Pu back.

Mitterrand, says Debray, is also surprised that the Chinese are so interested in this case of which he is barely aware. Once it is clear to Mitterrand that there is, in Debray's words, "nothing very important" about the case, the President decides to pardon Pei Pu. He seems to believe—and Debray agrees with him—that it is "very silly" to endanger relations between China and France over such an unimportant case. Shi Pei Pu is an artist; he may have been used by Chinese intelligence; but it is clear that he does not belong to the world of espionage. Debray himself is always suspicious of what he calls the paranoia of the secret security services.

Working under the President's orders, Debray moves to expedite the release of Shi Pei Pu. It is not so easy. The Chinese do not understand why if Mitterrand has agreed to pardon Pei Pu he cannot be released the next hour; they don't understand there are legal procedures that must be followed. Pei Pu's lawyers, as Debray recalls it, have to be convinced that once Shi Pei Pu is freed he will not be forced to leave France and that the French will never give him back to the Chinese. Pei Pu's trial attorney, François Morette, declines to discuss the case.

On April 6, 1987, Shi Pei Pu receives a presidential pardon. Once Pei Pu has been freed, Debray says, "it is impossible" that his co-defendant not also be freed.

Nonetheless, Bernard is not pardoned at once. His release does not come until four months later, on August 3, after his attorney makes an appeal and Bernard's own friends in government deliver a petition to the President. While Shi Pei Pu has served a total of a year and a half in prison, Bernard has served four years.

Bernard goes home to Thierry. The following weekend, joined by Bertrand, they go down to Vannes, where Bernard's parents and brothers are waiting. They drink champagne and celebrate Bernard's release from prison and the birthdays of Bernard and Bertrand. They drink well into the night and then Bernard's brothers Roland and Alain take him outside and ask him how he could have made such a stupid mistake. They demand a detailed explanation. Lionel, who has followed, cannot watch.

Back in Paris, Bernard goes to visit Pei Pu, who tells him he must write a thank-you letter to Mitterrand.

"I have already done that," Bernard says.

A feast has been prepared, but Bernard waits for Pei Pu to eat first. He knows it is crazy, but he keeps thinking the food is poisoned.

Bertrand visits often. Then one day, says Bernard, Bertrand arrives and tells Bernard he should leave Thierry and live with Pei Pu. Bertrand walks out and Bernard does not hear from him for several months. Then things go back to normal. Bertrand takes a job in a famous French restaurant, as an apprentice chef, and supports Pei Pu. They live, through the generosity of a wealthy friend, in a set of meagerly furnished maid's rooms, six floors up, on Boulevard Haussmann, on the Right Bank. When the weather is fair, Pei Pu goes into the well-ordered fantasy world of the Parc Monceau, with its clipped hedges and pagoda and miniature pyramid and faux Roman ruins. He works on a memoir of his life in the opera. Sometimes he lectures and sings, perhaps in the town hall of Versailles, and a few old friends from the diplomatic service from the time before the Cultural Revolution attend. They do not give their names to the press. There appears to be no lover in Pei Pu's life. At times, as was common in another age among those who suffered in love, he speaks of ending his days in a monastery. In March 1988, the play *M. Butterfly*, inspired by the case and written by American playwright David Henry Hwang, opens on Broadway and soon becomes an international hit. Pei Pu and Bernard hire American lawyers who argue that their clients' right to privacy has been invaded and their story exploited.

Bernard, after prison, does not work. When the weather in Paris is

poor, he takes off with Thierry and perhaps Mme. Lavalier and Basia.
Bernard rents a houseboat in India for several weeks. He goes to the
mountains of Crete and visits the Kazantzakis museum. Postcards from
cities with names like Paleochora and Bombay arrive at the offices of
Bernard's work-bound friends. "I believe you think I enjoy too much
life . . . ," one begins. Curiosity about how he supports this life rivals,
for some, curiosity about his affair with Pei Pu. He supports himself as
he always has: the sale of a rug here, a small inheritance there. When the
money runs out, Thierry takes a job as a hotel clerk for a few months.
Then they collect unemployment insurance. Their overhead is low.
Rent income from the little studio covers the two-hundred-dollar mort-
gage on the Paris apartment. When Bernard and Thierry dine out,
friends pick up the check; they reciprocate with dinner parties of pasta
and chicken. They do not waste funds. When *M. Butterfly* opens in April
1989 in London, with Anthony Hopkins portraying Bernard, the man
who has inspired the play stays at a friend's little house in Cambridge,
two hours outside of town, sleeping on the living room floor. Why spend
money on hotels? Bernard says.

In 1989, Bernard realizes the profits of his celebrity. The sale of a
book to an American publisher guarantees Bernard a percentage of the
royalties. An out-of-court settlement with the producers of *M. Butterfly*
the following year gives Bernard a share of the playwright's royalties as
well. The show goes on to be produced in thirty countries. Pei Pu
negotiates with the producers separately. According to Pei Pu's American lawyer, Terry Freiberg of Boston, he tries for three years and works
"hundreds of hours" to bring about a settlement before he gives up.
"The real Pei Pu was no better known to me than to Bernard," says
Freiberg. "He flows from one form to another—it's like trying to grab a
cloud." Freiberg has an additional frustration—Pei Pu does not pay him
for this work.

M. Louis Boursicot dies in Vannes in 1991, at age seventy-six, after
a series of strokes that he had survived for ten years.

Mme. Boursicot no longer hears from Pei Pu and Bertrand. Nonetheless, she keeps Bertrand's picture in the living room with those of
her other grandchildren and carefully tends the rubber plant he had sent
her when she had last gone to the hospital, when Bernard was in jail.

Five feet tall, it rests in the corner of the cluttered living room next to the tasseled lamps that were Kang's gift to Bernard, and it is treasured.

"When you see the plant growing, Mami," Bertrand had told her, "think of me."

The great adventurer Fernand Fournier-Aubry writes the story of his life five years after Bernard leaves him in the Amazon jungle. Published in the summer of 1972, *Don Fernando* sells over a quarter million copies in France and is translated into fourteen languages. Fournier-Aubry has little time to enjoy his success. He dies of cancer six months after his book comes out and is buried in the cemetery of Monte Carlo. On his first trip to the south of France with Thierry, Bernard visits the grave.

The French embassy in Mongolia is shut down in 1984. The embassy in Belize is closed one year later.

It is not known who Bernard's contact, the mysterious "Kang," might have been. French investigative journalists Rémi Kauffer and Roger Faligot, authors of *The Chinese Secret Service* and some half dozen books on international espionage, theorize that it might have been one Yu Zhensan, adopted son of Kang Sheng, the head of the Chinese intelligence service. Yu Zhensan was in charge of surveillance and counterintelligence of foreigners in China. The name, they say, provides no clue: the Chinese intelligence service sometimes followed the Comintern tradition of giving the name or code name of a section chief to his case officers and agents. It is supposed that the name "Kang" was a pseudonym. Or perhaps a private joke.

Catherine divorces in 1990, after sixteen years of marriage. A doctor specializing in geriatrics, she practices in a hospital in Paris and is the mother of a ten-year-old son and a thirteen-year-old daughter. Catherine's relationship with her mother is once again close; she and her children often spend weekends with her in an old stone farmhouse Mme. Lavalier has bought in the countryside. While Bernard considers Catherine his great woman love, the two rarely see each other. Catherine cannot believe Bernard did not know Pei Pu was a man. She is also angered and dismayed by her belief that Bernard has done nothing with his life but live on his story.

"He acts like he was this big spy. It was shown clearly at the trial, he was a spy of nothing," she says. "He refuses to take any responsibility for knowing Pei Pu was a man and throws it all on Pei Pu. What I think, it is a way to protect his *romanesque*, to protect himself from the mere mortals. If he doesn't keep this belief in Pei Pu being a woman, it becomes just another homosexual love story."

Catherine longs to discuss the affair with Bernard, but she cannot. When Bernard visits he never comes alone. It is clear to Catherine he does not want to talk with her about the case.

Bernard and Pei Pu remain in sporadic contact. They are, in fact, like a long-married couple now divorced but entwined for life. Meet Bernard for the first time, after meeting Pei Pu, and Bernard will ask what Pei Pu said about him and if you also met his son Bertrand. Is he not tall, is he not handsome, do you know that he happens to be an exceptionally talented cook? Return to Pei Pu after seeing Bernard and it will not be five minutes before he has questions.

"How *is* Bernard?" he asks. "Still drinking?"

Twice a year, on the occasion of the Chinese New Year and on the anniversary of his release from prison, Bernard goes to Pei Pu's home and has a drink.

Bernard has never asked Pei Pu how he was able to deceive him physically, nor do they ever discuss the case.

José Rambeau, the analyst who saw Bernard for three years in prison, does not care to discuss the case either, although Bernard has given his permission.

He will, however, address one or two issues:

Yes, he says, there is indeed a psychological condition in which, when reality is painful, a person alters that reality so quickly that he himself does not know he is doing it. Yes, it is his belief that Bernard did so.

"These are unconscious processes," the analyst says. "That is why such a person can believe certain things even if they are not so. I think Boursicot had this psychological condition: a personality split which allows one to stand an unbearable reality. It is not that one has a split personality to begin with; it is a defense: There are two things in front of me, one is bearable, the other is unbearable, I will not see that which is unbearable. Then, when he was in prison, Bernard found himself in a situation that destroyed the defense: the meeting with Shi Pei Pu when he was forced to see who Pei Pu really was and that he was not the father of his child. It is that reality he didn't want to see. . . ."

Did Bernard Boursicot, then, really believe when he was making love to Pei Pu he was making love to a woman?

"Consciously," the therapist says, "he believed."

Duet for Reporter and Spy
"I Got Lost in His Arms," Reprise
Paris, 1990

"Bernard, listen, I gotta tell you: We're waltzing on thin ice here. I mean, I believe it when you say you didn't know Pei Pu was a guy. Your shrink believed you. Maybe the interrogating judge and a few of the doctors who saw you for an hour in prison believed you; but your lawyer didn't believe you, Catherine doesn't believe you, none of your friends seem to believe you, your own mother, I have a feeling, doesn't believe you. . . ."

"If you don't believe me why do a book?"

"I *do* believe you. And I've told you: Even if I didn't, I think it's a story."

"Probably the reason I believe is I have seen so many times this business."

"But how did he do it?"

"The technical recipe, it is Shi Pei Pu who has it."

"But you never asked him. How could you never ask him?"

"Why? Do you think I would get an answer? After it was over, and we saw the results of the blood tests, he was still able to say to me, 'But Bertrand is *still* your son.' Lies, more lies."

"You realized Pei Pu was a man in February '84—over six years ago. Since that time have you spent much time wondering what the secret was?"

"Oh, he did it mentally. He screwed my head very well. And it was quite easy, when I was twenty. He planted some seeds to make me believe and he just had to put some fresh water on the seeds and the seeds grew by themselves."

"So you didn't wonder about it much."

"No. Even to the shrinks, the psychiatrists, in prison. I didn't ask this question in my delirium. It was not my main question. Now it is over, it is too late."

"You tormented yourself over other things—like why you confessed to the police."

"Yeah. For three and a half years I wondered about this: Why did I talk?"

"But the question of how come you didn't realize Pei Pu had a penis?"

"It didn't torment me."

"Why do you think that is?"

"It's difficult to answer. First when I learned I was angry. Then when I knew this I wanted to kill myself."

"Why did you want to kill yourself?"

"Because I was dispirited because of being cheated. The story was false. It became a nightmare in my head."

"But by then you were making love to men, so why did you feel so bad when Pei Pu turned out to be a man?"

"Because I was cheated."

"How were you cheated?"

"Because he told me for so many years that we had a family and about our child and his poor condition, 'As you know, Bernard, my difficult condition, my difficult condition'; making so many confidences which were pure invention. And I helped him as much as a donkey could carry a safe. If you trust somebody, you trust."

"Bernard, you told me you were comfortable making love with men when you turned thirty. You said when you went to the psychiatrists in 1980 in Tel Aviv and Paris it was just to get out of Israel and that you didn't discuss anything serious. But the psychiatrists who examined you in prison for the judge said you told them you went into therapy because you were unhappy about two things: the failed love affair with Basia and your homosexuality."

(No reply.)

"The word they use is 'tormented.' They said you told them that

you were tormented about your homosexuality. Do you remember telling the court-appointed psychiatrists that?"

"Oooh, I told them so many things, it is possible. They probably
interpreted it this way because they wanted to interpret things the way
they like, but it was not one of the main problems I had."

"In 1981 were you still upset about homosexuality?"

"I used to visit my family with Thierry. I was not shy. I introduced
Thierry to all my friends. It was not a big problem."

"Yeah, but your parents and brothers and a lot of other people
never knew he was your boyfriend. They thought he was just a friend."

"You don't have to be proud of it and have a T-shirt that says, 'I am
homosexual.' You can understand that if I was in the diplomatic area it
was better not to be an exhibitionist, but inside me it was not a big
problem. Particularly with Thierry. We had a very good relationship,
and when I was not with Thierry I was able to find men and women all
over, but men were easier to find."

"Why were you going to a psychiatrist?"

"My friend from Morocco was doing it. He said, 'Confession is
good for the soul. You go to a psychiatrist, you confess your crimes, it is
finished.' I heard the message but I was not ready to tell my crimes. I
was not understanding psychiatrists. I was not trusting anybody enough
to tell him I had been spying. Afterward when I was in prison, I regret-
ted this, because I thought that if I had told him he would have said, 'It
is not a psychiatrist you need, but a lawyer.' "

"Let's go back to the beginning for a second: You meet Pei Pu and
you know he has played women's roles in the theater?"

"Yes."

"You know he is a student of Mei Lanfang, who specialized in
playing women's roles. . . ."

"Yes. There was a stamp on the market with Mei Lanfang's picture
when I arrived. I even saw the stamps and I was thinking, 'What a nice
woman.' "

"My point is—"

"—Yeah, but I don't make this connection, that he is an actor and
he is doing it for me."

"I would say you don't make that connection because you didn't
want to."

"No. I was not prepared in my mind to make this connection. Not only would I not have admitted it, I had nothing in my mind to make me suspicious."

"Your friend Komaroff tells you in February, five months before you go to bed with Pei Pu, that he's a homosexual. Other friends tell you the same thing. You know Pei Pu's an actor. You never put these things together?"

"No. I was wanting to defend Pei Pu because I was knowing he was not homosexual. I thought people were jealous because he was so pure, so fine. . . ."

"Bernard, let me hit you with a psychological theory: You were attracted to boys at the time you met Shi Pei Pu, but you couldn't face it, and Shi knows it, and if he says he is a girl, you can have it both ways."

"No, this is not true, not to me."

"Can you explain why?"

"Consciously, first, I would never admit to sleeping with boys at that time. Consciously, if I had admitted to sleeping with a boy, Pei Pu was not my type."

"But unconsciously—"

"Unconsciously the thing that happened was I wanted to marry and have a normal life. When Pei Pu revealed he was a woman, for me it was more exotic in my unconscious. Another thing, it was very rare to have a girl as intelligent as Shi Pei Pu. Intellectually, he was very much higher than me. As soon as he revealed his secret, he was so feminine around me I had no doubt, plus he was so sick after his abortion and I was in a certain way attacked by the emotion. . . ."

"Hold on, let's get back to this femininity." (Reporter brings out papers.) "You've seen the medical report on how he did it."

"Yeah."

"Here—you look at this paragraph and explain to me what it's saying."

"It's well explained."

"No, it's not. I've had a million people look at these papers, including a French doctor who specializes in sex change surgery, and nobody knows what they're talking about. Here:

" 'During our examination, the indicted, without us having to make a request, wanted to give us an "explanation" and executed in front of us certain maneuvers with his external masculine organs, bringing back up his testicles and his penis under the fatty tissues of his pubic area, hiding the organs under the folds of his scrotum. This procedure, under the condition of holding one's thighs tightly together during any sort of sexual liaison, could in general terms produce something of a feminine appearance. This setup, being rather crude, can only fool or create an illusion for a partner who is totally ignorant of the female anatomy. Whatever the case, during sexual contact, only penetration of a small depth in these folds could have taken place.'

"I don't get it. Are they saying he put his penis under a roll of fat on his stomach or on his thigh?"

"No."

"Well, what is this fatty area of the body they're talking about?"

(No reply.)

"Okay, hold on." (Bringing out and opening small container.) "You guys got Play-Doh in France?"

(No reply.)

"See, it's like clay; you mold stuff with it—it comes in different colors—and when you're done with it, you put it back in the jar and then you can take it out and play with it again. Now, what I thought is, maybe you could mold one and show me what you think Pei Pu did. I know you don't know what he did, but I want you just to show me what you think he could have done."

"What?"

"You just take this dough and mold it into a little penis and show me what you think he did."

(Bernard shakes his head no.)

"Okay, look. Say we divide the dough in half and you make one and I'll make one."

(No response.)

"Okay, I'll make one."

(Reporter molds handful of yellow Play-Doh into the pelvis of a man, from waist to knees, legs apart, with two prominent testicles and erect penis.)

"You have a very exaggerated idea of what is a man."

"Look, you don't want to make one, don't criticize. I think it looks pretty good. I never made anything out of clay before. Now. You take this and you show me what you think Pei Pu did."

(Bernard sticks out one finger, shoves testicles up into the body cavity of the figure with one rough gesture, then bends the penis backward between the legs.)

"That's what you think he did? Jammed his balls up into his body and pushed his penis behind his legs?"

"Yeah. This is what is written and also I am sure."

"Looks painful."

"For love, you suffer."

"Why do you believe this is how he did it?"

"Because I was never able to see it [his penis]. And the day I saw it, I understood that he had not so much to hide. But you know, I never saw it when it was growing. And if he was taking hormones, which I believe he did, then maybe he was, um, *impuissant*. . . ."

"Impotent?"

"Mmmm."

"Why would he shove his balls into his body instead of pushing them behind his legs?"

"I don't know. If I had the opportunity of knowing I would not be here. He had the capability of great mystification. Maybe he was greasing himself, I believe so. . . ."

"Listen, a man's balls are hairy—"

"—A man's. But he's half a eunuch, this guy."

"Well, when you were penetrating him, what were you feeling on your penis? Balls, which would have been hairy, or the smooth skin of a penis?"

"I was feeling only confident. I am sure he was never in erection. This is what I never felt, an erection. Maybe he was excited but able to correct it."

"How?"

"I don't know."

"You feel he always had to shove it between his legs."

"Yes. When we were going to bed, it was not just like that. There was preparation, he was saying, 'Come to me. . . .' "

"But the point is, you really feel a man could stick his balls up in his body cavity and push his penis backward and pass as a girl?"

"I know a girl in Paris, I should present her to you, she is a man."

"A transvestite?"

"She told me, after I got out of prison, 'Oh, dear, you got caught. But what happened to you, we do this every evening in the Bois-de-Boulogne and people who are coming know nothing at all.'"

"Oh, yeah?"

"She knew my story. She said, 'Baby, what happened to you happens to many people. . . .'"

6

In a small prison hospital room outside Paris, sometime after the arrest of Bernard Boursicot in the summer of 1983, a Chinese man of middle age arrives for a court-ordered physical examination. He is a slightly built man, five feet four inches tall, one hundred and forty-six pounds. His face is smooth, he is balding. Prison conspires against a man's self-worth, but this man's dignity, even knowing what is before him, is unimpaired. He carries himself in such a way one knows he is not just another desperate émigré, fallen into some illicit game, but a person of importance: a member of a ruling family, a great actor, a master of his craft.

The details of his case, which have appeared in the newspapers, are known to everyone in the hospital. There is talk of a homosexual liaison, espionage, sexual duplicity. Many jokes have been made at the expense of this man. The written instructions of the court to the doctors, by contrast, are matter of fact:

Determine if the prisoner, in addition to his masculine organs, has external female organs. If he does not, determine whether he might have had female organs in the past.

Determine whether the prisoner shows any trace of surgical intervention of the sexual organs. If so, make a report of the nature of that intervention.

Determine whether the prisoner, as he has claimed, has the ability to withdraw his penis and testicles into his body cavity.

Examine the prisoner's anus for signs of sodomization.

The doctors make their examination. They find the prisoner is a man, with normal sexual organs which show no trace of surgical intervention. The anus shows no signs of sodomization. And while the patient has complained of chest pains in the night, and has a history of heart problems, his heartbeat now is normal.

Then, as the examination is ending, the prisoner, without being asked, says that he would like to explain something to the doctors. Easily, smoothly, he pushes his testicles up into his body cavity. The skin of the scrotal sack hangs slack, like curtains. The man now pushes his penis between his legs, toward his back, bisecting the skin of the scrotum, and squeezes his legs tightly together. The penis is hidden, while the skin of the scrotum resembles the vaginal lips, beneath a triangle of pubic hair. Pushed between the empty scrotal sac, the penis has also created a small cavity so that shallow penetration is possible. A naive or credulous lover, looking at this man now, might believe he was looking at a woman. Of course, one could not look too closely. It was only illusion. But ninety percent of love, even a man of science will volunteer, is illusion. In defense of love, a story we love, a person we love, is there anyone among us who has not closed his eyes and refused to see?

There are people, they hear my story, they don't believe. They think it is about a homosexual couple, they want to have a son. This is a normal situation, I agree, but this is not my story. My story is true, it is overwhelming, it is not a false story. It is not that I did not want to believe Shi Pei Pu was a man. I was stupefied when I learned. He was not like a homosexual man when he was with me; he was like a woman. One day we were visiting the Forbidden City, he had on a green jade bracelet and the bracelet fell and was broken. It was Sunday morning, we were alone. You have to know how it was, how cold and dry and beautiful a place was Beijing. He said, "It is a good thing. I will give you part and I will keep the other and one day when we are united we will fix it." I have known many homosexual people; not one would do this; this is exactly how a woman would do. I kept this bracelet for twenty-four years. Stories like this, he told me. Years and years of his beautiful lies. I went before the judge; he said to me, "Do you believe everything everybody tells you?" I said, "Yes, that is why I am here." What a violinist Pei Pu was. And before such a stupid man.

I was a diplomat—I was four years in prison; I am not proud of it—but I am not a criminal. I was breathing the same air as the bandits, but I was one of the persons who have not been contaminated. I was not there for the same reason as the others. I did not kill the French state, I did not kill any person. I was never paid any money for what they call spying. The police arrest me, I tell them everything. The next morning, they come for me in prison, I give them four sheets of paper. I say, "Here are some things I forgot." I talked to the police like they were my father. I wanted *to talk.*

I was a diplomat, I had a beautiful life: apartments, a house, a car, everywhere first class. In Mongolia, the ambassador would ask me on weekends, "Bernard, are you using the car this weekend or will it be free?" He is the ambassador, he is asking me. Now it is gone, the car, the life, everything. I made nine trips to Tegucigalpa with the diplomatic pouch the year I am arrested. . . . I miss my diplomatic pouch.

People ask do I hate Pei Pu. I don't say he's a bastard, no. I hate no man, not even the police. I have no regrets for what they call this spying. I am just sorry the story was not the one I was believing. Love is to trust; that is what was the fault of my friend Shi Pei Pu: to lie. It's better to be cheated than to cheat, there is no dishonor in being cheated. Anyway, let us not say anything against Pei Pu.

I had a lot of luck being posted over and over in China. But even if I had not, I would have come back. It was my destiny. Even when I was no longer in love with Pei Pu, I had made my promise, I was in love with my child. I traveled all over, but I was no longer free. Shi Pei Pu was always saying to me, "I know you will have to leave, but I know your heart is with me. So do whatever you like, sleep all over the world, but she who has provided you with a child you will always remember." And in this, Shi Pei Pu was smart. There was a bid in Shi Pei Pu's mind that worked:

"Never will you have with anyone such a beautiful story as you have with me."

In the spring of 1988, while I was working as a writer at *People* magazine, I saw a show on Broadway called *M. Butterfly*. It told the story of a middle-aged French diplomat, sexually insecure, who falls in love with a beautiful Beijing Opera singer, only to learn that the singer is a man.

I knew the play had been inspired by a real case—I remembered seeing a story a few years earlier in *The New York Times*—and now I wanted to know all about these people. How could a man make love to another man and believe he was a woman? Had the Frenchman been a closet homosexual? Where had the son come from? Was he in on the deception, too?

Looking over the French newspaper accounts, I became even more interested—particularly after learning that having been sentenced to prison for espionage in 1986, the men had been released in 1987, only the year before. And while I expected that Pei Pu would have been deported to China, he and his son were living in Paris.

I decided I had to talk to them. It wasn't easy. Convincing Pei Pu to do an interview took three months. What finally persuaded him was the opportunity to perform on American television. *(People,* at that time, was starting a TV show.) He arrived at our first meeting in Paris like an exiled princess, accompanied by a retinue of two or three friends. He was dressed conservatively, in a turtleneck and navy blazer and baggy men's trousers, yet there was something otherworldly about him. His hands were not only unusually small and delicate for a man, they were also strikingly mobile. He did not speak with his hands so much as use them to create an entire stage setting. He was a master of small talk, particularly in the arts, and had a gift for creating atmosphere—within moments we were all tiptoeing around him as if he were some rare *objet* from the Ming Dynasty. He was not, however, especially eager to discuss espionage or Bernard Boursicot.

Then, after four or five days, he began to talk. He talked about meeting Bernard at the party at Claude Chayet's, he talked about their arrest by the Red Guard, he talked about how he and Bernard sat across from one another on Changan Avenue for months, grateful for the opportunity to just see one another. As he talked about Changan Avenue, he cried. He was a fastidious man, but now he went into the kitchen of the apartment where we were meeting and returned with a dishcloth and sat weeping into it. I knew Pei Pu was an actor, but I never doubted his tears were genuine. I could also see Pei Pu was still in love with Bernard.

Bernard posed a different problem. Friends told me he was traveling in Morocco, but they did not know where. *People*'s editors weren't concerned. They sent me, photographer Peter Serling, a French cinematographer, and an interpreter to Morocco on spec, sort of like the vultures in *Ishtar*. We found Bernard, through a friend in Casablanca, living in a borrowed villa in Marrakesh. Thierry was with him. Unlike Pei Pu, Bernard wanted to talk. He started five minutes after we arrived in midafternoon and continued to midnight. He also cried, though at a different point in the story. He cried when he talked about how he had been portrayed in the newspapers; he cried about having been betrayed. Thierry, as Bernard cried, couldn't watch—he had to walk away.

I wrote the story for *People* and decided I wanted to do a book. I made Pei Pu and Bernard identical offers: In exchange for telling me their story, they would get a share of the royalties. They would not, however, have any control over the manuscript. Pei Pu declined the offer. Bernard accepted it.

In the spring of 1989, I arrived in Paris. I had one serious problem as a journalist: I could not speak French. I did have, however, a superb French-American interpreter and assistant named Stéphane Dujarric de la Rivière, and Bernard's English was fluent. We spent two and a half months talking. Inasmuch as it is possible to give another person complete access to one's life, Bernard did. He turned over his court records, which sometimes included very unflattering information, such as his personnel report from Foreign Affairs. He introduced me to his family, friends, and lovers. He gave his psychiatrists and attorneys clearance to talk about the case. Occasionally, as we talked, he directed me to people who he knew disliked him.

"You should talk to this one," he said of an acquaintance from Mongolia. "She hates me."

Independent of Bernard, I made contact with dozens of other sources, including members of the French foreign service, the family of Mei Lanfang, and members of the Chinese community in Paris. I had another problem there: I did not know Chinese. One afternoon at the Loo Tou restaurant, listening to the Beijing Opera group, I realized I was in reporters' hell: I was surrounded by people who were talking *two* languages I did not speak.

Over the three years I worked on this book, I interviewed approximately one hundred people. Most of the information in the book is drawn from those interviews. In some cases, usually when persons were deceased or declined to speak, I used information from court papers, including police reports. A number of names have been changed. Though the story is told largely from Bernard's point of view, attempts were always made to contact the people about whom he told a story. The assessment and interpretation of events is, of course, mine and not Bernard Boursicot's.

This book would not have been possible had it not been for Jim Gaines, the former editor of *People* magazine and current editor of *Time*, who first gave me the go-ahead to pursue the story and then gave me the leaves to research and write the book. As the project became increasingly complicated, his successor, Landon Jones, gave me additional time. Kathy Nolan, *People*'s Paris bureau chief, was essential in helping to locate Bernard and Pei Pu. I would also like to thank Stéphane Dujarric, who, after going off in the fall of 1989 to do his military service in the French navy, returned—during his leaves—to translate some particularly sensitive interviews. I am also grateful to Stef's Parisian successors, Laurie Ziesk and Catherine Godrèche.

I am chauvinistic about my profession. I have always felt that journalists, so often portrayed as competitive, are in fact a very generous group. My experience on this book reinforced that feeling. My thanks, then, to writer Christine Horko, who gave me a letter of introduction to Bernard; to French investigative journalists Rémi Kauffer and Roger Faligot, experts on international espionage; to Tiziano Terzani, the globe-trotting correspondent for *Der Spiegel,* at this writing based in Bangkok, and his wife Angela, author of *Chinese Days;* to Pierre Comparet of Agence France-Presse; and to Jean Leclerc du Sablon, presently reporting on China.

In the political world I would like to thank former French prime minister Maurice Couve de Murville; Ambassador and Mme. Claude Chayet; Ambassador and Mme. Aristide; Ambassador Étienne Manac'h; former presidential adviser Régis Debray; and General Henri Eyraud.

I would also like to thank Jean Rouch, president of the Cinémathèque Française, for his memories of Henri Langlois and Mary Meerson.

When I first approached Bernard about the book I warned him that in speaking about his life, he would not be the only one to reveal himself—he would be asking the people he loved to expose themselves also. For discussing some very intimate moments I would like to particularly thank Bernard; his mother Mme. Jeanne Boursicot; his brother Lionel Boursicot; Mme. Cécile Lavalier and her daughter, Catherine; Basia and Thierry.

Personally, this book was not easy for me. I arrived in Paris having two friends: John Morris, former picture editor of *The New York Times,* and his wife, photographer Tana Hoban. I was not as frightened as I might have been, however, because I knew that the Morrises, famous for looking after journalistic strays, would look after me. They did and I thank them. I am also grateful for the hospitality and help of Martha Shulman and Bill Grantham; Ruby and Jack Monet; S. Sarzana; John Simmons; Jianghong Chen; Simon and Marie-Dominique Thornton; and Lucy and Robert Szekely, of Budapest.

For support at home I thank Carol Ardman, Veronica Bennett, Christina Emanuel, John Goldman, Heidi Handman, Sheenah Hankin, Noah Kimerling, Susan Beth Pfeffer, Jesse Rosenthal, Stephen Sheppard, Alana Verber-Fein, and the many members of the Wadler family. My thanks to the staff of the New Courtney Coffee Shop, in Greenwich Village, who, when letters and documents arrived in French, hollered down the breakfast counter until they found somebody to translate; and to Scott Collins, of the Embassy of France Press and Information Service in Washington D.C., who sent along countless pages from the *Annuaire Diplomatique*. Thanks to my agent, Amanda Urban, who made it possible for me to have the means to do this book; to my editor, Genevieve Young, for loving the project and making the book take life.

Finally, I would like to thank my friend Lewis Grossberger, who put me on the plane to Paris and was there when I got home.

—Joyce Wadler
New York, 1993

INDEX